# INFORMATION SCIENCE

*Information Science: The Basics* provides an accessible introduction to the multifaceted field of Information Science (IS).

Inviting readers to explore a modern field of study with deep historical foundations, the book begins by considering the complexities of the term "information" and the information life cycle from classification to preservation. Each chapter examines a different area within IS, surveying its history, technologies, and practices with a critical eye. This interdisciplinary field incorporates a wide range of approaches which it shares with humanities, social science, and technology fields. What makes IS unique is its emphasis on the connections between information, technology, and society. The need to share information more effectively in response to social, environmental, and biomedical challenges has never been so urgent; the volume discusses the risks as well as benefits that come with the emerging technologies that make it possible. The book also explores how IS, with its long-standing commitment to intellectual freedom and digital inclusion, and its keen attention to the protection of privacy, data ethics, and algorithmic transparency, can contribute to the creation of a more open and equitable society.

*Information Science: The Basics* is essential reading for anyone who wishes to know more about information and the impact it has on our world. It will be particularly useful for anyone intending to study IS at the undergraduate level or considering a shift to a career in the information professions.

**Judith Pintar** is a faculty member and directs the Game Studies & Design program in the School of Information Sciences at the University of Illinois Urbana-Champaign. In 2020, she was named a University of Illinois Distinguished Teacher/Scholar. She teaches introduction to information sciences, and interactive narrative design. Her research interests include game studies, gameful pedagogy, digital literacies, immersive storytelling, narrative AI, the digital afterlife, propaganda, persuasion, and disinformation.

**David Hopping** is a faculty member and Director of Workforce Development/Continuing Education in the School of Information Sciences at the University of Illinois Urbana-Champaign. He teaches web design, information architecture, and web content strategies. His research interests include social and community informatics, sociological theories of human rights, action research and public policy relating to digital inclusion and digital literacy, and biofeedback game design in virtual environments.

# THE BASICS SERIES

*The Basics* is a highly successful series of accessible guidebooks which provide an overview of the fundamental principles of a subject area in a jargon-free and undaunting format.

Intended for students approaching a subject for the first time, the books both introduce the essentials of a subject and provide an ideal springboard for further study. With over 50 titles spanning subjects from artificial intelligence (AI) to women's studies, *The Basics* are an ideal starting point for students seeking to understand a subject area.

Each text comes with recommendations for further study and gradually introduces the complexities and nuances within a subject.

For a full list of titles in this series, please visit www.routledge.com/The-Basics/book-series/B

# INFORMATION SCIENCE

# THE BASICS

**Judith Pintar and David Hopping**

Routledge
Taylor & Francis Group

LONDON AND NEW YORK

Cover image: © Getty Images

First published 2023
by Routledge
4 Park Square, Milton Park, Abingdon, Oxon OX14 4RN

and by Routledge
605 Third Avenue, New York, NY 10158

*Routledge is an imprint of the Taylor & Francis Group, an informa business*

© 2023 Judith Pintar and David Hopping

*British Library Cataloguing-in-Publication Data*
A catalogue record for this book is available from the British Library

*Library of Congress Cataloging-in-Publication Data*
Names: Pintar, Judith, author. | Hopping, David, author.
Title: Information science : the basics / Judith Pintar and David Hopping.
Description: Milton Park, Abingdon, Oxon ; New York, NY : Routledge, 2023. |
Series: The basics | Includes bibliographical references and index. |
Identifiers: LCCN 2022042213 (print) | LCCN 2022042214 (ebook) |
ISBN 9780367725204 (hardback) | ISBN 9780367725181 (paperback) |
ISBN 9781003155119 (ebook)
Subjects: LCSH: Information science.
Classification: LCC Z665 P56 2022 (print) | LCC Z665 (ebook) |
DDC 020--dc23/eng/20221020
LC record available at https://lccn.loc.gov/2022042213
LC ebook record available at https://lccn.loc.gov/2022042214

ISBN: 978-0-367-72520-4 (hbk)
ISBN: 978-0-367-72518-1 (pbk)
ISBN: 978-1-003-15511-9 (ebk)

DOI: 10.4324/9781003155119

Typeset in Bembo
by Deanta Global Publishing Services, Chennai, India

# CONTENTS

# PREFACE

*Information Science: The Basics* provides an accessible introduction to a complex field. Some readers may (justly) feel that important topics were left out, or that others do not belong in the chapters where they were placed. If a history book is a sonnet, a basics book is a haiku! We have chosen to take a narrative approach to the material. We tell stories about historical figures in the text, but credit most contemporary scholars, even luminaries, in the endnotes unless they are the subject of the tale being told. We encourage our readers to follow the trails suggested by the notes to learn more about the people whose ideas spark their curiosity.

We are fortunate that information science is rich with histories, textbooks, and encyclopedias which trace the professional accomplishments of important scholars, map the controversies, and provide technical details of the tools and practices of information science in a more detailed and comprehensive way than we can do here. We direct readers, in particular, to the work of Marcia Bates, Michael Buckland, David Bawden, Lyn Robinson, and William Aspray whose long arc perspectives on the history of information science illuminate the field's complexity and promise.

We are grateful to our colleagues Lisa Bievenue, Maria Bonn, Lisa Hinchliffe, Kathryn LaBarre, Emily Knox, Melissa Ocepek, Madelyn Sanfilippo, Jodi Schneider, Linda Smith, and Mike Twidale for their moral support and editorial suggestions. We also wish to acknowledge our anonymous reviewers whose productive comments narrowed our narrative at key points, and broadened it at others, with special thanks to the one who will immediately recognize their contribution to the introduction.

The book is dedicated to the memory of Jerome "Jerry" McDonough (1963–2021) who never let us forget that information science is a network of relations. Both consciousness and responsibility are a requirement of that belonging:

> The technological web and the social web cannot be regarded as separate. The threads of technology cannot be rewoven without altering the social web, and vice versa. If designers wish to build a better world, they will need to fully comprehend the webs which they weave, and those in which they are entangled.[1]

## NOTE

1 Jerome Patrick McDonough, *Under Construction: The Application of a Feminist Sociology to Information Systems Design* (Berkeley, CA: University of California, 2000): 228–229.

# INTRODUCTION

In the first months of the Covid-19 pandemic, schools across the world found themselves suddenly faced with quarantine conditions. Still needing to serve their students, they hastened to put their classrooms online. A photograph captured that moment and its dramatic contradictions: two young girls sit cross-legged on a public sidewalk outside of a Taco Bell restaurant in Salinas California, using its public WiFi connection in order to attend school.[1] An impressive array of technologies had made it possible to transition rapidly from physical classrooms to online learning spaces, but it was also clear that the benefits of those technologies were unequally distributed. The educational experiences of some students, and their ability to access the information they needed during the early months of the pandemic, were dramatically different from the experiences of other young people, located in different geographic and socioeconomic places across town and across the globe.

> Two students sit outside a Taco Bell to use Wi-Fi so they can "go to school" online.
> This is California, home to Silicon Valley...but where the digital divide is as deep as ever.
> Where 40% of all Latinos don't have internet access. This generation deserves better.[2]

As public sympathy poured out towards the family, commentators noted that the problem was actually widespread. California Senator

Kevin de León tweeted the viral photo, noting that 40% of Latino families in the state lacked access to the Internet.[3]

The Salinas City Elementary School district subsequently provided their students with 1,500 WiFi hotspots, along with 10,000 Chromebooks. The girls' case was used to spearhead California Senate Bill 156, "Broadband for All," which passed the following year. The legislation allocated six billion dollars for broadband infrastructure in California, noting that two million Californians were without high-speed internet access, including 50% of rural housing units.[4]

Uneven distribution of *information and communication technologies* (ICTs), including access to the Internet through local infrastructure, and to the devices able to make use of high-speed connections, reflects other information stratifications that exist within and between nations. The sociotechnical issues associated with the digital divide are only one part of a more complicated set of global information challenges. Even when people have access to the Internet, not everything that they find through their computers, phones, and other devices is accurate, nor is it necessarily placed there for their benefit or on behalf of any greater good.

Disinformation is proving to be an effective strategy for use in pursuit of political power or financial gain. During collective crises, like pandemics and environmental disasters, information becomes an issue of life and death. In a time of war, information is weaponized both for offense and defense. This was clearly demonstrated during Russia's invasion of Ukraine where the Internet provided a sociotechnical front for an accompanying information war.[5]

Corporations and governments have unprecedented access to private data at scale, and the people from whom it is taken have little control over how it is used. There is a pressing need to foster information literacy globally, a literacy that includes knowing how to critically assess the origin of information, becoming more skeptical of requests for private information, and understanding the risks that come with sharing it.

The quality of education in a community will either support or undermine the ability of its members to locate online information, ascertain its accuracy, and protect their privacy. In fact, education has emerged as one of the key factors driving information inequity and the growing divide between the "information rich" and the "information poor."

The digital divide is just one of many pressing information-related challenges. News headlines on any given day will offer stories pertaining to conspiracy theories and election interference, privacy and surveillance, disaster response and health disparities, structural inequalities, and algorithmic biases. These are all challenges that information science is uniquely positioned to address.

The practices of information science include the classification, organization, retrieval, analysis, utilization, governance, management, study, design, expression, and preservation of information. Information professionals may be librarians, records managers, analysts, programmers, researchers, administrators, technicians, designers, curators, or archivists, among other traditional, related, and evolving professions. Their titles may or may not include the term "information." They may have been trained within any number of different intellectual traditions and degree programs, and make use of a wide array of tools, methods, practices, and technologies.

As scholars, information scientists conduct interdisciplinary research, both quantitative and qualitative, in lab and community settings, asking and seeking answers to questions across all domains of human knowledge and experience. In this introduction to the volume we begin by discussing the complexities of the term "information," and the challenges of defining the field of information science. Then we lay out the organization of the book, and let readers know what they can expect to find here.

## WHAT IS INFORMATION?

Information flows continuously around us, into us, and through us, and yet we may be unconscious of the role it plays in creating the worlds in which we live. Our bodies themselves are full of information; every moment of the day we take in and process sensory experiences that we sort and store in different parts of our brain depending on whether they are temporary working memories, episodic memories about things that have happened, or semantic memories relating to facts that we pick up about the world.

Procedural memories (the things we know how to do) are stored in both brain and body. Our DNA encodes genetic information, the instructions that guide our growth, development, and eventual decline. Human knowledge may one day be stored on synthesized DNA molecules, which can hold mind-boggling amounts of information in a space the size of the period at the end of this sentence.[6]

Everyone may agree that the phenomenon of study for the field of information science is *information*, but it is surprisingly difficult to define. The term is chimerical, with multiple academic definitions and commonsense usages. As a noun, it describes physical objects (books) or digital documents (files) that contain meaningful content encoded in text or images, but we also use the word to describe casual speech in which information is passed (gossip). We typically refer to both the container of information (an instruction sheet) and the meaning it conveys (the instructions) as information. The term sometimes serves as an adjective describing an attribute (an informational video) or a value (an informative meeting), but it also defines subjective states related to understanding (being well-informed) or status (being an informant). As a verb, information may be a relational act (informing someone else) or be implicated in complex social processes (the political, psychological, and social effects of dis/misinformation upon public opinion and behavior).

Information is sometimes conceptualized as a metaphorical living thing, which moves and grows, and which can be analyzed much as other living things are. It is situated within networks of relations, and changes through predictable life cycles. Information can be observed to have an identifiable moment of birth (a press release); from there it may change in unexpected ways (a conspiracy theory); it can be acted upon (an executive order), or suppressed (book banning), but sometimes it seems to have a life of its own (going viral). It has a life span (the news cycle), after which it may be forgotten (dementia-related memory loss), literally lost (phone dropped over a cliff), or destroyed (intentional, unrecoverable file deletion). Information management professionals use the metaphor of the information life cycle to organize the policies and practices involved with steering an organization's information resources through all their stages from creation to retirement (or destruction).

A more computational way of thinking about information comes from *information theory*, a branch of mathematics that models the processing, storage, and transmission of information. It understands the term "information" narrowly, as signals that can be distinguished from random noise. In this model, communication occurs when an encoded signal is transmitted to a receiver which successfully decodes it, despite it being corrupted by noise en route.[7] Developed further by others, but first proposed by Claude Shannon, the model remains fundamental to modern communication systems. Because it treats information as a resolution of uncertainty, it is directly relevant to probability theory, pattern recognition, data compression, and cryptography. Further along this track is *quantum information science,* a theoretical and experimental field within physics that combines computational models with quantum mechanics.

Any attempt to define information comprehensively would have to contend not only with dramatically different academic understandings, but also commonsense notions that further muddy the water. Even if a definition were to be agreed upon and applied across disciplines, it would be unlikely to have much effect on everyday usage. For example, "information" is often presented as a discrete stage between "data" and "knowledge" on a path towards "wisdom." This hierarchical progression is visualized in the data-information-knowledge-wisdom (DIKW) pyramid, which places data at the bottom and wisdom at the top.[8] The *DIKW hierarchy* solidified a generally accepted idea that data is potential information, lacking meaning until analysis extracts meaningful information from it. Even so, the words "data" and "information" are often used as synonyms, even in scholarly writing. Likewise, knowledge is sometimes understood as emerging when information is applied to accomplish a practical task (knowledge about how to do something), but it is common to find the words "knowledge" used interchangeably with "information" as well.

The idea that knowledge is derived from information (rather than, say, the other way around) is disputed; since knowledge is a subjective experience, "knowable only to the knower," only *information about* knowledge can be collected and shared.[9] "Knowledge" and "wisdom" each have multiple context-bound cultural meanings as well, further complicating the situation. The DIKW model as a whole has been criticized for assuming a direct hierarchical relationship between sociotechnical processes that are non-linear and entangled[10] but it shows few signs of disappearing; it has been productively reinterpreted and applied within particular domains.[11]

In the absence of consensus on how to define information, scholars face the ongoing work of classifying and mapping the definitions. Lyn Robinson and David Bawden productively analyze the "gap" between five distinct approaches to information: technological, physical, biological, social, and philosophical.[12] Marcia Bates suggests six broad approaches to defining information: semiotic, activity-based, propositional, structural, social, multi-type, and deconstructionist. Many information scientists and theorists from other disciplines have contributed to these various strains of thought.[13]

We are left to conclude that the contradictions attending the term information don't seem to be particularly problematic for the field. Robinson and Bawden agree, concluding that there is insight to be found in attempts to bridge the gaps in understanding, even between dramatically different approaches. The practical consequence of the complexity, as Michael Buckland counsels, is that when it matters, we have to be precise.[14] The rest of the time, contentious discussions around a key term can be productive and even on-point; consider how "society" and "culture" simultaneously bedevil and invigorate the fields of sociology and anthropology respectively.

The theoretical and practical work of information science is relevant across all domains of human understanding, from the artistic to the legal to the psychological to the astrophysical; each one understands information in relation to its domain. Far from being a liability, it is this extraordinary *breadth of relevance* that allows the interdisciplinary field of information science to respond to some of the world's most vexing problems.

## THE CHALLENGE OF DEFINING THE FIELD

In an ambitious study conducted from 2003 to 2005 an international panel of 57 scholars from 16 countries all weighed in on the question. They ended up producing 50 definitions of information science.[15] The problem (or the opportunity, depending on one's point of view), is that information science shares foundational histories, skills, methods, and practices not only with library science and other longstanding disciplines including archival science, history, computer science, communication, and statistics, among others, but also with more recent interdisciplinary fields such as informatics, science and technology studies (STS), media studies, and data science. Courses and degree programs with the word "information" in their name may exist within, above, or alongside any of these programs, or they may be housed idiosyncratically within newly devised interdisciplinary units.

The information technologies that emerged during the 20th century fell under the purview of multiple academic disciplines, triggering a sometimes contentious interplay between information theory as it was embraced by computer science and engineering, and the fields of library science and documentation, which became the discipline of library and information science (LIS) in the middle of the 20th century. Efforts to synthesize LIS with information theory largely foundered, leaving inquiry into the meaningful content, classification, and organization of information and information-related technologies on one side, and the structure and engineering of those technologies largely on the other.[16]

Academic boundary-making is an ongoing process; in the 21st century, programs offering information-related degrees vary greatly in their pedagogical missions. There is also significant international variation. In France for example, information science has been part of *information and communication sciences* since the 1970s, a circumstance that has challenged French information scientists to carve out an identity that is distinct both from computer science and from communication.[17]

The schools that teach information science may differ greatly, or hardly at all from one another. Some programs offer graduate degrees that include library certification and licensure, but some do not. Some include human-centered design practices and user experience research, but some do not; some focus on information organization and knowledge management as central concerns, but some do not; some view developments in data science which incorporate artificial intelligence and machine learning to be essential areas of inquiry, but some do not; some include training in archival methods of information conservation and preservation, but some do not; an increasing number place diversity, equity, inclusion and critical approaches to data, information, and librarianship at the heart of their programs, but some do not. There are also schools that consider information science to be inclusive of all of these areas.

As a result, faculty employed in degree-granting information science programs tend to be methodologically diverse. They may or may not call themselves "information scientists." They may retain multiple professional identities, making use of diverse theoretical and methodological approaches originating in STEM disciplines, the social sciences, the humanities, and the arts. They may have backgrounds in interdisciplinary fields such as informatics, which combines computational and information-related skills and practices with deeper study and application of those practices within a particular domain, or in science and technology studies (STS), in which historical, sociological, and theoretical frameworks shed light on sociotechnical processes. They may also be engaged in a transformation of traditional disciplines, creating new fields within which to study information.[18]

These unusually generative circumstances have the effect of shifting curricular conversations from the capacity (what are various programs on a particular campus able to teach) to the territory (which programs have the *right* to offer courses about which information-related topics, skills, and practices).[19] So, the question of what information science *is* cannot be separated from the politics and economics of the academe. How the institutional title of Information Science(s) appears within any given institutional structure today will reflect national, regional, and local campus politics, and the pressing realities of limited resources.

Systems of higher education without long-term, sustainable funding models, are increasingly vulnerable to the shifting priorities of government and the marketplace. The relative prosperity of programs related to science and technology, compared to alarmingly defunded arts and humanities units, may be guiding the strategic naming of programs, rather than substantive discussions about how, in some more ideal situation, an interdisciplinary program should be organized, institutionally situated, and governed.

It is often suggested that, because of its heterogeneity, information science should forego the label of "discipline" altogether, and simply refer to itself as a "field of study," a term that designates a broad intellectual area closely associated with the skills and practices of the professions that compose it.[20] Some degree-granting programs organize themselves around the mission of training students to take up positions in information-related professions, referring to the field as "Information Studies." The truncation of "Library and Information Science" down to "Information Science" sometimes goes one step further to refer to the field as "Information." Another strategy is to cast information science into the plural form, "information sciences," signaling wider inclusivity of interest and practice.

Because of the breadth of application of information science to all domains of human inquiry, enterprise, and creativity, it has also been described as a *metadiscipline*, much like education, which gives its pedagogical consideration to every academic discipline, including its own. The institutional solidity and longevity of education provide information science with the assurance that as a discipline it can be capacious while remaining a coherent intellectual enterprise.[21]

The question of what information science is, and where it belongs in the greater academic community, has been under discussion for the last half-century within national and international professional organizations, including the Association for Library and Information Science Education (ALISE) and the Association for Information Science and Technology (ASIS&T).

The iSchool Movement was sparked by conversations during a 1988 ALISE meeting which proposed centering the field on the needs of the information professions. It began as a consortium of academic institutions, with a founding "Gang of Three" (University of Pittsburgh, Syracuse University, and Drexel University), expanding into gangs of increasing numbers until it became a caucus. Over 100 institutions across the globe now refer to themselves as iSchools.

The consensus opinion of the iSchool Caucus is that humanities, social science, and STEM approaches are all necessary aspects of academic training for information professionals. This is typically expressed through value statements referring to the relationships between "information, technology, and people." While the offi- cial iSchool website refers to the field as "information," individual iSchools go their own ways in naming themselves. The iSchool movement is just one way that information science is evolving,[22] and even among iSchools there is significant variation in the spe- cific courses of study, professional licensures, and academic degrees offered.

The authors of this book are faculty in a college at the University of Illinois Urbana-Champaign that was long known as the Graduate School of Library and Information Science (GSLS). After it joined the iSchool caucus it renamed itself the "School of Information Sciences." It remains a global leader in library science graduate edu- cation, deeply involved in the intellectual communities of LIS. The name change, which did not occur without contention, reflects the argument that the field of information science must increase its reach if it is to respond effectively to rapidly evolving information systems, technologies, and sociotechnical practices, and to provide comprehensive training for all information professions: the tradi- tional, the emerging, and the yet-to-be-imagined.

## AN INVITATION TO INFORMATION SCIENCE

Sociologist C. Wright Mills described the "sociological imagina- tion" as a lens through which individuals can view their individual lives within broader social contexts. During the social upheav- als of the 1960s, sociology issued an invitation to students, and to the public at large, to try looking through that lens. In his book *Invitation to Sociology* Peter Berger described the unique methodolo- gies of sociology, which were trained on social factors rather than on individual metrics, as a vantage from which to understand the socially constructed nature of the world and its persistent stratifica- tions. Generations of social theorists across many disciplines who responded to that call have had a profound effect on intellectual conversations still ongoing today.[23]

The lens of the sociological imagination is as relevant now as it ever was. As continuously evolving information technologies reshape our social practices and norms, there is a critical need for a shared consciousness of the ways in which information practices, processes, systems, and technologies are shaped by, and shape, our shared social worlds. It is commonplace to say that we are in an *Information Age*. For some, this age is defined by the dramatic transformations in information and communication technologies that occurred over the last century, in the leap from analog to digital storage, which produced the Internet, cellular phones, and then faster (and smaller and stranger) methods of information sharing, storage, search, and retrieval. But for others, what marks this moment are the social changes that have driven those technologies, and the consequences that have resulted from them.

We have more information of every kind at our (literal) fingertips than we can digest. It has become less an insight than a truism that we can feel that we are drowning in information. And there are other dangers as well; the technologies that enable crucial flows of information to meet contemporary crises, have also produced vulnerabilities that enable bad actors to take advantage of the 21st-century information cornucopia heralded as "Big Data."

We have arrived at another game-changing intellectual moment, in which students and scholars are being called to study the swiftly evolving information challenges of our time. In crucial capacities, the interdisciplinary agility of information science can well serve. By making information and its processes visible, information professionals can refine the tools, technologies, and networks through which information is collected and organized, is impeded or flows, and is accessed within and between systems, domains, organizations, and nations. At the same time, information science works to mitigate biases within information systems, identifying inequities in access to information, in who benefits from new technologies, and in who pays the social and environmental costs.

We accept the view, shared by many, that information science is best described as an interdisciplinary field of study, closely associated with, and reflecting the needs of, its professions. But we are also persuaded that information science is more than its practices, professions, tools, and technologies, and that it may also be productively understood as a metadiscipline, with its unique lens trained on every domain of human inquiry, including its own.

In this book, we invite readers to enter a complex intellectual terrain. All maps are partial; we acknowledge that others, situated differently, would chart a different route and highlight different points of interest along the way. Information science is here understood to have emerged from the field of library and information science, enlivened by information-related technologies, skills, and practices shared with many other disciplines and interdisciplinary fields. We take an inclusive approach which situates the study of information at the conceptual, virtual, and material places where information, technology, and society meet, embracing multiple methodological, theoretical, and domain-specific approaches to understanding what takes place there. We refer to *information science* in the singular when referring to the field, to its expression within information professions, and to information-related concepts and practices. In thinking about its institutional expressions, we recognize that the complexity and contradictions of its manifestations make it rest more comfortably within the inclusive plural: *Information Sciences*.

Narratively, we trace the path of information across its metaphorical life cycle. The body of this book follows the life of information as it is collected (Chapter 1), classified (Chapter 2), organized (Chapter 3), retrieved (Chapter 4), utilized (Chapter 5), governed (Chapter 6), studied (Chapter 7), designed (Chapter 8), and preserved (Chapter 9). In the book's concluding discussion, we address imagined futures for information and information science (Chapter 10). Throughout the book we highlight the contributions that the field can make toward addressing the serious information challenges of our day, and present critical perspectives on the ideas and practices described.

*Information Science: The Basics* invites a new generation to the work of making visible (and legible to all) the contexts through which information flows powerfully and continuously through the backgrounds, and the foregrounds, of our lives.

## NOTES

1 Jesse Gary, "Photo of Girls Using Taco Bell Wifi become Symbol of Digital Divide," 31 August 2020, KTVU FOX, 2. https://www.ktvu.com/news/photo-of-girls-using-taco-bell-wifi-becomes-symbol-of-digital-divide.

2 Kevin de León, @kdeleon, *Twitter*, 28 August 2020. https://pic.twitter.com/iJPXvcxsLQ.

3   Kevin de León. https://twitter.com/kdeleon/status/12993869698734
    61248. Retrieved 12 May 2022.
4   "Monumental Broadband Legislation by Senator Lena Gonzalez and
    Assemblymember Cecilia Aguiar-Curry Signed Into Law," 8 October
    2021. https://sd33.senate.ca.gov/news/2021-10-08-monumental-broad-
    band-legislation-senator-lena-gonzalez-and-assemblymember-cecilia.
5   Jim Allsop, "The Ongoing Information War over Ukraine," The Media
    Today, *Columbia Journalism Review*, 9 May 2022.
6   Ed Yong, "This Speck of DNA Contains a Movie, a Computer Virus, and
    an Amazon Gift Card," *The Atlantic*, 2 March 2017.
7   William F. Aspray, "The Scientific Conceptualization of Information: A
    Survey," *IEEE Annals of the History of Computing* 7, no. 2 (1985): 117–140.
8   Russell L. Ackoff, "From Data to Wisdom," *Journal of Applied Systems
    Analysis* 16, no. 1 (1989): 3–9.
9   Thomas D. Wilson, "Human Information Behavior," *Informing Science* 3,
    no. 2 (2000): 50.
10  David Weinberger, "The Problem with the Data-Information-
    Knowledge-Wisdom Hierarchy," *Harvard Business Review* 2 (2010).
    https://hbr.org/2010/02/data-is-to-info-as-info-is-not.
11  See for example Kate McDowell, "Storytelling Wisdom: Story,
    Information, and DIKW." *Journal of the Association for Information Science
    and Technology* 72, no. 10 (2021): 1223–1233.
12  Lyn Robinson and David Bawden, "Mind the Gap: Transitions between
    Concepts of Information in Varied Domains," in *Theories of Information,
    Communication and Knowledge* (Dordrecht: Springer, 2014): 121–141.
13  Marcia J. Bates, "Information," *Encyclopedia of Library and Information
    Sciences* 3 (2010): 2048–2063.
14  Michael Buckland, *Information and Society* (Cambridge, MA: MIT Press,
    2017): 4.
15  Chaim Zins, "Conceptions of Information Science," *Journal of the American
    Society for Information Science and Technology* 58, no. 3 (2007): 335–350.
16  Ronald R. Kline. "What is Information Theory a Theory of? Boundary
    Work among Information Theorists and Information Scientists in the
    United States and Britain during the Cold War," in *The History and Heritage
    of Scientific and Technological Information Systems*, eds. W. B. Rayward and
    M. E. Bowden (Medford, NJ: American Society of Information Science
    and Technology and the Chemical Heritage Foundation, 2004): 15–28.
17  Fidelia Ibekwe-Sanjuan, "Whither Information Science in France?" in
    *International Perspectives on the History of Information Science and Technology*
    (Baltimore, MD: Association of the American Society for Information
    Science and Technology, 2012): 83–95.
18  See Luciano Floridi, *The Philosophy of Information* (Oxford: OUP, 2013).
19  See Lili Luo, "Being Interdisciplinary: A Look into the Background
    and Experiences of iSchool Faculty Members," *LIBRES: Library and
    Information Science Research Electronic Journal* 23, no. 2 (2013): 1–20.

20 David Bawden and Lyn Robinson. *Introduction to Information Science* (London: Facet Publishing, 2015): 3; Charles H. Davis, and Debora Shaw, eds. *Introduction to Information Science and Technology* (Medford, NJ: American Society for Information Science and Technology, 2011): 16.

21 Marcia J. Bates, "The Information Professions: Knowledge, Memory, Heritage." *Information Research* 20, no. 1 (2015). Retrieved from http://InformationR.net/ir/20-1/paper655.html.

22 See Joacim Hansson, *Educating Librarians in the Contemporary University: An Essay on iSchools and Emancipatory Resilience in Library and Information Science* (Sacramento, CA: Library Juice Press, 2019).

23 Peter Berger, *Invitation to Sociology* (New York, NY: Anchor Books, 1963).

# COLLECTING INFORMATION

In the summer of 2012 in the city of Timbuktu, a library housing hundreds of thousands of rare, handwritten manuscripts was threatened by an Al Qaeda-allied terrorist group intent on burning it to the ground. Nearly a half-century earlier, the United Nations Educational, Scientific, and Cultural Organization (UNESCO) had helped to create the Mamma Haidara Institute, named after a self-taught scholar whose family had been collecting manuscripts since the 15th century. Haidara's son, Abdel Kader Haidara, inherited the family mission, sought professional training, and continued the effort, shared by many others, to locate and preserve the manuscripts that are the priceless heritage of the nation of Mali.[1]

Timbuktu was founded in the 11th and 12th centuries by Tuareg tribes. By the 15th century the city had become a trading center on the trans-Saharan caravan route, and by the 16th had a thriving intellectual community centered around a mosque and a university that attracted scholars from across Africa and the known world. The city's collections, written mostly in Arabic, contained works of broad and liberal subject matter, from history to theology, to astronomy to poetry. Even when the city's geopolitical prominence waned, these manuscripts were preserved, copied, and held by the city's first families, which passed them down through the generations in their private homes.

There had been enough warning of the impending attack that the institute's librarians, with the help of friends, family members,

DOI: 10.4324/9781003155119-1

and library volunteers, were able to secretly pack thousands of items from the collections into small metal boxes before the library was destroyed.[2] The boxes were moved via donkey cart and ATV, by twos and threes, hidden under fruit and vegetable crates, and then transported by bus, truck, or canoe along the Niger River to Mali's capital city, Bamako, or to safe houses throughout the region. Reports vary, but it is possible that as many as 300,000 manuscripts were saved.[3]

Collecting, preserving, and transmitting information across time is an ancient human project. What we think of as the *right* of access to information rests upon a set of human practices and values which are far older and more global than the rapid technological changes of recent history would make it seem. That longer arc narrative is part of the foundational history of information science.

More than 30,000 clay tablets inscribed with cuneiform script have been unearthed from the ruins of the city of Nineveh, in the Mesopotamian kingdom of Assyria, now located in present-day Iraq. By a fortuitous twist of fate, clay tablets become stronger when they are burned or baked in sand, rather than disintegrating as papyrus scrolls, wood, and paper do over time. Their survival is the enduring legacy of King Ashurbanipal, a fourth eldest son who had not expected to succeed his father and was trained instead to be a scholar. When he did become King of Assyria, ruling from 668 to 631 BCE, Ashurbanipal had the wealth, power, intelligence, curiosity, and ambition that were needed for the task of acquiring all the written knowledge of his day, much of it by that time already ancient.

Modern information-related activities have their roots in the evolution of skilled memory techniques necessary for practices of storytelling, which passed on the collective memories of families and cultural groups from generation to generation. The earliest indirect evidence of storytelling among our most ancient ancestors comes from cave paintings, which provide vivid images of their worlds. In a cave on the Indonesian island of Sulawesi, a life-sized image of a Sulawesi warty pig (*Sus celebensis*) was discovered in 2017, one of several detailed and life-like animal figures interacting in a complicated scene. The images are estimated to have been created as early as 44,000 years ago, which would make them the oldest figurative paintings to have been found.[4]

Scholars make use of archeological, genetic, geological, linguistic, and other types of evidence to understand the past in the absence of written records. Some of this evidence also provides clues about the form, content, and purpose of humanity's oldest stories. Stories travel from storytellers to their communities; listeners become the storytellers in the next generation. It is true that in the absence of a written record, knowledge transmitted through oral tradition is lost when the continuity across generations is broken. But it would be a mistake to conclude from that vulnerability that storytelling, as a memory technology, is ineffective at communicating across time. The *Vedas*, religious texts written in Vedic Sanskrit, have been orally transmitted in India since the 2nd Millennium BCE, and continued to be shared from teacher to student in the traditional way, even after it was possible to write them down, into the present day. Although some texts may have been physically recorded as early as 500 BCE, the sources of modern printed texts of the *Vedas* for the most part originated in the 16th century.[5]

A study in Australia suggests that its indigenous peoples may have successfully transmitted some stories over many thousands of years. Cultural stories still being told along the Australian coast have been found to contain descriptions of the coastline that do not resemble what it looks like today; but geological evidence indicates that the stories accurately describe the coastline as it existed 7000 years ago. Stories collected from discretely different indigenous groups describe the specific ancient shorelines of their local territories, providing additional evidence of narrative continuity.[6]

Collective memories of events that happened in the distant past, which are communicated through stories, cultural beliefs, and religious practices, become lost as a result of the same kinds of environmental crises and sociopolitical conflicts that lead to the burning of libraries. The written word is vulnerable too.

More familiar to schoolchildren than the creation of King Ashurbanipal's library is the burning of the Library of Alexandria, which was reputed to hold all the knowledge of the known world. Planned in the 3rd century BCE by the Egyptian King, Ptolemy I, the library project was taken up by his son, Ptolemy II Philadelphus, who acquired or created papyrus copies of originals to build a collection that may have held as many as 400,000 scrolls. The Library at Alexandria is unlikely to have been destroyed in a single tragic conflagration. It suffered a succession of unfortunate events, beginning with politicization that led to defunding, followed by a (probably accidental) fire, and then a final purging of intellectuals during the Roman period.

A more systemic problem arose because of the nature of the scrolls themselves. In a humid climate, papyri have a shelf life of about 150 years. A library of scrolls needs to be engaged in a continuous process of recopying the oldest texts, requiring funds to pay the scribes to do the work, if it is to survive.[7] All of these circumstances: disaster, politics, war, preservation challenges, and lack of funding continue to threaten vulnerable collections today.

In this chapter we consider information as a form of collective remembering. After examining the aspirations of libraries towards becoming universal collections, we focus on the requirements for such endeavors: their completeness, accessibility, and searchability, before examining the context surrounding each one.

## INFORMATION AS COLLECTIVE MEMORY

The *idea* of collecting information did not emerge spontaneously out of the sands of ancient Mesopotamia, which at that time was not a desert. The Tigris and Euphrates rivers made the semi-arid climate humid, and the land nutrient-rich and well-suited to agricultural settlement. History is traditionally said to begin with the existence of written records. Writing emerged in parts of the world that had already been transformed by agriculture, which brought new domains of knowledge and practice related to the domestication of animals and farming. The concept of ownership, which swept up women, children, and slaves as well as land and animals into the category of things-that-can-be-owned, inevitably followed the accumulation of surplus and wealth in those societies. Keeping track of property required recordkeeping, and someone able to keep the records.

The appearance of written records in human history did not immediately (or ever completely) replace storytelling as a method of transmitting information. The advent of writing is celebrated by scholars because of the wealth of clues it provides about the past.

The reason why we, in the 21st century CE, can enjoy the adventures of Gilgamesh, the hero-king of Uruk who may have ruled in Mesopotamia during the Early Dynastic Period (c. 2900–2350 BCE), is because Sumerian tales about him were recorded on clay in Sumerian and Akkadian by the time of the Neo-Sumerian Empire in the 22nd to 21st centuries. The stories were copied and recopied, surviving to be collected by the Assyrian King Ashurbanipal more than a millennium later. But during all this time, they were likely also being told, sung, illustrated, and enacted for entertainment as well as religious instruction. Only a very narrow literate class could have accessed the story of Gilgamesh by reading engraved tablets.[8]

The transition from oral to written traditions across the globe was a process and not an event, though it is sometimes remembered that way. In a Sumerian epic poem, "Enmerkar and the Lord of Aratta," estimated to have been recorded in about 1800 BCE, there is an account of the creation of writing, including a clear description of why it was considered necessary. The poem describes in detail the tense back-and-forth negotiation between a ruler, Enmerkar, king of Unug-Kulaba, and a neighboring lord, the King of Aratta, who Enmerkar wanted to make into his vassal. It would have been important to both sides that their communications, which included flattery, threats, and bona fide offers, were transmitted accurately:

> Enmerkar's speech was very grand; its meaning very profound. But the messenger's mouth was too heavy, and he could not repeat the message. Because the messenger's mouth was too heavy, and he could not repeat it, the lord of Kulab (that is, Enmerkar) patted some clay and put the words on it as on a tablet. Before that day, words put on clay had never existed. But now, when the sun rose on that very day—so it was! The lord of Kulab had put words as on a tablet—so it was![9]

Later in the poem, the messenger successfully delivers Enmerkar's message by handing over the clay tablet and explaining to its recipient that he must read the tablet to receive the information it contains. This poem is remarkable, since it illuminates for us the historical period during which writing, as an information technology, was evolving, and how cultural understandings and practices had to change along with it. Message recipients had to be taught (and to adjust) to the new way of receiving information.

We can imagine that for a period of time the written record might not have been considered to be as authoritative or trustworthy as a message transferred from a speaker's ear to a trained listener, with the content faithfully delivered. As writing became accepted as authoritative, the situation would have gradually reversed, so that it was spoken messages that were seen to be more susceptible to error, as this poem suggests. Of course, this may also have been a self-fulfilling prophecy; the memory training that messengers would have received prior to the advent of writing would have become less rigorous as it became less necessary.

Other ancient libraries existed in present-day Syria, Iran, Egypt, Turkey, Greece, India, Ethiopia, and China. Surviving from the oldest library in Syria are the *Ebla Tablets*. When the palace that held them burned the tablets were buried where they were stored, with their identifying tags still attached, preserving their order. Within the collection can be found an incantation against insomnia, documents relating to the beer trade, travelers' accounts of distant places, proverbs, songs, and translations of Sumerian works.[10] The life worlds documented in these documents are rich, sometimes even capturing the experiences of those who wrote them. Surviving copybooks and practice tablets used by scribes-in-training humanize these information professionals of the distant past.[11]

In order to imagine that it would be possible to gather up and store *all* the information in the world, not just the accumulated knowledge of one's own tribe or culture, one must have an elevated sense of one's place in the order of things. Assyrian King Ashurbanipal certainly did, proclaiming himself to be ruler not just of Assyria but of "the World."

His title was aspirational—he had to defend himself against anyone who might seek to displace him, including his elder brother Shamash-shum-ukin who had been appointed by their father to a lesser position as King of Babylon. Viewing himself as owning everything in the world, he thus had the right to take whatever he wanted for his library collection, as well as having the right to decide what was worth preserving. We are fortunate to have a letter written by Ashurbanipal to one of his agents in the field, directing him to contact a certain group of scholars who held a collection of clay tablets that he particularly wished to acquire. He lent his authority to the task:

> No one is allowed to hold back a tablet from you; and as for any tablet or instruction that I did not write to you about but you discover to be good for the palace, you must take it as well and send it to me.[12]

One of the scholars contacted by the agent sent back a message to the King saying that he would promptly begin *copying onto wood* all the requested texts. The King had asked for the originals. We do not know what happened next, but Ashurbanipal had the power to do things that today are understood to be illegal or unethical, such as taking tablets from sacred shrines by force, or copying secret knowledge never intended to be shared outside its community. It is no coincidence that the largest ancient libraries were founded within empires, where military conquest broadened the known world.

In China, imperial libraries began to appear as early as the 16th century BCE during the Shang dynasty, which ruled over a network of warlords that it had to keep under control. Maintaining an empire requires not only recordkeeping (of taxes and tributes), but also information management.[13] The imperial library held proclamations, genealogies, and records of historical and political events and natural disasters, as well as religious, cultural, and artistic content. "Oracular bones" were inscribed with questions before they were burned; answers would be read in the pattern of cracks that formed. That these were collected and preserved suggests that they were believed to contain informational value even after their immediate interpretation.[14]

In the ancient world, most library collections were both scholarly and strategic, part of the practical necessity of empire building for the rulers who ordered them. But some projects such as the libraries of Ashurbanipal and the Ptolemaic Pharaohs appear to have resulted from a ruler's wish to collect all recorded human knowledge. That vision of information is still with us today.

It is beyond the scope of this book to trace the many-branched path from the libraries of the ancient world down to the printing press, which transformed the way that information was reproduced.

The social and cultural impacts of print technology not only widened the reach of information by increasing access to it (at least for literate sectors of the world's societies); it also dramatically increased the magnitude of what there was to read, and for information professionals, what there was to collect, classify, organize, and curate.[15]

Swiss naturalist Conrad Gessner (1516–1565) is best known for his *Historiae animalium*, an illustrated multi-volume compendium of knowledge (and myth) about the natural world. His interests were expansive; he had previously stopped one volume short of completing a 20-volume collection of what he ambitiously considered to be all human knowledge. Before embarking on these encyclopedic projects, he compiled the *Bibliotheca Universalis*, an alphabetical list of 1800 authors, detailing their works, with annotations regarding their content and intellectual value.

In 1627, one of the first statements to express the vision of a universal library collection was published in a treatise entitled *Advice on Establishing a Library*. In this book Gabriel Naudé (1600–1653), a French librarian sometimes referred to as the "Father of Library Management," provides advice for readers interested in creating their own collections:

> a Library which is erected for the public benefit, ought to be universal; but which it can never be, unless it comprehend all the principal authors, that have written upon the great diversity of particular subjects, and chiefly upon all the arts and sciences...For certainly there is nothing which renders a Library more recommendable, then when every man findes in it that which he is in search of.[16]

Our modern public libraries developed in the way that they did, in part because of the advice of Naudé, that a library's collection should be *complete* (by which he means comprehensive), *accessible* (available for the benefit of the public), and *searchable* (so users can easily find what they are looking for).

Conceptually, there is little difference between a cave painting, a well-told tale, a clay tablet, and a digital photo posted on social media. In each, four aspects come into play. Information can simultaneously be understood as:

- a meaning-bearing form or *object, tangible or intangible (a* spoken story, a visual painting, a written tablet, or a digital text)
- the meaningful *content* that the object contains (the image's shape and color, the plot's twists and turns, a message's details, the post's ironic stance)
- the *process* through which the object and its meaning are accessed (entering the lighted cave, listening to a story, receiving a clay tablet, or scrolling through a feed)
- the social *contexts* within which the object is created, its meaningful content is understood, and its accessibility is determined (religious beliefs about the cave and who may enter, the audience considered appropriate for a particular storytelling event, the secrecy around the delivery of message-bearing tablet, or the privacy settings on a media post).

The different aspects of information—object, content, process, and context—are of central importance to all the practices and professions of information science.[17] These aspects can be seen across the entire information life cycle: in the organization of collected information, in refinements of the techniques and technologies associated with information search and retrieval, in the task of expanding digital literacy, in the analysis and use of information, in the creation of information policies for privacy and protection, in the best practices of information design, and in the curation and preservation of information of all kinds.

Thinking about information simultaneously as object, content, process, and context sheds light on the practicalities of the three-part vision of Universal Information, that collection should be comprehensive (a qualified completeness), accessible, and searchable. The completeness of a collection and its searchability pertain to both the *object* and the *content* of what is being collected, classified, and organized. Accessibility relates most directly to the *processes*, including the technologies and practices through which items in a collection are shared and used, though censorship may prevent access to the physical items themselves, as well limiting the content they contain.

The *context* of information is essential to all three. Attending to the context requires asking what it means for a collection to be *complete.* Since it isn't possible to collect all the information in the world, what is collected? For a collection to be considered *accessible,* does it have to be accessible to everyone, or does it count if it is accessible only to certain classes of people? When a collection is made *searchable,* whose interests and priorities take precedence in that classification process? Each part of the vision of universal information requires examination through a critical frame; and no part can exist outside of its historical, sociocultural, and sociotechnical contexts.

## THE CONTEXT OF COMPLETENESS

King Ashurbanipal would not have collected the stories and traditions of peoples that were vanquished during his military exploits if these undermined his right to rule them. Nor would he have collected much beyond the sectors he valued within his own society. The personal experiences of marginalized people, such as slaves or non-elite women and children, would have provided less material to be collected, though historians are good at gleaning details about such lives from what does survive; fortunately, Mesopotamian women could train as scribes.[18]

Apart from Ashurbanipal's collecting bias, there were also physical limitations that likely frustrated him. Many of the oldest written records of his day would already have been damaged or copied inaccurately. Historical records might also have been destroyed for political reasons during previous regimes. In the 15th century BCE, for example, images of Egyptian Queen Hatshepsut, engraved or painted on monuments, statues, and cartouches, were removed by her stepson, Thutmose III (for whom she had been regent), when he came to power. His son Amenhotep II continued the effort, even removing her name from lists of kings. The Romans called this kind of erasure *damnatio memoriae* and practiced it on the living as well as on the dead, as punishment for crime, scandal, or disfavor. This also happens in a more limited way in the present day, when paintings and monuments are removed from public buildings and squares.[19]

Depending on the thoroughness of such actions, political actors in the past may well have succeeded in disinforming us in ways that have shaped our understanding of history. We can't know *about* what we can't know *of*, which is the point of the practice.

Maurice Halbwachs (1877–1945) was a French philosopher and sociologist whose most famous work, *The Collective Memory*, gave us the idea that social groups (and not just individuals) remember the past and pass those memories on. Commemorations and monuments are expressions of that group memory process, which helps to explain why people feel so strongly about tearing down or preserving certain historic statues. Halbwachs' research on memory was part of ongoing interdisciplinary and collaborative work with social psychologist Charles Blondel, whose contributions to their shared preoccupation is frequently overlooked in the English-speaking world, perhaps because most of it has not been translated from French to English.[20] This is ironic and on point, since collective remembering requires forgetting alternative ways of understanding the past.

Recently, forgotten figures in science are being recalled and credited for their work, but the problem is endemic; structural inequalities lead to making the work of lower-status people (students, lab assistants, wives) invisible, with credit going to the person with the highest status in a partnership or on a team. Each time one person is uniquely honored for a complex scientific discovery that required the work of many others, information about how that discovery came about is lost.

Historians and other scholars engage in productive, evidence-based debates over the past as a matter of professional interest, curiosity, and reputation. Outside academia, people also disagree about the past and how it should be remembered, but the tenor of the disagreements may be quite different in situations where the past provides personal and collective identity. The context within which a statue or historical monument is viewed in the present is as important as the context in which it was originally commissioned and erected. Old forms get new meanings as contexts change over time, which can lead to violence upon the steps of those monuments as some seek to tear them down, and others strive to make sure they remain where they are.

This question becomes a practical one in memorialization debates. What should be done with statues that were erected to honor individuals that history has reassessed and found to no longer represent the values of their current society? In the 20th century, after World War II, newly Communist countries tore down statues of nationalist heroes and replaced them with statues of war heroes. After the fall of communism, some of the original statues were hauled out of storage and reseated in public squares. Around the world, there are discussions about what should be done with the awkward memorials of past eras, even where there is a broad consensus that they need to come down. Should they be put on display in museums, with historical context? Should they be destroyed? Do some ideas deserve to be forgotten? Is it worth preserving objects such as Nazi paraphernalia that are fetishized and eagerly collected by the next authoritarian generation?

Debates over school curricula and how they should cover problematic eras of national history, including legacies of colonialism, slavery, and racism, sometimes conflate personal memory and interpersonal relations with collective memory and structural relations: can't we just forget about the past and move on? Memorialization conflicts are rife with apparent contradictions. Politicians in the United States who claim that removing Confederate monuments is an "erasure of history" support the censorship of textbooks that present slavery, accurately, as the cause of the Civil War.

The connection between the control of knowledge and political power has been articulated by French historian and philosopher Michel Foucault (1926–1984). His work suggests that what counts as *all the information in the world* will always be a reflection of power inequalities from the past, which determine what information will survive into the present. Structures of power in the present will also shape how the past is taught, and how current events will be remembered in the future.

From the perspective of information science, as for historians, all accounts are important to preserve, even the fabricated and self-serving ones.

## THE CONTEXT OF ACCESSIBILITY

If the goal of building a universal collection is undercut by social stratifications, this is just as true for the second goal of Naudé's vision, that a library collection should be *accessible*. We can surmise that one reason King Ashurbanipal wanted to centralize his collection of tablets was to make it easier for the scribes, priests, and scholars of his day to read and copy them. The majority of people in his society were non-literate, including most of his own royal household. Even apart from the limitations of literacy, physical access to library collections has historically been constrained by social class. Wealthy and aristocratic families in many eras and across the globe have assembled private libraries in their homes and educated their children in elite institutions where printed information is available to them that would not be accessible to the lower classes, or to women, or to the public at large.

In the United States, during the centuries when the ownership of human beings was legal, what was *illegal* was teaching a slave to read. That slaveowners and their apologists felt it necessary to create such a law is evidence that they knew that the racial stratification that they were creating in their society required control of information; why otherwise would they be afraid of literate slaves?[21] In thinking about the ways in which historical injustices were transformed into modern inequalities, we may well ask why, across the globe, education is funded in such a way that schools attended by poor children have dramatically fewer resources of all kinds than schools attended by wealthy children.[22] Why do the Taliban when they are in power in Afghanistan immediately deprive girls of the right to education?[23] Even in educational systems with high levels of educational attainment, like the Nordic system, stratifications continue to exist.[24]

The United Nations General Assembly passed the Freedom of Information Resolution in 1946. Two years later the 58 members of the General Assembly adopted the Universal Declaration of Human Rights, which included the right of children to be educated. Elementary education was directed to be free and compulsory; and while parents had the right to choose the kind of education their children received, the UN agreed that they could not deprive their children of their right as human beings to the knowledge and skills that education provides.

The issue of information accessibility is not only about social inequalities which affect literacy and access to education; it is also about broader issues related to the *value* of intellectual freedom and the *right* to information. The idea of a truly public library, embraced

by libraries and championed by librarians, has always been in conflict with those sectors of society that seek to censor information,
to lock it up behind a paywall, or to surveil its use. The American
Library Association (ALA) code of ethics includes statements of
commitment to intellectual freedom, resistance to censorship of
library resources, and protection of library users' rights to privacy
and confidentiality."[25] Inclusion, accessibility, and privacy protection are all areas of professional training and continuing study
within information science.

Censorship, from an information science point of view, must be
understood in the context of authority, power, and control, since
a deliberate restriction of access to information only works when
it is enforced.[26] Censorship sometimes involves symbolic or actual
destruction of information objects such as books, or of the buildings
where books are held, as occurred in Timbuktu, but sometimes it
is a restriction of specific words, images, or ideas. Censorship has
been productively categorized as having both active and passive
forms. In passive form, individuals may self-censor because they
are afraid of the repercussions of not conforming to their community's values. The actions of censorship lie along a continuum of
increasing severity in which materials may be redacted, restricted,
relocated, or completely removed.[27]

Information Scientists study censorship to learn more about
attempts to limit access to information. Reasons for censoring may
include protection (usually of children, but sometimes of society);
prejudice (to maintain social inequalities, or to promote particular
worldviews); or power (to limit dissent). Legislation aimed at controlling what children may read and discuss in school (eliminating,
for example, texts about the theory of evolution, or gender and
queer studies, or racial history) reflects a politicization of information that is bound up in religious, nationalist, or other political
projects.

The attack on the libraries of Timbuktu can be understood to
be an attack on freedom of information, a brute-force attempt at
censorship and control of thought within the Islamic world by the
destruction of the evidence of a more tolerant Islam. In Bosnia,
the lack of consensus over who is responsible for the violence
that occurred during the dissolution of Yugoslavia in the 1990s is

particularly marked. Bosnia is an ethnically divided state, with power shared uneasily between Bosnians who are ethnically Croatian and Roman Catholic, Bosnians who are Muslim, and Bosnians who are ethnically Serbian and Orthodox Christian. Within a single high school, students of different ethnic groups may attend separate classrooms and be taught from textbooks that refer to the country's history in different ways, with alternative views censored.[28]

Similarly, in textbooks used in the United States to teach U.S. history, the historical significance of slavery can be presented quite differently from state to state. Social panic around "critical race theory" led some conservative-led states to scour discussions of slavery from textbooks and library shelves, and especially of its legacies in the systemic and structural racism that still powerfully impact Black people's lives today. In contrast, textbooks in progressive states continue to present the country's racial history in a critical and comprehensive way.[29] Regardless of its stated intent, this censorship provides an excellent example of structural racism. The use of state power to wrest control of decisions on textbook content away from educators has the immediate effect of erasing Black history and experience. Attempts to shut down academic departments of ethnic or area studies, and the censoring of books addressing ethnic and racial history from prisons, schools, and libraries reoccur when the political winds make anti-minority or anti-immigration sentiment expedient again.

The American Library Association has released a statement that communicates its opposition to "any legislative proposal or local initiative intended to ban instruction, consideration, or discussion about the role of racism in the history of the United States, or how systemic racism manifests itself in our schools, workplaces, and government agencies."[30] In statements such as these, information science, as a field, communicates its commitment to widening and protecting access to information as a core value, and a collective goal towards which to work.

## THE CONTEXT OF SEARCHABILITY

The third part of the vision of a universal library is that users, having been granted access to all the available information in the world, should be able to find what they are looking for. The effective search of collections has been a central task of information science throughout its history.

Argentinian translator, essayist, and poet Jorge Luis Borges (1899–1986) had a penchant for writing satirical short stories touching on themes related to classification and memory; some of these are prescient, appearing to speak directly to the information challenges of the digital era.[31] In his short story "The Library of Babel," Borges asks us to imagine the creation of a library, infinitely large, with books that contain every possible combination of the letters of the alphabet. Within the collection it would become possible to find any book ever written or that ever could be written, every sentence ever spoken, or that might ever be spoken, including "the true story of your death, the translation of every book into every language, the interpolations of every book into all books, the treatise Bede could have written (but did not) on the mythology of the Saxon people, the lost books of Tacitus."[32]

Humankind would have reacted with joy and hopefulness at the idea that the solutions to all problems, personal and collective, must lie within the library, if only they could be found. But there's the rub. The Library of Babel could not be searched. Although somewhere in its chaos must exist "the faithful catalog of the Library," there would also be "thousands and thousands of false catalogs, the proof of the falsity of those false catalogs, a proof of the falsity of the true catalog." Hope would turn to depression when people understood that nothing in the library could ever be found: "The certainty that some bookshelf in some hexagon contained precious books, yet that those precious books were forever out of reach, was almost unbearable.[33]

Because the Library of Babel is a computational construct, it could *in theory* exist. And in a less-than-infinite digital form, it now does. You will be able to find your name, and every word you have ever written, and every word you will ever write, through a website that brings Borges' wry dystopian fable to life.[34] It is less cruel than the original, because it is searchable (though it has no catalog or index—actually it does have one, but just like the one in Borges' story, it can't be found).

It is a strange and unsettling experience to type, say, the sentence you just spoke, or your most guarded secret, into the virtual Library of Babel, and have the text turn up on your screen. It was not produced by your input—it already existed in the digital library in its own unique location, along with every possible variation of the same text with words or letters missing or disarranged. The online Library of Babel is not truly infinite; it contains all possible pages of only 3200 characters each, which amounts to about $10^{4677}$ "books." So although the website doesn't contain the entire text of your as-yet-unwritten novel in a single string, you could find all the pieces of it there, 3200 characters at a time, along with every possible revision and parody and bastardization and terrible translation that could possibly follow—if you knew what text to input in order to find them.

To get closer to the experience of Borges' Library of Babel, you can simply try browsing through the website. You can spend hours and hours looking randomly through it and never find anything but garble.

The title of Borges' story refers to the ancient tale of the Tower of Babel, which relates an attempt by human beings to build a tower all the way to heaven. As the story goes, God struck down the builders for their hubris, causing them to speak in different languages. Unable to communicate, they could no longer work together, and their tower soon fell to ruin. The builders of the tower of Babel had not lost the *form* of their communication—they could still hear each other—but they could no longer access the *content* of the spoken words. Without a dictionary and grammar to guide a process of translation, they also lacked any *context* from which to find shared understanding.

It is a common experience to come across, in an antique store or resale shop, a box of random photographs that are unidentifiable because there are no names written on the back. Having been separated from any historical documents that could provide clues to their identities, such as marriage records or a family bible, these photographs now retain only aesthetic or iconic value. The photographs lack information about the information in them: they lack *metadata*.

When we inherit old family photographs, it is tempting to be irritated at our ancestors for failing to write names on the backs of their photos to tell us who they are. But really why would they have? They knew who the people were when the pictures were taken. And perhaps we shouldn't throw stones. How many of us give meaningful file names to our digital photographs that would allow our future great-grandchildren to identify the people in them?

Imagine a Library of Babel digital resale shop, with all the photographs taken on all the cameras and phones and digital cameras of everyone in the entire world, all gathered in one place, all without identifying information. Future facial recognition technologies may evolve to the point that any single photograph in that collection could be identified through algorithms that compare them to all the other images. But a match would not provide identification; the program would still need to access other types of information linked to the matching photo, as there would be on a passport, or in a high school yearbook, or on a social media site. To identify all the random faces in that infinite collection, it would need to have access to all the public and private information about everyone in the world.

Researchers, governments, and corporations are collecting ever-increasing amounts (and kinds) of data to fuel AI-driven technologies for a variety of purposes, from the scientific to the entrepreneurial. Governments pursue facial recognition technologies for the purpose of surveillance, but they could also be used to instantly identify random photographs. If everyone gave up their private data on behalf of the goal of being instantly able to put a name on any face, that might be cool, but whom would it serve? Who would be harmed? The answers to these questions also constitute the context of searchability.

The actual collecting of all the information in the world is more complicated in practice than it might seem to be when viewed as a utopian ideal. In "The Total Library" (a short essay written two years before "The Library of Babel") Borges opens with that very thought: "The fancy or the imagination or the utopia of the Total Library has certain characteristics that are easily confused with virtues."[35]

# NOTES

1 "Timbuktu's 'Badass Librarians': Checking Out Books Under Al-Qaida's Nose," 23 April 2016, in *All Things Considered*, produced by National Public Radio, https://www.npr.org/2016/04/23/475420855/timbuktus-badass-librarians-checking-out-books-under-al-qaidas-nose.

2 Yochi Dreazen, "The Brazen Bibliophiles of Timbuktu: How a Sneaky Team of Librarians Duped Al Qaeda," *The New Republic*, April 24, 2013.

3 Hammer, Joshua. "The Brave Sage of Timbuktu: Abdel Kader Haidara," *The Innovators Project*, *National Geographic*, 21 April 2014, https://www.npr.org/2016/04/23/475420855/timbuktus-badass-librarians-checking-out-books-under-al-qaidas-nose.

4 Adam Brumm et al., "Oldest Cave Art Found in Sulawesi," *Science Advances* 7, no. 3 (2021): https://doi.org/10.1126/sciadv.abd4648.

5 Michael Witzel, "Vedas and Upaniṣads," in *The Blackwell Companion to Hinduism*, ed. Gavin Flood (Oxford and Malden, MA: Blackwell, 2003): 68–101.

6 Patrick D. Nunn and Nicholas J. Reid, "Aboriginal Memories of Inundation of the Australian Coast Dating from more than 7000 Years Ago," *Australian Geographer* 47, no. 1 (2016): 11–47.

7 Rico, Christophe. "The Destruction of the Library of Alexandria: A Reassessment," in *The Library of Alexandria: A Cultural Crossroads of the Ancient World*, eds. Chrostopher Rico and Anca Dan (Jerusalem: Polis Institute Press, 2017): 330.

8 Jeanette C. Fincke, "The British Museum's Ashurbanipal Library Project," *Iraq* 66 (2004): 55–60.

9 Lines 500–506 of *Enmerkar and the Lord of Aratta*, as rendered by Christopher Woods, "The Earliest Mesopotamian Writing," in *Visible Language: Inventions of Writing in the Ancient Middle East and Beyond*, eds. Christopher Woods, et al (Chicago: IL: Oriental Institute Museum Publications 32, 2010): 34.

10 Alfonso Archi, *Ebla and Its Archives: Texts, History, and Society* (Berlin: De Gruyter, 2015).

11 See Wiebke Beyer, "Teaching in Old Babylonian Nippur, Learning in Old Assyrian Aššur?" in *Education Materialised: Reconstructing Teaching and Learning Contexts Through Manuscripts*, eds. Eva Maria Wilden, Giovanni Ciotti, Stefanie Brinkmann, and Stefano Valente (Berlin: De Gruyter, 2021): 15.

12 Fincke, Ashurbanipal, p. 57.

13 Wei Lu and Max Aiken, "Origins and Evolution of Chinese Writing Systems and Preliminary Counting Relationships," *Accounting History* 9, no. 3 (2004): 25–51.

14 Adam C. Schwartz, *The Oracle Bone Inscriptions from Huayuanzhuang East* (Berlin: De Gruyter, 2020).

15 Leo Lahti, Jani Marjanen, Hege Roivainen, and Mikko Tolonen, "Bibliographic Data Science and the History of the Book (c. 1500–1800),"

*Cataloging & Classification Quarterly* 57, no. 1 (2019): 5–23. See also Sarah Werner, "Working towards a Feminist Printing History," *Printing History* (2020): 11–25.

16  Gabriel Naudé, *Advis pour dresser une bibliotheque*, Paris, 1627, translated by John Evelyn as *Instructions Concerning Erecting of a Library*, London, 1661, 19–20. See also Thomas Ash, "Naudé, Mazarin and the Origins of France's Oldest Public Library," 2017, https://thomasash.wordpress.com/2017/03/09/naude-mazarin-and-the-origins-of-frances-oldest-public-library/.

17  Michael K. Buckland, "Information as Thing," *Journal of the American Society for Information Science* 42, no. 5 (1991): 351–360; and Buckland, *Information Society*, p. 22.

18  Kathryn R Raign, "Finding Our Missing Pieces—Women Technical Writers in Ancient Mesopotamia," *Journal of Technical Writing and Communication* 49, no. 3 (2019): 338–364.

19  Sarah E. Bond, "Erasing the Face of History," *New York Times*, 14 May 2011.

20  Annette Becker, "Memory Gaps: Maurice Halbwachs, Memory and the Great War," *Journal of European Studies* 35, no. 1 (2005): 102–113.

21  Grey Gundaker, "Hidden Education among African Americans during Slavery," *Teachers College Record* 109, no. 7 (2007): 1591–1612.

22  Sol Gamsu, "Why are Some Children Worth More Than Others? The Private-State School Funding Gap in England," *Common-Wealth Thinktank, Durham University* (2021), https://www.common-wealth.co.uk/reports/why-are-some-children-worth-more-than-others.

23  Fatima Faizi, "Afghan Students Run Underground Book Club to Keep Dreams Alive, *Al Jazeera*, 9 May 2022.

24  Ulpukka Isopahkala-Bouret et al., "Access and Stratification in Nordic Higher Education: A Review of Cross-Cutting Research Themes and Issues," *Education Inquiry* 9, no. 1 (2018): 142–154.

25  Trina J. Magi and Martin Garnar, *Intellectual Freedom Manual* (9th ed., Chicago, IL: American Library Association and Office for Intellectual Freedom, 2015).

26  Emily J. M. Knox, *Book Banning in 21st-Century America* (Lanham, MD: Rowman & Littlefield, 2015): 87.

27  Emily J. M. Knox, "Opposing Censorship in Difficult Times," *The Library Quarterly* 87, no. 3 (2017): 269.

28  Goran Šimić, "To Believe or Not to Believe: Current History Textbooks in Bosnia and Herzegovina," in *Nationhood and Politicization of History in School Textbooks*, eds. Gorana Ognjenović and Jasna Jozelić (Cham: Palgrave Macmillan, 2020): 155–179.

29  Dana Goldstein, "Two States. Eight Textbooks. Two American Stories," *The New York Times*, 12 January 2020.

30  American Library Association, "ALA Statement on Censorship of Information Addressing Racial Injustice, Black American History, and Diversity Education," https://www.ala.org/advocacy/intfreedom/

statement/opposition-censorship-racial-injustice-black-history-diversity
-education. Retrieved 17 May 2022.

31  Stefan Herbrechter and Ivan Callus, *Cy-Borges: Memories of the Posthuman in the Work of Jorge Luis Borges* (Lewisburg, PA: Bucknell University Press, 2009).

32  Jorge Luis Borges, *The Library of Babel*, trans. Andrew Hurley (Boston, MA: David R Godine Press, 2000).

33  Ibid.

34  Basile, Jonathan. *Tar for Mortar: "The Library of Babel" and the Dream of Totality* (Santa Barbara, CA: Punctum Books, 2018). See also *Library of Babel* (website), https://libraryofbabel.info/About.html. Retrieved 17 May 2022.

35  Jorge Louis Borges, "The Total Library," trans. Eliot Weinberger, in *Selected Non-Fictions*, eds. Esther Allen, Suzanne Jill Levine, and Eliot Weinberger (New York, NY: Viking, 1999): 214.

# CLASSIFYING INFORMATION

A 16th-century Spanish book that had been lost for centuries turned up in Denmark. Ironically, it was found in a library. No one who cared about the book would ever have thought to search for it in Denmark, much less in the place where it was found, which was the Arnamagnæan Collection at the University of Copenhagen. The collection holds Icelandic and other Nordic manuscripts, with only about 100 works from other countries in total, of which only 20 originated in Spain.

It could not be accurately classified, except by language (it was written in Latin, but had Spanish passages). The cover and the first section of the enormous 2000-page tome were missing; it had been rebound in plain gray cardboard in the 18th century.[1] So there was no title, no author, no identifying information of any kind. To make things worse, at some point in the past, it may have been put on the wrong shelf.[2]

When the unidentified book turned up, it presented scholars at the University of Copenhagen with a puzzle. Eventually a visiting historian recognized it as a book that had been lost for 500 years: the *Libro de los Epítomes* (*Book of Abstracts*), created by Hernando Colón (1488–1539), whose father was the controversial Italian explorer, Christopher Columbus.[3]

Like King of Assyria two thousand years earlier, Colón wanted to create a universal library, containing all the knowledge in the world, a world much bigger than it had been when Ashurbanipal

DOI: 10.4324/9781003155119-2

had ruled. Colón's hubris in his endeavor was as great as the ancient king's had been, even if he lacked a king's power. He wasn't without resources, however. Despite being one of Columbus's two sons born out of wedlock, Colón's association with his famous father provided him with social status, wealth, and connections sufficient to indulge his ambition to collect "every book on every subject and in every language, from within Christendom and without."[4] Historians have noted that his ambitions were not free of the colonizing ideologies that sent his father out to violently plunder the New World.[5]

Hernando accompanied his father on his disastrous fourth trip to Central America and the Caribbean, in which all ships were lost but one, leaving the surviving crew stranded in Jamaica. Although the fourth voyage marked the end of exploration for Columbus, his son's ambitions continued. By the end of his life Colón had acquired between 15,000 and 20,000 volumes, many of them not found in other collections. In addition to books, he acquired popular works and ephemera, newspapers, pamphlets, brochures, ballads, and academic treatises. The contents of his collection ranged from erotica to the classics of ancient Greece and Rome. In his era, it was the largest collection of printed material in the world.

Not surprisingly, Colón's library suffered the same fate as other libraries through time. They are vulnerable to theft, fire, war, and weather. Their collections are valuable, sometimes immeasurably so, which means their books will be stolen, or sold to pay debts or to make a profit. Sometimes the value is not evident, and books are thrown away, or used as kindling. They may also become collateral damage in violent conflicts that have nothing to do with them or serve as symbolic targets. In August 1992, the Yugoslav army shelled Bosnia's National and University Library, burning close to two million books, including 155,000 rare books and manuscripts; this act was understood to be an attempt to destroy the memory of a peaceful, multiethnic Bosnia.[6]

Only about a quarter of Colón's collection has survived into the present, but among what does remain are a series of bound indexes, created by Colón's team of librarians, which describe what the entire collection once contained. These indexes provide a record of the system of classification that Colón developed to organize his holdings. He kept a list of all of his acquisitions, and from this created a bibliography that included collected works organized by author. A second volume sorted the works by broad topic. A third sorted them by keywords. These indexing volumes can today be found in the *Biblioteca Colombina* of the *Institución Colombina* in the Spanish city of Seville. It is because of Colón's meticulous classification that scholars know the titles, authors, and subjects of the books in the collection that did not survive.

But the *Book of Abstracts*, which summarized the *content* of each work in the collection at some point in the last 500 years, disappeared from Spain and from the eyes of the world. Its absence was felt by historians; in its 1,964 pages were recorded almost 2,000 detailed abstracts of the books and other texts collected by Colón in the late 15th and early 16th centuries, many of which no longer exist.

Historians have traced the book's adventures; they believe that it left Spain in the hands of a Danish envoy in the 17th century who brought it back to Denmark. It was auctioned off at his death and then purchased by the Icelandic scholar, librarian, and collector Árni Magnússon (1663–1730). Magnússon's collection of Icelandic works was the largest of its kind in the world, and the central focus of his interest and acquisitions. Remarkably, the *Libro de los Epítomes* survived the Copenhagen fire of 1728, in which the University Library was completely destroyed, except for some works that had been copied by Magnússon. His printed book collection also burned, but his copied manuscripts and some of his books were moved before the fire reached them. Among them was the *Libro de los Epítomes*.[7] After his death his book collection was divided between the Árni Magnússon Institute for Icelandic Studies in Reykjavík and the Arnamagnæan Institute in Copenhagen, where the *Libro de los Epítomes* was sent. There the book lay, unrecognized for nearly 400 years.

Colón had indexed his books nearly a century before Naudé asserted the importance of completeness, accessibility, and searchability in a library collection. But neither of these men invented the idea of library classification. For that, we must go back again to the ancient world.

In this chapter we explore the earliest known classification systems, and the history of the development of modern library cataloging. We survey the parallel development of special libraries in the United States and the international documentation movement before examining challenges to traditional classification and the identification of bias within information frameworks and systems.

## THE ORIGINS OF CLASSIFICATION

Ancient Sumerians created lists of their collections, perhaps as early as 2500 BCE. Among the clay tablets found at the Sumerian city of Nippur, now located in present-day Iraq, are two indexing tablets, dating to about 2000 BCE. The discrepancies between the two lists suggest that they were made at different times, or represented separate, incomplete attempts to account for what was in their collection.[8] Indexing tablets from Hattusa, the capital of the Hittite empire in the 14th century BCE (in modern Boğazkale, Turkey), are more detailed, including a summary of the content that provides the names of authors or transcribers, as well the number of tablets across which a text was written.[9] Given that long texts required multiple clay tablets to record them, it was the practice to include at the end of each tablet some text to aid the reader. This might include the next few lines to be found at the beginning of the next tablet, a kind of ancient hyperlink. Information such as this, which is not part of the text, but *about* the text, is referred to as a *colophon*. On a modern book, the spine serves as a colophon, providing the title, author, and sometimes the publisher's name or identifying logo. On ancient cuneiform tablets the colophon sometimes recorded the name of the scribe, the library where the tablet would be held, or the owner of the collection.

The creation of the classification system used in the ancient Egyptian Library of Alexandra is attributed to a man named Kallimachos (Callimachus in Latin), a poet, scholar, and librarian who lived circa 200 BCE. He was responsible for maintaining the *Pinakes*, the catalog of the library's collections, which eventually grew so large that it required 120 papyrus scrolls to record it. Although it did not survive intact, the 480 surviving fragments give us a wealth of information about the system. The word *pinakes*, plural for *pinax*, or wooden tablet, also referred to the clay markers that hung above the pots that contained the scrolls. The library's collections were classified into two familiar categories: literature and nonfiction. Works listed as literature were subdivided into the categories of epic, elegy, iambics, melodrama, tragedy, or comedy. The nonfiction texts were categorized as history, rhetoric, philosophy, medicine, or law.[10]

Although Kallimachos is credited with creating the "world's first bibliography," his system was influenced by Aristotle's approach to list-making, and by the work of Aristotle's pupil, Theophrastus, who created and organized summaries of the opinions and ideas of philosophers. These were recorded, without additional commentary or analysis, into documents called doxographies, which could serve as the basis for scholarly discussion. The system also made use of the new and evolving practice of alphabetization.[11]

Kallimachos was an information professional in a startlingly modern sense. He organized the physical scrolls that were collected, he evaluated their content so that he could classify them accurately, and he recorded information about the scrolls in the kinds of metadata categories that we still use today: length, name of the author, content summary, review of a work's contributions to its field, and the author's other works. Although the *Pinakes* provided a detailed list of the library's scrolls, it did so as a bibliography rather than an index. What his bibliographic catalog did *not* provide was a way to locate the scrolls in the library. To find what they were looking for, scholars still needed to ask the librarians where to look.[12]

We know less about the workings of the Imperial Library of China during the Han dynasty. A cataloger by the name of Liu Xin (c.50 BCE–23 CE), a relative of the royal family, continuing a work begun by his father, produced a catalog of the library's collections. *The Seven Epitomes*, which included extensive editorial commentary on the items in the collection did not survive, but a shortened version was included as a chapter in a history of the Han dynasty written a generation later.[13] The chapter, entitled "Treatise on Classics and other Texts," listed 631 works from the Imperial Library, none of which still exist, and of only 20% is there any knowledge beyond their titles. We can glean a little more about what they contained from their classification into six categories and 38 subcategories. The main categories were Six Arts, Various Masters, Poems and Rhapsodies, Military Writings, Calculations and Methods, and Recipes and Techniques. Missing from the catalog are laws and statutes, which were collected separately.[14]

## LIBRARIES AND CATALOGS

Organizational tools that help people discover what they are looking for in collections are called *finding aids*. We may say that we are "searching for a book" in the library, but we aren't actually searching the contents of its collections, unless the library is very small, or we already have some idea on which shelf to look. What we are searching is the finding aid. Catalogs and indexes are two common kinds. The difference between them reflects the difference between information understood as a container of meaningful content, and the meaningful content that it contains.

A *catalog* is a list of the names (or other identifying labels) of items in a collection. A *bibliography* is a common kind of catalog that lists written works organized by author. In contrast, an *index* is often organized by the topics in a collection (or within a single work). An index at the back of a book, for example, is typically an alphabetized list of topics with page numbers indicating where that content shows up in the text. Sometimes a book will have more than one index, one that lists the names of people who appear in the book, one for place names, and one for subjects.

Before the era of digital storage, and even after indexing began to be digitized and accomplished through networks, the most common finding aid in a library was the long wooden filing cabinet, containing stacked drawers full of alphabetized 3" × 5" cards. The location of any book on any shelf in the library could be determined through a few different searching paths, because card catalogs included multiple cards for any single book, indexed in different ways. One card would be in a drawer alphabetized by the author's last name, another one could be found by searching for the title of the book, and a third would be sorted by subject area.

This multiple-index strategy increased the chances that library patrons would be successful in locating what they were looking for in the catalog, even if they only knew one of those three pieces of information.

The cards contained descriptive information about the book and its contents. The *technical description* of a book related to its physical form. This would typically include its size, the number of its pages, or its type of binding.

The *identifying description* of a book was related to its meaningful content. This would include the author's full name and birthdate (death date if deceased), the name of any co-author, illustrator, or translator, the work's title and subtitle, its publication and printing dates, its table of content and genre category, and a summary of its theme or plot. Sometimes additional information would be provided describing the significance of the work, such as published book reviews or literary awards received.

The *administrative description* of a book was related to the third aspect of information, the process of accessing the physical book. This might indicate whether it could be borrowed locally, or could be requested through interlibrary loan, or if it was located in the rare book room and could not be borrowed at all. The administrative description would also include its shelf location, or a notification that it was missing from the shelf.

Physical card catalogs were built to hold rectangles of cardstock paper five inches long and three inches wide. The story of the 3" × 5" card usually begins with Carl Linnaeus (1707–1778), the Swedish botanist and taxonomist who invented *binomial nomenclature*, the Latinized two-word naming system for biological species.[15] His system not only simplified the names of plants and animals, it also created the hierarchical classification system that we still use today, which begins with kingdom and goes down through phylum to class, order, family, genus, and species.

When Linnaeus was collecting and cataloging butterflies, he used whatever slips of paper were near at hand to take notes about his specimens, and to sort them by their various characteristics. He didn't invent this practice. Two centuries earlier, the Swiss naturalist Conrad Gessner had used paper slips to organize his notes as he created his 1545 *Bibliotheca universalis*.

Linnaeus's innovation was to standardize the size of his slips by employing playing cards. In that era, the backs of playing cards were blank, so people used them for sundry purposes. Eventually standardized into the 3" × 5" light card stock that is familiar to us now, this powerful, low-tech information technology has been used for more than two and a half centuries to classify everything in the world.

The first physical card catalog was created in 1780 by Dutch-born Austrian librarian Gottfried van Swieten (1733–1803).[16] By the 19th century, "index cards" had been fully adopted by cataloging librarians. *Dewey Decimal Classification* (DDC), usually referred to as the "Dewey Decimal System," was developed in the late 19th and early 20th centuries. It established the systematic use of index cards and provided a standardized template for the classification of library holdings. Named after Melvil Dewey (1851–1931), who first proposed the system in 1876, it was developed and amended by generations of librarians, and would eventually spread to libraries around the world

Dewey's legacy has been tarnished in recent years, following a collective reassessment of his behavior and character. It was an open secret during his lifetime that he was a serial sexual harasser, engaging in unwanted touching and kissing of subordinate women. He was also criticized for racially segregating the private resort that he owned and ran with his wife in the Adirondacks in New York. They disallowed the membership of racial minorities and Jews, and once refused entry even to the renowned African-American educator, Booker T. Washington. Segregation was not illegal, but it did not reflect the values of the American Library Association (ALA). The scandals accumulated, and Dewey was eventually dismissed as a New York City librarian, and his membership in the ALA was revoked.[17]

After his death, Dewey's official biographies sanitized these aspects of his character and career. It wasn't until 2019, during the #MeToo movement, that his name was removed from the Melvil Dewey medal awarded annually by the ALA, 100 years after they had first censured him.[18]

The second half of the 19th century was an exciting time for women who were able to pursue professional training as catalogers and librarians, during a period when there were few other fields open to them. Many young women trained by Dewey went on to have remarkable careers. One of the most well-known was Katherine Sharp (1865–1914), who in 1897 founded and directed the Library School at the University of Illinois as well as directing the University Library. As the story goes, when Dewey was asked to provide names of some men who might be able to take up the challenging position in Illinois, he replied that the best man for the job was a woman; and that woman was Katherine Sharp. Sharp was responsible for training a generation of women who subsequently "went West" to jobs in public and academic libraries across the United States in the early 20th century, taking the DDC with them.[19]

The opportunities offered to white women in the library profession were also available to other women, though limited by the same stratifications and prejudices that affected their ability to rise in other sectors of society. Black women in the field of Library Science in the United States made significant contributions to the institutions and communities in which they lived and worked.

Vivian Harsh (1880–1960), the first Black woman to be a credentialed librarian in Chicago, developed an important archival collection related to the African American experience in that city. Naomi Willie Pollard Dobson (1883–1971), the first Black woman to graduate from Northwestern University in 1905, served as head librarian of Wilberforce College, where she also served as the director of its Library Science program, and was an active civic leader.[20] Historically Black Colleges were instrumental in supporting and training Black librarians during the first half of the 20th century.

## CLASSIFICATION SYSTEMS

The Dewey Decimal system standardized the practice of assigning a four-part code to every work in a library collection. The most important part of that code is the identifying number, created by matching a book's content to the closest matching subject categories and subcategories. The system classifies all human knowledge into only ten categories:

000 Computer science, information & general works
100 Philosophy and psychology
200 Religion
300 Social sciences

400 Language
500 Science
600 Technology
700 Arts and recreation
800 Literature
900 History and geography

Each of these ten categories has ten subcategories, and those ten subcategories have subcategories. Beyond this level, additional decimals can be added as the categories become more specific. There is (theoretically) no limit to how many subcategories could be added to classify a given work. The system gave early catalogers the power to classify any domain of knowledge with extraordinary specificity.

In the DDS, the *Call Number* is the code that allows it to be shelved correctly and found when needed. It is composed of four parts: Size Designation, Dewey Decimal Number, Cutter Number, and Work Mark. The *Size Designation* is a technical description, which is used to indicate a physically oversized book. The letter F (standing for *Folio*) or the letter Q (for *Quarto*) will begin the code if the book is a standard Folio size of 12" × 19," or a Quarto, measuring 9.5" × 12."

The *Work Mark*, which comes at the end, is another optional designation. It is an administrative description which ensures that multiple copies of the same book will have a unique identifying number, (the first, second, or third copy, and so on). Between the Size Designation and the Work Mark are the Dewey Decimal number and the Cutter Number; both provide identifying descriptions. The Dewey Decimal number encodes the book's subject matter with as much specificity as is needed.

The *Cutter Number* encodes the author of the work, and was named after the man who devised it, Charles Ammi Cutter (1837–1903). Like Dewey, Cutter was an early and influential librarian, as well as a founding member of the ALA, but the two men had very different personalities and professional ambitions. Cutter criticized Dewey's system, wanting a more flexible classification system that could be tailored to different-sized collections.

Cutter was part of a group of American librarians who were engaged in developing cataloging standards. The group also included Charles Coffin Jewett (1816–1868), Librarian of the Smithsonian Institution and Superintendent of the Boston Public Museum. They collaborated with cataloging librarians in the U.K. and Ireland, including Antonio Panizzi (1797–1879), principal librarian from 1856 to 1866 at the British Museum (which also served as the national library). The Library Association of the United Kingdom (created in 1877) worked together with the ALA to form an Anglo-American cataloging alliance, which was codified in 1906.[21]

Cutter anticipated the growth of community-based public libraries and the activities that would continue to shape them through the 20th century into the 21st. He believed people should be able to wander freely in public libraries, browsing the shelves by category, to find books of interest. He insisted that children should be welcome and that their art should hang on library walls. Cutter is responsible for the card pouches we may find on the inside of library books that held cards marked with their due dates. He is credited with producing the first public card catalog. He also invented inter-library loan and the practice of home delivery of library books, being particularly concerned with the accessibility of library collections.[22]

In 1868 Cutter was named Librarian at the Boston Athenaeum. In an essay he penned in 1883, he mused about what his library might become after the passage of a century:

> Our library is not a mere cemetery of dead books, but a living power, which supplies amusement for dull times, recreation for the tired, information for the curious, inspires the love of research in youth, and furnishes the materials for it in mature age, enables and induces the scholar not to let his study end with his school days...Its mottos are always "plus ultra" and "excelsior."[23]

In the essay, "The Buffalo Public Library in 1983," he glimpsed the information future that dawned with the digital age—he was reaching towards future technologies that would allow information to be retrieved with greater speed and accuracy:

> The desks had every convenience that could facilitate study; but what most caught my eye was a little key-board at each, connected by a wire

with the librarian's desk. The reader had only to find the mark of his book in the catalog, touch a few lettered or numbered keys, and on the instant a runner at the central desk started for the volume and, appearing after an astonishingly short interval at the door nearest his desk, brought him his book and took his acknowledgment without disturbing any of the neighboring readers.[24]

Cutter died at 66 without finishing his system, which had been eclipsed by DDC. But it was Cutter's approach, *Expansive Classification*, which became the basis for the Library of Congress classification system. It had 20 broad categories, and one general category, in contrast to DDC's ten. Cutter eventually developed seven expanding versions of the system, tailored to libraries of different sizes. He published guides to the first six of these but died before completing the seventh.[25]

Julia Pettee (1872–1967) was another significant figure in the history of cataloging. She was trained at the Pratt Institute, a private college in Brooklyn, New York, the third of the important early library training institutions in the U.S. after Albany and the University of Illinois. In her autobiography, Pettee tells a story about the low standards for cataloging that existed in the University of Philadelphia library when she arrived, and how difficult that made her job. She complains of "the misery of being told to do things your own judgment refused to sanction" and provides an illustration:

The subject headings given by other people form a continual sore point. I have a spasm nearly when I have to write a subject card headed *aleta xylantia* for a two-page analytical for some obscure butterfly no one ever heard of but once and never will again. They scatter their butterflies under 1104 possible headings throughout the catalogue.[26]

Moving on from this unhappy position, Pettee was to serve for 30 years as head cataloger for the Union Theological Library in New York City, where she developed a hybrid system for the cataloging of theological writing. *Union Classification*, as she named it, dispensed with the aspects of Dewey's system that she found unworkable for cataloging religious documents, made additionally complex because authorship of historical religious texts was often obscure or entirely lacking.[27]

Pettee spent most of her career working in a theological library, one example of what is termed a *Special Library*, a collection that is not intended to be complete across all areas of human inquiry, but serves a narrowly defined community of interest, like law, or medicine, local history, or children's books. Special libraries must be responsive to the changing needs of the community that makes use of their collection.

Julia Pettee advised her fellow catalogers that they must create classification standards that are flexible enough to change as society changes: "The best that a book classification can do," she said, "is to plan its outline with an eye prophetic, so that it will serve the coming as well as the present generation; and then to provide, by a flexible notation, for inevitable future readjustments."[28]

Pettee helped to professionalize the field of cataloging by publishing subject headings, inviting feedback and debate among catalogers and librarians. Her careful, collaborative approach raised the profile of cataloging as scholarly work, requiring broad knowledge and specialized training.

Working a generation later, Mary "Paul" Pollard (1922–2005), librarian at the Library of Trinity College Dublin, made similar contributions in a different domain—the cataloging of early printed books.[29] She was a specialist in early children's literature, but was also a collector; at her death she left more than 11,500 pre-1914 children's books to the Trinity College Library, along with her documenting notebooks.[30]

The professional growth of cataloging, inspired by the needs of special library collections, coincided with the *documentation movement* taking place in Europe. One of the best-known figures in this movement was a Belgian lawyer named Paul Otlet (1868–1944). Inspired but also frustrated by the Dewey Decimal system's focus on books, Otlet developed *Universal Decimal Classification* (UDC) which could handle many kinds of media: photographs, videos, advertisements, brochures, letters, and miscellaneous ephemera.[31]

Setting out with the goal to catalog everything published in the world, he called his cataloging project the *Répertoire Bibliographique Universel* (Universal Bibliographic Repertory). He made use of hundreds of thousands (and eventually millions) of index cards. Otlet's staff functioned as an "analog search engine," answering queries from people around the world by letter or telegraph, after searching for and locating answers in their indexed collections.[32]

Otlet's partner in many of his visionary endeavors was Henri La Fontaine (1854–1943), a Belgian lawyer, peace activist, and feminist whose Nobel Peace Prize in 1913 funded some of their projects. In collaboration with futurists and architects, they began to organize a networked alliance between international organizations that were working towards similar goals. They gathered cultural artifacts as well, storing, and curating them in a 150-room museum they named the *Palais Mondial*. Convinced that universal access to information was the key to world peace, Otlet and La Fontaine were actively engaged with the League of Nations, organized after World War I to work toward global cooperation. They named their larger project, which encompassed the classification system, their physical collections, their network of organizations, and their futuristic aspirations, the *Mundaneum*.[33]

In the generation following Paul Otlet, Suzanne Briet (1894–1989), a French librarian at the *Bibliothèque Nationale* (the National Library of France) helped to professionalize the field of documentation in Europe. She was the founding director of the *Union Française des Organismes de Documentation*, the French equivalent of the American Documentation Institute, which would later become the Association for Information Science and Technology (ASIS&T). After a visit to the United States, Briet recognized that the specialized cataloging work happening in special libraries was similar to what was happening in Europe in the field of documentation. She saw no need to merge the professions of librarianship and documentation, nor to formally separate them.[34]

Expanding on Otlet's treatment of non-textual materials as documents, Briet's classic article, "What is Documentation?" has become a foundational text in information science. It explains that anything that conveys information can be understood to be a document. As an example, Briet asks the reader to imagine a previously uncatalogued species of antelope captured in Africa and brought to Europe. The antelope in the wild is not a document; but as soon as it has begun to be observed, analyzed, cataloged, and put on display, documents begin proliferating: text descriptions, publications from those descriptions, reprints, and translations of the publications some of which have photographs that are then reprinted in newspapers and magazine articles, which in turn are microfilmed. When the antelope dies, it may even be stuffed and put on display in a museum, completing its final transformation from animal to document.[35] Briet brought both humanistic insights and theoretical frameworks from the social sciences to the professional field of documentation.[36]

## CLASSIFYING INFORMATION IN CONTEXT

Jorge Luis Borges was well aware of the work of Paul Otlet; some of his short stories must be read as a commentary on what was happening in the early documentation movement. Ironically, while *The Library of Babel* underscored the importance of an index to search a collection, he was also skeptical of the project of classification needed to make one. In "The Analytical Language of John Wilkins," Borges discusses the real-life 17th-century Anglican clergyman and Oxford professor who attempted to create a universal language, using a logical numerical system. Borges makes fun of Wilkins by comparing his efforts to a book, supposedly entitled *Celestial Empire of Benevolent Knowledge* (but in fact wholly imaginary) which was translated by Franz Kuhn, an actual German translator of Chinese. Borges tells us that in this encyclopedia, animals are divided into these categories:

(a) belonging to the emperor, (b) embalmed, (c) tame, (d) sucking pigs, (e) sirens, (f) fabulous, (g) stray dogs, (h) included in the present classification, (i) frenzied, (j) innumerable, (k) drawn with a very fine camelhair brush, (l) et cetera, (m) having just broken the water pitcher, (n) that from a long way off look like flies.[37]

Since the story was first published, some readers periodically have believed that the *Celestial Empire of Benevolent Knowledge* and its list really existed, though it was meant to be absurd. Borges reveals in the story that the real target of his criticism is the "Bibliographic Institute of Brussels," which is to say Paul Otlet, whose classification systems seem to be just as arbitrary as Wilkins's numerical language, or that of the imagined Chinese encyclopedia. Borges concludes by saying that it is not possible to come up with a classification system that is not arbitrary. The reason for this, he says, is very simple: "we do not know what thing the universe is."[38]

This is a very old human insight. The founder of Taoism, Lao Tse, said that "the name that can be named is not the eternal name."[39] The moment we give a name to something, information is lost. After we name something, we can classify it, which moves it even further from what it was in and of itself: the antelope before it becomes a document.

When catalogers classify documents, they are ordering the world, and everything in it. They do this when they decide what subject headings to use, and also when they criticize those categories and propose others. When Julia Pettee went to work in the library of the Rochester Theological Seminary, before being hired as head cataloger at Union Theological Seminary in New York City, she discovered that "women" were classified in a category labeled "Minor Morals":

> Men have never known what to do with women. These theologians had an idea. They considered women a moral problem. And, as women were not very great consequence anyway, they fitted very well under the caption "Minor Morals." And actually on the shelves here at Union under "minor Morals" were these topics, in this order: first came Profanity; then came Drunkenness; Drunkenness was followed by Lotteries; Lotteries was followed by Women, and after Women came Dueling. The whole series of Minor Morals was climaxed by: War.[40]

This may seem an outlying example, but classification systems cannot avoid bias, since they emerge from within particular historical and social contexts.

The *Library of Congress Subject Headings* (LCSH) are used not only in the U.S. Library of Congress, but in libraries across the English-speaking world, as well as nations that use English as a second or common language.[41] The words used as subject headings were meant to be easy to understand by the "average" users of the information, and it's not hard to imagine who that means. Beginning in 1802 when the first Librarian of Congress, John Beckley, was appointed by Thomas Jefferson, everyone who held the position was a white man until David Mao was appointed by President Barack Obama as Acting Librarian in 2015, the first Asian-American

Librarian of Congress. In 2016, Carla Hayden became both the first woman and the first African-American Librarian of Congress.

When Librarian Sanford Berman published his famous 1971 article, "Prejudices and Antipathies: A Tract on the LC Subject Heads Concerning People," he unearthed the following subject headings: "Sexual perversion—see also Homosexuality" and "Child Nurses—see also Mammies." Lynching was listed as a form of "Criminal Justice," and Roma, referred to in the headings as "Gipsies," were classified with "Vagabonds and Rogues."[42]

Following the publication of Berman's article and the attention it brought to problems in the LCSH, "Epilepsy" was removed as a cross-listing for "Idiocy," which was changed to "Mental Retardation."[43] This term was changed again later—the work of categorizing is never done. What appears (to some) in a given generation to be an acceptable sorting of the world becomes unacceptable, even to the mainstream public, in the next.

Critical librarians who study cataloging from a social justice perspective have explored the history of how LGBTQ+ people have been classified and categorized over time, and how these processes have engaged (or not) with changing terms referring to sexual orientation and gender identity. The LCSH have in the past reflected: psychiatric diagnostic categories, rejections of those diagnoses, stereotypes, updated stereotypes, and, more recently and more slowly, reflections of how LGBTQ+ individuals and communities understand themselves. Another, deeper, problem is that hierarchical classification systems are not well-suited to non-binary, non-linear, or fluid conceptualizations or identities.[44]

The term *radical cataloging* emerged in the early 21st century to describe a suite of issues, including the inherent hierarchical nature of classification, the challenges associated with the LCSH, and the use of cataloging as a kind of activism.[45] Changes in the LCSH happen, but they can come slowly, and inconsistently. They can also be politicized. A coalition of advocacy groups in 2015–2016 lobbied to replace the LCSH terms "Illegal Aliens" and "Illegal Immigration" with "Noncitizens" and "Unauthorized Immigration." Shortly after the decision was made to effect the change, conservative members of the U.S. Congress got wind of it. They added a provision to an appropriations bill that put limitations on the Library of Congress, preventing them from using language in the LCSH which was different from that used in the U.S. legal code.

The provision wasn't enacted, but to give some sense what a step backward this would have been, while the LCSH had ceased using the terms "Negro" and "Oriental" in 1975, the U.S. legal code contained these words until 2016.[46] The Library of Congress decided not to go forward with the change, given the politicized climate, to the frustration of the scholars and activists who had lobbied for it. It wasn't until November 2021 that the Policy and Standards Division of the Library of Congress, which maintains Library of Congress Subject Headings, announced that they would replace "Aliens" and "Illegal Aliens" with "Noncitizens" and "Illegal Immigration." The decision to retain the term "illegal" rather than using less-stigmatizing words like "unauthorized" or "undocumented" was met with another round of disappointment and critique.[47]

It has been argued that the work of cataloging can be emancipatory as well as narrowing.[48] But transformative change requires a collective acceptance of responsibility and oversight for the frameworks used to classify and sort the world, especially if the goal is to make information universally accessible.

Among the earliest and most important 20th-century critics of cataloging was librarian and bibliographer Dorothy B. Porter Wesley (1905–1995). Wesley was the first African-American to earn a Master of Science in Library Science degree from Columbia University. She served as the Chief Librarian of Howard University from 1930 until 1973, during which time she facilitated the development of an internationally recognized collection of works related to global Black history and culture.

When first tasked with cataloging Howard's collections, she found Dewey Decimal Classification wholly inadequate. It provided only two numbers under which everything about or authored by an African-American, from poetry to sermons to historical study was supposed to fit: the choices were "colonialism" or "slavery." The literature in the collections was so rich and varied that it needed to be classified across all possible categories of human knowledge, experience, and expression.[49] By facilitating the creation of a system that evaded racist stereotypes, Wesley challenged the biased and Eurocentric ontology at the heart of the DDS system, creating instead what has been described as a "catalog of Black Imaginaries," a classification that reflected how Black people understood themselves in relationship to the world.[50]

## NOTES

1  N. Kıvılcım Yavuz, "Hernando Colón's Book of Books: AM 377 fol.," https://nkyavuz.com/blog/ams-am-377-fol/. Retrieved 17 May 2022.
2  "Christopher Columbus' Son Had an Enormous Library. Its Catalog Was Just Found," *All Things Considered*, National Public Radio, 24 April 2019.
3  Sharon Hill, "U of W Prof Gets 'Indiana Jones Feeling' with Discovery of Historic Manuscript," *Windsor Star*, 12 April 2019.
4  "The Book of Books: Hernando Colón's Libro de los Epítomes," Department of Nordic Studies and Linguistics, University of Copenhagen, https://nors.ku.dk/english/research/arnamagnaean/the-book-of-books /e. Retrieved 17 May 2022.
5  José María Pérez Fernández and Edward Wilson-Lee, *Hernando Colon's New World of Books: Toward a Cartography of Knowledge* (New Haven, CT: Yale University Press, 2021).
6  Andras Riedlmayer, "Erasing the Past: The Destruction of Libraries and Archives in Bosnia-Herzegovina," *Review of Middle East Studies* 29, no. 1 (1995): 7–11.
7  Yavuz, "Book of Books."
8  Lionel Casson, *Libraries in the Ancient World* (New Haven, CT: Yale University Press, 2001): 3.
9  Ibid., 4.
10  Casson, *Libraries*, pp. 39–40.
11  Ann M. Blair, *Too Much to Know* (New Haven, CT: Yale University Press, 2010): 201.
12  Casson, *Libraries*: 39f, 13f.
13  Max Jakob Fölster, "Libraries and Archives in the Former Han Dynasty (206 BCE–9 CE): Arguing for a Distinction," in *Manuscripts and Archives: Comparative Views on Record-Keeping*, eds. Sabine Kienitz, Michael Friedrich, Christian Brockmann and Alessandro Bausi (Berlin: de Gruyter, 2018): 201.
14  Ibid., 206–207
15  Daniela Blei, "How the Index Card Cataloged the World," *The Atlantic*, 1 December 2017.
16  Bernhard Rieder, *Engines of Order: A Mechanology of Algorithmic Techniques* (Amsterdam: Amsterdam University Press, 2020): 151.
17  Anne Ford, "Bringing Harassment Out of the History Books," *American Libraries* 49, no. 6 (2018): 48–53.
18  Wayne A. Wiegand, "Sanitizing American Library History: Reflections of a Library Historian." *The Library Quarterly* 90, no. 2 (2020): 108–120.

19  Walter C. Allen and Robert F. Delzell, *Ideals and Standards: The History of the University of Illinois Graduate School of Library and Information Science, 1893–1993* (Champaign, IL: The Graduate School of Library and Information Science, University of Illinois at Urbana-Champaign, 1992).

20  LaVerne Gray, "Naomi Willie Pollard Dobson: A Pioneering Black Librarian," *Libraries: Culture, History, and Society* 6, no. 1 (2022): 1–20.

21  Virgil L. P. Blake, "Forging the Anglo-American Cataloging Alliance: Descriptive Cataloging, 1830–1908," *Cataloging & Classification Quarterly* 35, no. 1–2 (2002): 3–22.

22  Pip Stromgren, "Charles Ammi Cutter: Library Systematizer Extraordinaire," *Daily Hampshire Gazette*, 26 June 2004, https://forbeslibrary.org/info/library-history/charles-ammi-cutter/.

23  Charles Ammi Cutter, "The Buffalo Public Library in 1983," *Papers and Proceedings of the Sixth General Meeting of the American Library Association, Held at Buffalo, August 14 to 17, 1883* (Boston, MA: Press of Rockwell and Churchill, 1883): 49–55.

24  Ibid.

25  Charles Ammi Cutter, *Expansive Classification: Part I: The First Six Classifications* (Boston, MA: C. A. Cutter, 1891–93).

26  Christopher Walker and Ann Copeland, "The Eye Prophetic: Julia Pettee," *Libraries & The Cultural Record* 44, no. 2 (2009): 166.

27  Julia Pettee, "The Development of Authorship Entry and the Formulation of Authorship Rules as Found in the Anglo-American Code," *The Library Quarterly* 6, no. 3 (1936): 270–290.

28  Julia Pettee, "A Classification for a Theological Library," *Library Journal* 36 (2011): 623; cited by Walker and Copeland, "The Eye Prophetic: Julia Pettee."

29  David McKitterick, "That Woman! Studies in Irish Bibliography: A Festschrift for Mary Paul Pollard," *The Library: The Transactions of the Bibliographical Society* 7, no. 2 (2006): 210–211.

30  In 2018 the Pollard Collection of Children's Books was digitized by the Department of Early Printed Books & Special Collections. "Pollard Collection of Children's Books Now Fully Available for Online Searching!" *The Library of Trinity College Dublin News & Alerts*, 19 February 2018. https://www.tcd.ie/library/news/pollard-collection-of-childrens-books-now-fully-available-for-online-searching/.

31  Michael K. Buckland, "Information Retrieval of More than Text," *Journal of the American Society for Information Science* 42, no. 8 (1991): 586–588.

32  Alex Wright, "The Web Time Forgot," *New York Times*, 17 June 2008. See also *The Man Who Wanted to Classify the World*, directed by Francoise Levie (New York: Filmakers Library, 2004).

33  See Alex Wright, *Cataloging the World: Paul Otlet and the Birth of the Information Age* (Oxford: Oxford University Press, 2014); and W. Boyd Rayward, "Knowledge Organisation and a New World Polity: The Rise and Fall and Rise of the Ideas of Paul Otlet," *Transnational Associations* 55, no. 1–2 (2003): 4–15.

34 Mary Niles Maack, "The Lady and the Antelope: Suzanne Briet's Contribution to the French Documentation Movement," *Library Trends* 52, no. 4 (2004): 737.

35 Suzanne Briet and Laurent Martinet, *What Is Documentation?: English Translation of the Classic French Text* (Lanham, MD: Scarecrow Press, 2006).

36 Michael Buckland, "A Brief Biography of Suzanne Renée Briet," *Science* 42, no. 5 (1991): 351–360.

37 Jorge Luis Borges, "The Analytical Language of John Wilkins," *Other Inquisitions* 1952 (1937): 103, https://ccrma.stanford.edu/courses/155/assignment/ex1/Borges.pdf.

38 Ibid., 104.

39 Paul J. Lin, *A Translation of Lao-tzu's Tao Te Ching and Wang Pi's Commentary* (Ann Arbor, MI: University of Michigan Press, 2020).

40 Walker and Copeland, "Eye Prophetic," 169.

41 Hope A. Olson, "Difference, Culture and Change: The Untapped Potential of LCSH," *Cataloging & Classification Quarterly* 29, no. 1–2 (2000): 54–55.

42 Sanford Berman, *Prejudices and Antipathies: A Tract on the LC Subject Heads Concerning People* (Metuchen, NJ: Scarecrow Press, 1971).

43 Steven A. Knowlton, "Three Decades since Prejudices and Antipathies: A Study of Changes in the Library of Congress Subject Headings," *Cataloging & Classification Quarterly* 40, no. 2 (2005): 123–145.

44 K. R. Roberto, "Inflexible Bodies: Metadata for Transgender Identities," *Journal of Information Ethics* 20, no. 2 (2011): 56.

45 Heather Lember, Suzanne Lipkin, and Richard Jung Lee. "Radical Cataloging: From Words to Action," *Urban Library Journal* 19, no. 1 (2013): 7.

46 "ARLIS/NA Statement on Removal of Library of Congress—Illegal Aliens—Subject Headings," *Art Libraries Association of North America*, 21 January 2022.

47 Jill E. Baron and Tina Gross, "Sorrow, Fury, Helplessness, and Cynicism: An Account of the Library of Congress Subject Heading 'Illegal Aliens,'" in *Borders and Belonging: Critical Examinations of Library Approaches toward Immigrants*, ed. Ana Ndumu (Sacramento, CA: Library Juice Press, 2021).

48 Olson, "Difference," 69.

49 Zita Cristina Nunes, "Remembering the Howard University Librarian Who Decolonized the Way Books Were Catalogued," *The Smithsonian Magazine*, 26 November 2018.

50 Laura E. Helton, "On Decimals, Catalogs, and Racial Imaginaries of Reading," *PMLA* 134, no. 1 (2019): 105.

# 3

# ORGANIZING INFORMATION

The Whanganui river on the North Island of New Zealand is a legal person under the law. The relationship between the Whanganui Māori tribe and the river that bears their name is estimated to be at least 800 years old. The tribe began their fight for its protection nearly a century ago, the longest-running litigation in New Zealand's history. The Whanganui Māori view the river as inseparable from themselves, a belief expressed in the saying *Ko au te awa. Ko te awa ko au* ("I am the river. The river is me").[1] The practical result of the 2017 legal ruling is that if the state wants to take action that affects the river, they have to ask the tribe. This is not because the tribe *owns* the river but because, in the tribe's view, they are its kin.[2]

A decade earlier, Ecuador became the first nation to put into its constitution recognition of the rights of "nature." The amendment that established the rights of *Pachamama* not to suffer "the extinction of species, the destruction of ecosystems and the permanent alteration of natural cycles" was approved in 2008.[3] Mexico, Bolivia, Brazil, Columbia, and Panama followed Ecuador in establishing rights for natural areas. Uganda is the first African country to do so, granting nature the right "to exist, persist, maintain and regenerate its vital cycles, structure, functions and its processes in evolution," and giving Ugandan citizens the authority to sue for infringement of these rights.[4]

DOI: 10.4324/9781003155119-3

After New Zealand, the nations of Bangladesh, India, and Canada granted personhood to rivers. In Canada this was the Magpie River in Eastern Quebec, known as *Muteshekau-shipu* in the language of the Innu people, who consider the river sacred. It was granted nine separate rights under Canadian law.[5] In 2020 the Menominee Indian Tribe of Wisconsin recognized the rights of the Menominee River, joining other native tribes in the U.S. which have given legal protection to nature within their sovereign territories as well.[6]

The legal arguments supporting personhood for non-humans can be traced back to a 1972 article, "Should Trees Have Standing," by American law professor Christopher Stone.[7] The paper explored the legal and practical implications of granting rights to nature— for example, to whom would corporations pay damages, and how would costs be calculated?[8] In the conclusion of the paper, Stone asserts that the protection of nature requires "a radical new theory or myth—felt as well as intellectualized—of man's relationships to the rest of nature." In other words, the problem was framed, from its beginning, as an ontological one, an issue of how human beings sort the world.[9]

Epistemologies (ways of knowing and understanding the world), and ontologies (ways of classifying the world) are tied to one another. Epistemological understandings lead to different ontologies, because how human beings *classify* the world is necessarily shaped by assumptions about *the nature of* the world.

Rather than viewing humans to be distinct from and higher than other creatures within a hierarchy of importance and power, a view predominating across our planet today, many indigenous peoples consider human beings to be just another part of the planet, a relative in need of lessons the earth provides.[10] Rather than believing that only humans *create* knowledge (achieved through classificatory scientific study and modeling of the natural world), indigenous people may view knowledge as a gift to humans from plants, animals, wind, and water, making little distinction between "living" and "non-living" things.[11] Regarding the earth's resources, what the predominant worldview judges to be property, indigenous people may understand as a common good to be shared, with relationality between humans and the earth leading to responsibility of humans for the earth.[12]

The legal conflict between the Māori tribe and the government of New Zealand took almost a century to resolve, because they could not align their incompatible ontologies.[13] Granting legal personhood to the river provided a workaround that didn't require any resolution of the deeper differences. It acknowledges the Māori worldview and *mātauranga Māori* (a modern Māori term used to describe Māori traditional knowledge), without having to accept Māori cultural values. By granting the river a privileged place within the Western hierarchical ontology, it reclassifies the river, removing it from the category of *things that can be owned by people* (which have no rights under the law), and putting it into the category of *persons* (who do have such rights).

*Indigenous knowledge* is a term that refers to the cultural beliefs, languages, and practices of indigenous people across the planet. The gulf is wide between the leaders of environmental protection movements, who come from indigenous communities and whose epistemologies and ontologies lend themselves to environmental preservation, and the national and international corporations who use Western values to justify the destruction of environments and the extinction of species. Indigenous people looking at the West criticize it for valuing non-humans only to the extent that they serve or are profitable to humans. The fight over water governance has become a flashpoint in North America in conflicts over oil pipelines that endanger waterways.[14]

There is nothing eternal or inevitable about epistemologies. Western cultural traditions have included alternative ways of knowing which were historically displaced or lost. "Wood libraries" for example, created in the 18th and 19th centuries, were buildings that housed collections of preserved specimens from trees—including bark, seed, flowers, and fruit—which had been crafted in the shape of books, with all the specimen parts inside. The approach to studying and *knowing* about trees and forests through direct experience of it, as exemplified by wood libraries, provides a contrast to prevailing taxonomic ways of creating scientific knowledge, which keep humans artificially separate from, and above, the nature that they study.[15]

Information science is interested in studying and understanding how different knowledge systems impact the ways in which information is created, understood, classified, analyzed, and applied in the world. These questions are pertinent to multiple domains and challenges, including environmental sustainability and social justice. They are also important to consider because information professionals are tasked with the ontological work of sorting the world.

This chapter begins with an exploration of knowledge organization as an area of professional practice. It surveys a variety of tools used, including documentary language and metadata of many kinds, before returning to the consideration of indigenous knowledge and the context of organizing information.

## KNOWLEDGE ORGANIZATION

There are many ways to organize the world and the things that are in it. Imagine that someone is tasked with sorting a tiger, a cup of coffee, a tennis match, and an earthquake into two groups. They might consider the *attributes* that the four items possess: size, color, shape, condition, existence, edibility, tangibility, function, temporal state, and so on. But let's say the classifier remembers having once made the mistake of resting their coffee on a toppling pile of papers, which reminds them of another occasion when they tried to play tennis on un-mowed grass. This personal association suggests this category for sorting: "requiring a flat surface for best results" which groups the coffee cup with the tennis match. The tiger and the earthquake correspondingly share the attribute of "being unbothered by uneven surfaces." This works to sort these four things, but it isn't likely to be useful at scale.

If the items are instead classified by *type*, reflecting the kind of thing they are, the tiger might end up grouped with the earthquake because they are both "nature-related" and the cup with the tennis match because they are "human-related." The classifier wouldn't necessarily recognize that this classification reflects a prevailing worldview that sees humans as something apart from nature. Our cultural and personal beliefs about the nature of the world, and the relationships between the things that are in it, can operate upon us without our being aware of it, a phenomenon known as unconscious bias.[16]

Technical, identifying, and administrative descriptions corresponding to form, content, and process of information are used to catalog and index documents of all kinds. Libraries may sort their physical collections differently at different points in time and for different reasons. They might separate magazines from books (a technical sort) or move young adult books away from children's books (an identifying sort), but they may place all of those items in a separate room together while they wait to be reshelved or to be sent back after an interlibrary loan (an administrative sort).

Online digital catalogs allow searchers to change the method of sorting with a single click, so that they can view a list of one author's works, or all works on a single topic, or all items intended for a particular audience. Much organizational and data collection work has gone on behind the scenes to make this quick and seamless sorting experience possible. Technical, identifying, and administrative descriptions of items in a collection are referred to collectively as *descriptive metadata*.

You will come across the term "metadata" defined as "data about information," but also as "data about data," or "information about information," or even "information about data." Sometimes the specific usage is a vain attempt to be precise, but in most cases the terms are being used synonymously. In an academic setting, distinguishing the two concepts is more important, because information is understood to hold meaningful content in ways that data does not. Data is derived *from* an information source, and it has the potential to *become* information again. Whether it will (or not) depends a lot on the quality of the organizing that preceded and followed its collection.

The International Organization for Standardization's Online Browsing Platform (ISO OBP), which is tasked with recognizing metadata standards, accepts widely different definitions for metadata listed within their accepted standards—by one count 46 definitions in 96 different standards.[17] Speaking generally, metadata provides context for information. But metadata is itself a kind of information, so it also has form, content, process, and context. Metadata can be sorted, classified, cataloged, and indexed, and metadata also *has* metadata—its own context—which might have metadata too. For example, bibliographies contain metadata about the collection of works that they describe. If a collection of several bibliographies was assembled, the names of the people who put it together would be metadata about that metadata. If there were a footnote attached to the names, indicating their institutional affiliations, that would be meta-meta-metadata.

A *knowledge organization system* (KOS) is the comprehensive organizational plan for the management of a collection (which might hold anything from artifacts in a public museum, to books in an academic library, to digital resources on a corporate website). There are a variety of approaches to knowledge organization, which may produce, for example, metadata classification systems, categorization schemes, or taxonomies.

The organizational work associated with KOS is done by information professionals within the long-standing and complex field of *knowledge organization* (KO). It involves, among other things, the practices of creating or selecting appropriate classification systems and finding aids, working with communities and clients to collect and understand the context of materials being collected, and then organizing the collection, producing metadata to facilitate search and retrieval.[18]

Knowledge organization as an active field within information science is broader and more eclectic than the tasks that it performs. It engages with theoretical issues surrounding classification within their sociocultural, political, and global contexts. It also explores the consequences of classifications within particular domains.

One paradigm for theorizing and improving classification work is *facet analysis*, which involves distinguishing the component parts, features of interest, or "facets," of a complex topic within a field of knowledge, which then become the basis for sorting a collection. These facets might be attributes, characteristics, or functions.[19] The roots of facet analysis can be traced to discontent with Dewey Decimal Classification in the early 20th century. The problems were addressed by Paul Otlet, who designed *Universal Decimal Classification* (UDC), Henry E. Bliss who developed *Bliss* or *Bibliographic Classification* (BC), and S. R. Ranganathan who created *Colon Classification* (CC). Ranganathan's system has been influential in the modern development of facet analysis, but it has also been robustly critiqued, including for its failure to acknowledge the earlier work of Otlet and the premises it borrowed from his classification system.[20]

In its application within knowledge organization, the structure of a faceted classification is distinguished from the technique of facet analysis. Together they constitute the *facet analytical approach.*[21] The approach has been applied in Online Public Access (OPAC) catalogs, which allow the public to access library services and collections. In an online search, for example, a faceted approach allows users to select attributes through a drop-down menu, and these choices will affect what they are shown next, narrowing their search interactively.[22] Because facet classification can improve the construction of syntactical structures, it has much to offer for the future of online search, which requires sophisticated vocabulary control, consistency, and interoperability across international borders.[23]

## DOCUMENTARY LANGUAGE

A wide variety of techniques can be employed to aid in the classification of information and its effective search and retrieval. Knowledge organization systems provide users with handles to facilitate the process, but searchers must first communicate their desires effectively, and the collection has to understand the queries accurately. *Documentary language* is a broad term used to describe a wide range of tools that help with these processes.

The most common technique in the documentary language toolkit is *notation*, which refers to the practice of identifying works using numbers or codes rather than words. Numbers or alphanumeric codes are preferable as identifiers, as it is easier to ensure that they will be unique. People's names function poorly as a way to identify individuals, in a dataset or in the world. Headlines on any given week will turn up stories of people who happen to have the same name as a criminal and are trolled and harassed as a result.

In one story that reached the international press, a 51-year-old Kashmiri farmer with no history of criminal activity was detained in Najaf, Iraq while on pilgrimage with a large tour group. He was taken into custody and imprisoned because his name appeared on an Interpol list. He and this other man who shared his name had been born in the same year as well. Despite evidence of his citizenship and place of birth presented by his anguished family (and the embarrassed tour agency, and the furious Indian embassy), it still took a month before they concluded that they had detained the wrong person, and he was released.[24]

Better channels of information between international and national investigative agencies would have helped the Kashmiri farmer, but we can also say their search lacked specificity. When searching collections, ambiguity is not a friend—nor are common misspellings, contradictory usages, synonyms, or language variations. These can all be dealt with through the use of *vocabulary control*, a technique of listing words understood by the system to ensure that users will find what they are looking for.

Accounting for synonyms and alternative language forms are also forms of vocabulary control. An American or Australian English language book that discusses water fountains would need to include in its index the word "bubbler" which is used in some parts of the United States and Australia. *Bubbler. See Water Fountain* would direct searchers of either term to the information they want. Of course, some people also call them "drinking fountains" (and other things), which might need to be accounted for as well. Redirection is good for more than synonyms and language variations; it can also chart paths between topics that are in relationship to one another.

In Flint, Michigan in 2019, local government mismanagement caused poor and mostly Black communities to receive unsafe water in their homes. If someone wanted to find out about that event, but they didn't remember the name of the town or state, they could be helped by a subject listing like this: "Water pollution, see also Flint, Michigan."

This technique, called *coordination*, links two or more elements together into one subject heading, in anticipation of what searchers are trying to find. If a chain of topics is defined while the index is being prepared, this is referred to as *pre-coordinated indexing*. The more complicated chain "Water pollution – Michigan – Flint – 2019 Water Crisis" provides the searcher with a path towards increasingly more specific information. Of course, it is also making a guess about users' interests. In 2019 that interest might well have been the events in Flint. A year and a half later, interest in "water crisis" might have been Covid-related. As this book was being written, a web search on "water crisis" brought up stories of drought across Africa, the Middle East, and South Asia. As it was being edited, what was in the headlines was flooding in Pakistan and unsafe water in the city of Jackson, Mississippi. How is an indexer to cope with the changing interests of searchers across time, and the unpredictability of social and environmental changes which shift the salience of associations between terms?

In contrast to pre-coordinated indexing as typically done in physical card catalogs and print indexes, more flexibility is provided by *post-coordinated indexing* (also called post-combination indexing), which began to be developed in the 1940s.[25] In this approach, chains of topics are not created in advance as single index entries; instead, different parts of complex topics are divided into several different headings. The practical effect is that searchers have to provide their own keywords, but they can input them in any order.

Online indexes have the advantage of being updated more easily and frequently than printed indexes can be, but they still may use either pre- or post-coordinated indexing. The Library of Congress has found several advantages in using pre-coordinated indexing: it allows for complicated syntax, provides richer context, and appears to enhance browsability.[26] Although post-coordinated indexing allows users' digital queries to follow many more search paths, that doesn't mean that a search using post-coordinated indexing will always be more successful.

What if, for example, a searcher is looking for information about the Flint, Michigan water crisis many years after it occurred, and doesn't remember the name of the city and state where it happened? Without the keyword "Flint" included in their search, they may receive irrelevant results. Post-coordinated indexing thus trades precision for flexibility. Increasingly, new approaches are using machine learning techniques to try to get beyond the dichotomous choice between pre- and post-coordination.[27]

## CLASSIFYING METADATA

The set of categories (the metadata terms) within a metadata classification system, along with the allowable values that can be assigned in each category, is called a *metadata schema*. A schema might become a *metadata standard* when it becomes so widely accepted and frequently used that it is formally adopted by the International Organization for Standardization (ISO), or another such organization, lending it professional credibility and increasing its popularity.[28] There are many different metadata standards in use, and new schema are in development all the time.

A Knowledge Organization System for a collection must decide which existing metadata standards are most appropriate for the information in the collection being organized, or whether it will be necessary to create a new schema that can be tailored more exactly for its needs. There are so many standards, and so many kinds of standards, that it can be difficult to decide which is best.

The simplest classification of metadata divides all its kinds into four broad types: descriptive metadata, administrative metadata, structural metadata, and markup languages. Descriptive metadata is used in information classification and search. Administrative metadata might be technical, having to do with decoding in digital files; it might relate to preservation for long-term management; or it might address issues of intellectual property rights. Structural metadata specifies the attributes, internal structure and relationship *between parts* of a digital object (for example, the length and order of pages), as well as the external structure and relationship *between digital objects* (for example, the file size and series order of a set of documents). Markup languages integrate metadata into text documents, to identify their components, control their formatting, and facilitate their use.[29]

Metadata has also been productively classified by analyzing its domain and community on one hand, and its purpose and function on the other. Metadata domain and metadata community both pertain to the *kinds of information* being organized and where that information is held. In contrast, metadata function and purpose pertain to the *kinds of metadata* that are needed to organize the information.[30]

More specifically, a *metadata domain* reflects the kind of information held in a collection that needs to be sorted and curated: musical scores, films, datasets, and pottery all need their own specific meta–data standards. A *metadata community* refers to the physical (or digital) place where a particular kind of collection is held. The Assyrian Collection in the British Museum in London is a different kind of metadata community from the Louvre in Paris, which is different from the Winter Palace of the Bogd Khan in Ulaanbaatar, Mongolia, and different again from the Kite Museum in Ahmedabad, India or the Star Trek Original Series Set in Ticonderoga, New York. Certain metadata standards work best for one or another community, which reflect the kinds of information contained in their collections (cuneiform tablets, works of art, historical premises and their domestic artifacts, kites, or television sets and props). Each metadata domain collected in a particular metadata community is described through appropriate metadata standards, which won't work to describe other collections within other communities, because they have been developed specifically for their domain.

*Metadata function* refers to the specific tasks that the meta-data is being used for. A mark-up language, which might attach metadata to fragments of digital text in order to distinguish headings from paragraphs, is functionally different from a controlled vocabulary, which provides a list of terms that limit the choices for keywords in order to optimize a search.[31] *Metadata purpose*, is less about the specific task that is being accomplished than about the broader goals being served—its "higher" purpose, so to speak. The standards needed for "Rights Metadata" used in keeping track of copyright information, as part of its service to the Law. This is different from what is needed for "Preservation Metadata," which records a document's preservation history *after* being collected and archived; in service, we might say, to History.

The best-known descriptive metadata standard is the *Dublin Core*. The name does not refer to the Irish city, but to a town in the state of Ohio in the U.S., where the Online Computer Library Center in Dublin in collaboration with the National Center for Supercomputing Applications (NCSA) at the University of Illinois, hosted a meeting of information scientists to talk about metadata for the web. NCSA had just released *Mosaic*, the first application for the World Wide Web that could display more than one file at a time, including both texts and images. The problem is that much of the information being passed across the web, including websites themselves, lacked adequate or systematic metadata, which prevented the development of effective search engines.[32]

Although it took years to create a stable, standardized set of metadata standards, the basic principles of the Dublin Core were hammered out in Dublin, Ohio in 1995. The first metadata categories included in the Dublin Core, in alphabetical order, were Contributor, Coverage, Creator, Date, Description, Format, Identifier, Language, Publisher, Relation, Rights, Source, Subject, Title, and Type.[33]

The challenge that faced the group who came up with this list of terms was this: they needed categories that could collect the minimum necessary kinds of metadata for each item in a collection that would ensure effective digital searching. They wanted the minimum because they needed them to be simple, and general enough to be broadly useful and widely adopted. But they also wanted to make sure that every single necessary category was included, because they wanted their standard to be complete. Metadata standards are said to be better balanced when they provide more relevant, and less irrelevant, search results.

Criticism of the Dublin Core arises from that tension between *simplicity* (the minimum needed) and *completeness* (all that are necessary). Any standard not devised with a specific collection in mind will contain unnecessary terms and be missing important ones.

The usefulness of the Dublin Core has also been extended by translating and encoding text-based metadata into a numeric schema. Certain *qualifiers* for particular use cases were added to the Dublin Core to further refine the categories and make them more useful for specific collections or purposes. For example, the term, "date" is qualified by the date created, available, or modified. The term "relation" is qualified by being a version of, or a replacement for, or referenced by, another document.[34] The development of the Dublin Core is facilitated by the Dublin Core Metadata Initiative (DCMI), a membership-based organization supporting innovation in metadata design and best practices.[35]

The Dublin Core is only one of many metadata standards in use. Someone responsible for organizing information for a collection that has needs beyond what the Dublin Core can give, even with qualifiers, may create a whole new set of terms.

The *Darwin Core*, for example, was devised specifically for classifying data pertaining to environmental research. In the metadata term "BasisOfRecord" in the Darwin Core, the following possible values may be assigned: PreservedSpecimen, FossilSpecimen, LivingSpecimen, MaterialSample, Event, HumanObservation, MachineObservation, Taxon, Occurrence, or MaterialCitation. As with the Dublin Core, a community was involved in the development of the Darwin Core. The Darwin Core Maintenance Interest Group is supported by a non-profit association, Biodiversity Standards, which ratifies and promotes standards in the field of biodiversity.[36]

There are metadata tools and terms that are applicable to whatever standards are being used. Discussed previously was vocabulary control, which limits the words that people can use for assigning descriptions or names to objects being indexed. Vocabulary control for digital collections works somewhat differently from how it is used for physical collections, in that it also limits the range of metadata tags that characterize the content of web pages. *Authority lists* keep track of allowable or preferred category names, as well as non-preferred synonyms, near-synonyms, and common misspellings.

Finally, *Domain Analysis* is an approach to organizing information which asserts that the subject knowledge which arises from communities of knowledge should be made explicit and central in the creation of knowledge organization systems. This approach stands in contrast to traditional classification systems, which give preference to breadth of relevance rather than specificity.[37]

A knowledge organization system has to take into account the kind of information that needs to be organized, the domain of interest, who will be using it, and what will need to be done with it, in order to determine what kinds of metadata and which metadata standards to employ, or whether a new schema for the collection will be needed. Knowledge organization is a key component of *information infrastructure*, a broad term that refers to institutions such as libraries which facilitate the creation of bibliographies, catalogs, and indexes, academic societies which collaborate to create scholarly norms, and academic publishers which facilitate the distribution of research. Traditional patterns of information infrastructure were extended, and in certain aspects transformed, when it became necessary to classify digitized and born-digital documents.

What is happening behind the scenes as information is delivered every day, and all around us, is not typically at the forefront of people's minds. It is labor that is invisible to most users of information, but without it they would be hard-pressed to find what they seek.

## ORGANIZING INFORMATION IN CONTEXT

The practice of classifying information is always a political act, whether that is its conscious intention or not, because while a system is organizing information, it is also sorting the world. It is because classification systems produce infrastructure, that they have the power to shape people's actions in the world.[38] This is particularly true where societies are most stratified, since stratifications require ontologies, which are easily obscured beneath habit and tradition. Metadata invariably reflects the ontologies, and the biases, of our societies.

An illustrative example is provided by the Citing Slavery Project at the Michigan State College of Law. The project team has compiled a database of U.S. court cases dating back to the slavery era that are still being cited as precedents in modern cases.[39] Until very recently, the *Bluebook*, a finding aid that helps lawyers identify citations (a form of metadata) in support of arguments, did not include any indication that the "property" being discussed in a given case was *human* property.[40]

A new *Bluebook* citation rule requires that this fact be included. A case in which there was a dispute between a widow and her brother-in-law about the inheritance of her deceased husband's slaves, which was previously listed in the *Bluebook* as "Wall v. Wall, 30 Miss. 91 (1855)," now reads "Wall v. Wall, 30 Miss. 91 (1855) (enslaved person at issue)."[41] This new rule makes sure that lawyers who wish to cite these cases as precedents are alerted to the racial context. Correcting the metadata does not prevent lawyers from building upon these cases, but it forces public recognition of the normalization of racial bias that lies at the historical foundations of property-related case law.

The database being assembled by the Citing Slavery Project casts light on how the ontologies that allowed white people to treat Black people as property continue to operate, unremarked, within information systems and institutional practices today. *Racial profiling*, a technique of law enforcement that lends itself to mistaken identifications and false arrests, sometimes with fatal results, has an information problem at its heart.

False arrests are more likely to occur when a police officer does a quick cognitive sort by the category "skin color" and treats someone as a suspect without any additional identifying facets to justify questioning or arrest. The justification "he fit the description," is an admission that the number of categories matched prior to identifying a suspect and placing them under arrest turned out to be inadequate to make a correct identification.[42]

When approached by a police officer, a white child holding a real gun and a Black child holding a cell phone are not at equal risk, in the United States, of the use of excessive force, or even of death. For the white child their *age* might be viewed as the salient category, while for the Black child, *race* becomes the overpowering facet that guides an officer's split-second decision to shoot.[43]

Our biases are often unconscious. The claim of a police officer who kills an unarmed Black person that they do not espouse racist beliefs may well be true. Most people are also unaware that their biases reflect the ways in which they sort the world, or that the way they were taught to sort the world reflects specific historical events.

Thinking about the issues through the lens of classification, it becomes clear that in order to justify the global slave trade, in which non-white people could be bought, sold, and willed to others, *as property*, it was necessary to classify dark-skinned people as non-persons, along with animals, farm tools, and furniture within a hierarchy which placed white Christians at the very top.

In the colonial era, European ships traveled the globe, in competition with one another to claim and take possession of inhabited lands and their wealth, after killing, subjugating, and violating the indigenous people they found there. All of these actions were justified by the *Doctrine of Discovery*, set out in the Papal Bull *Inter Caetera*, issued by the Catholic Pope Alexander VI in 1493. It declared that lands occupied by non-Christians should be considered empty and free to be discovered. The U.S. Supreme Court unanimously validated the doctrine in the 1823 Supreme Court Case *Johnson vs. McIntosh*, ruling that Native Americans had the right of occupancy, but not the right of ownership, of the lands where they lived, because "the principle of discovery gave European nations an absolute right to New World lands."[44]

Conversion of indigenous people to Christianity in the colonial period typically involved the systematic destruction of stories, rituals, practices, artifacts, and written records which held indigenous memories, religious beliefs and identities; this process is recognized as *cultural genocide*.[45] The practice of removing indigenous children from their parents and educating them in boarding schools in the language of settler colonizers is particularly damaging to both individuals and their communities.[46] When children are deprived of their mother tongue, they lose the ability to understand the stories told by their elders and to pass them on in turn. In recent years, the discovery of extensive unmarked graves on the sites of boarding schools in Canada and the U.S. demonstrate the extent of the physical abuse and deprivation experienced by children in these institutions, on top of the psychological harm they suffered.[47]

The term *epistemicide* is used to refer to the deliberate destruction of indigenous knowledge systems and their replacement by other ideas about how knowledge is created, classified, and understood.[48] Indigenous librarians and their allies are critical of the Dublin Core, and other metadata standards, which accept as normative ways of knowing that were imposed by colonizing powers. These are inflicted upon indigenous knowledge collections, even though they don't map well to indigenous views of how knowledge is created and shared.[49] The Dublin Core category of "Creator," for example, doesn't allow for shared authorship with ancestors, clan, or tribe.

The long-term consequences of colonial-era violence, trauma, and loss have been entrenched poverty, regional unrest, and in some places, recurring ethnic conflict. In our post-colonial era, the drive for geopolitical power and wealth continues to endanger the connections between people and their remembered past. The persistence of white supremacist beliefs and practices across the globe is testimony to the fact that it was easier to end slavery as legal commerce through legislation and decree, than to change the way people sort the world.

The increasing presence and respect in New Zealand mainstream society for *mātauranga Māori* has provoked pushback. In 2021, a group of University of Auckland professors wrote a letter to the *New Zealand Listener* objecting to a plan to revise secondary school curriculum. The plan proposed to give equal status to *mātauranga Māori* alongside the teaching of science. The objectors were concerned that students would be less likely to pursue the study of science if they learned how science had been used, historically, to justify colonialism and to suppress traditional knowledge systems. In defense of science, they also rejected the elevation of *mātauranga Māori* within the curriculum.[50]

Response to the letter was swift and emotional. The vice-chancellor of the University of Auckland said that the letter had caused "hurt and dismay" and that it did not reflect the views of the university, which understood empirical science and *mātauranga Māori* as complementary and not in competition with each other. Māori scientists objected to the letter's assumption that empirical science is always objective and value-free, and that *mātauranga Māori* is never empirical.

Ecologist Tara McAllister pointed out that the Māori people had had enough scientific knowledge of the oceans and the stars to navigate safely to *Aotearoa* (New Zealand), and that science allowed them to live in balance with the environment. Other academic responses to the letter pushed back against the idea that teaching students history would cause them to mistrust science. Physicist Ocean Mercier, whose work involves applying both scientific methods and *mātauranga Māori* to real-world problems, told *Radio New Zealand* that attempts to delegitimize indigenous knowledge come up recurringly, reflecting old scientific norms that are rooted in colonialism, but that most scientists in New Zealand have moved past them: "If there's any mistrust in science, it comes from those historical legacies of research that have been harmful to indigenous peoples, to Māori, to minorities, to women."[51]

Geologist Dan Hikuroa has also argued that evaluating the relative worth of science above *mātauranga Māori* is out of step with the ways that scientists in New Zealand are making use of indigenous knowledge to solve ecological problems. Green crayfish are coming back to Lake Rotomā, on New Zealand's north island, for example, after a Māori technique for food gathering in swamps using woven flax mats was applied to suppress the weed and provide migration routes for the crayfish to get to their feeding grounds.[52]

Critical librarianship warns of the risks of *technocratic ideologies* that view themselves as rational and universal, even when they rest on patriarchal or white supremacist traditions.[53] Such ideologies are associated with solutionism—the tendency to view technology as being able to solve any problem, no matter how socially complex.

In the case of the crayfish in Rotomā, the low-tech solution of woven mats turned out to be more successful than herbicides or imported rubber mats; the problem was solved because the scientific team respected indigenous knowledge of the ecosystem.

Challenges to traditional practices of library cataloging and knowledge organization are important, not only because they shed light on historical and present-day wrongs, but because they bring attention to the fact that all information systems have cultural presumptions about how we know what we know, from which our ways of sorting are derived. Invariably, these will shape how we structure and organize information.

## NOTES

1  Aaron Smale. "'Ko au te awa, ko te awa ko au,'" *New Zealand Radio*, 17 March 2017.
2  Shannon Haunui-Thompson, "Whanganui to Gain Legal Personhood," *New Zealand Radio*, 16 March 2017.
3  "Constitution of the Republic of Ecuador," *Political Database of the Americas*, https://pdba.georgetown.edu/Constitutions/Ecuador/english08.html. Retrieved 19 May 2022.
4  "Local, State, and National Laws and Constitutional Frameworks, Uganda," *Right to Nature Law Library*, Center for Democratic and Environmental Rights, https://www.centerforenvironmentalrights.org/rights-of-nature-law-library. Retrieved 19 May 2022.
5  "Local, State, and National Laws and Constitutional Frameworks, Canada," *Right to Nature Law Library*, Center for Democratic and Environmental Rights, https://www.centerforenvironmentalrights.org/rights-of-nature-law-library. Retrieved 19 May 2022.
6  "Our Partnership with Menominee Tribal Members on the Rights of the Menominee River," *Center for Democratic and Environmental Rights*, https://www.centerforenvironmentalrights.org/news/our-partnership-with-menominee-tribal-members-z    -the-rights-of-the-menominee-river. Retrieved 20 May 2022.

7   Christopher D. Stone, "Should Trees Have Standing? Towards Legal Rights for Natural Objects," *Southern California Law Review* 45 (1972): 450–501.

8   Ibid., 460.

9   Ibid., 498.

10  Robin Kimmerer, *Braiding Sweetgrass: Indigenous Wisdom, Scientific Knowledge and the Teachings of Plants* (Minneapolis, MN: Milkweed Editions, 2013): 208.

11  Sarah Wright et al., "Telling Stories in, through and with Country: Engaging with Indigenous and More-Than-Human Methodologies at Bawaka, NE Australia," *Journal of Cultural Geography* 29, no. 1 (2012): 39–60.

12  Lauren Tynan, "What Is Relationality? Indigenous Knowledges, Practices and Responsibilities with Kin," *Cultural Geographies* 28, no. 4 (2021): 597–610.

13  Ella Henry and Hone Pene, "Kaupapa Maori: Locating Indigenous Ontology, Epistemology and Methodology in the Academy," *Organization* 8, no. 2 (2001): 234–242.

14  Ryan E. Emanuel and David E. Wilkins, "Breaching Barriers: The Fight for Indigenous Participation in Water Governance," *Water* 12, no. 8 (2020): 2113.

15  Bonnie Mak, "Wood Libraries: Knowing with Wood," *Caxtonian*, May–June, 2021.

16  R. R. Banks and R. T. Ford, "(How) Does Unconscious Bias Matter: Law, Politics, and Racial Inequality," *Emory LJ* 58 (2008): 1053.

17  Jonathan Furner, "Definitions of 'Metadata': A Brief Survey of International Standards," *Journal of the Association for Information Science and Technology* 71, no. 6 (2020): E33–E42.

18  Birger Hjørland, "Knowledge Organization (KO)," *KO Knowledge Organization* 43, no. 6 (2016): 475–484.

19  Kathryn La Barre, "Facet Analysis," *Annual Review of Information Science and Technology* 44, no. 1 (2010): 243.

20  La Barre, "Facet Analysis," 251, citing John Metcalfe, *Subject Classifying and Indexing of Libraries and Literature* (Sydney, NSW: Angus and Robertson, 1959).

21  Ibid., 244.

22  Marek Nahotko, "Knowledge Organization Affordances in a Faceted Online Public Access Catalog (OPAC)," *Cataloging & Classification Quarterly* 60, no. 1 (2022): 86–111.

23  La Barre, "Facet Analysis," 269.

24  Safwat Zargar, "Mistaken Identity: A Kashmiri Farmer on Pilgrimage in Iraq has been Detained on an Interpol Notice," *Scroll.In*, 12 January 2020.

25  F. W. Lancaster, *Indexing and Abstracting in Theory and Practice* (2nd ed., Champaign, IL: University of Illinois Graduate School of Library and Information Science, 1998).

26 Cataloging Policy and Support Office, "Library of Congress Subject Headings Pre- vs. Post-Coordination and Related Issues: Report for Beacher Wiggins, Director, Acquisitions & Bibliographic Access Directorate" (Library Services, Library of Congress, 2007): 1.

27 See Mārīte Apenīte, "Subject Indexing at the National Library of Latvia: New Approach, Challenges, and Benefits," *Cataloging & Classification Quarterly* 59, no. 4 (2021): 334–354.

28 Furner, "Definitions of 'Metadata.'"

29 Jenn Riley, "Understanding Metadata," Washington DC, United States: *National Information Standards Organization* 23 (2017): 6.

30 Jenn Riley, "Seeing Standards: A Visualization of the Metadata Universe," http://jennriley.com/metadatamap/. Retrieved 20 May 2022.

31 Ibid.

32 Jeffrey Pomerantz, *Metadata* (Cambridge, MA: MIT Press, 2015): 66–67.

33 Ibid., 72.

34 Ibid., 81.

35 "About DCMI," Dublin Core Metadata Initiative Website, https://www.dublincore.org/about/. Retrieved 20 May 2020.

36 "Darwin Core," Taxonomic Databases Working Group, https://www.tdwg.org/community/dwc/. Retrieved 21 May 2022.

37 Birger Hjørland and Hanne Albrechtsen, "Toward a New Horizon in Information Science: Domain-Analysis," *Journal of the American Society for Information Science* 46, no. 6 (1995): 400–425.

38 See Gregory H. Leazer and Robert Montoya, "The Politics of Knowledge Organization: Introduction to the Special Issue," *Knowledge Organization* 47, no. 5 (2020): 367–371.

39 Justin Simard. "Citing Slavery Project," https://www.citingslavery.org/. Retrieved 20 May 2022.

40 Justin Wm. Moyer, "Fighting Racial Bias with an Unlikely Weapon: Footnotes," *The Washington Post*, 18 January 2022.

41 Ibid.

42 Wayne A. Logan and Andrew Guthrie Ferguson, "Policing Criminal Justice Data," *Minnesota Law Review* 101 (2016): 541.

43 Diann Cameron Kelly and Rani Varghese, "Four Contexts of Institutional Oppression: Examining the Experiences of Blacks in Education, Criminal Justice and Child Welfare," *Journal of Human Behavior in the Social Environment* 28, no. 7 (2018): 874–888.

44 "The Doctrine of Discovery, 1943," The Gilder Lehrman Institute of American History, https://www.gilderlehrman.org/history-resources/spotlight-primary-source/doctrine-discovery-1493. Retrieved 17 May 2022.

45 Shawn Clark and Ruth Wylie, "Surviving a Cultural Genocide: Perspectives of Indigenous Elders on the Transfer of Traditional Values," *Journal of Ethnic and Cultural Studies* 8, no. 2 (2021): 316–346.

46 Margaret D. Jacobs, "Indian Boarding Schools in Comparative Perspective: The Removal of Indigenous Children in the United States and Australia, 1880–1940," Digital Commons at the University of Nebraska, Lincoln (2006), https://digitalcommons.unl.edu/historyfacpub/20/.

47 Rachel L. Burrage, Sandra L. Momper, and Joseph P. Gone, "Beyond Trauma: Decolonizing Understandings of Loss and Healing in the Indian Residential School System of Canada," *Journal of Social Issues* 78, no. 1 (2022): 27–52.

48 B. Patin, M. Sebastian, J. Yeon, D. Bertolini, and A. Grimm, "Interrupting Epistemicide: A Practical Framework for Naming, Identifying, and Ending Epistemic Injustice in the Information Professions," *Journal of the Association for Information Science and Technology* 72, no. 10 (2021): 1306–1318.

49 María Montenegro, "Subverting the Universality of Metadata Standards: The TK Labels as a Tool to Promote Indigenous Data Sovereignty," *Journal of Documentation* 75, no. 4 (2019): 737.

50 Sam Sachdeva, "Royal Society Investigation into Mātauranga Māori Letter Sparks Academic Debate," *Newsroom*, 17 November 2021.

51 Māni Dunlop, "University Academics' Claim Mātauranga Māori 'Not Science' Sparks Controversy," *Radio New Zealand*, 28 July 2021.

52 Pete McKenzie, "Can Ancient Maori Knowledge Aid Science? Ask These Freshwater Crayfish," *New York Times*, 1 June 2022.

53 Rafia Mirza and Maura Seale, "Who Killed the World? White Masculinity and the Technocratic Library of the Future," in *Topographies of Whiteness: Mapping Whiteness in Library and Information Science*, ed. Gina Schlesselman-Tarango (Sacramento, CA: Library Juice Press, 2017): 172.

# 4

# RETRIEVING INFORMATION

One evening in the late 1920s Hungarian writer Frigyes Karinthy mused to his friends how small the world had become. He wondered how quickly it would take a single thought or experience to be known by everyone in the world. Someone suggested that the question might be answered through an experiment in the form of a game: choose any random individual in the world and try to connect to them through a chain of acquaintance. He bet that it would be possible to make the connection in no more than five steps. As they played the game that evening, the bet was never lost.

Karinthy was given the challenge to connect himself to an anonymous riveter at the Ford Motor Company. He happened to have a close friend who was acquainted with William Randolph Hearst, owner of the biggest publishing network in the world, who could easily call up Henry Ford, who could then contact the foreman who supervised the riveter. "And so the game went on," remembered Karinthy. "Our friend was absolutely correct: nobody from the group needed more than five links in the chain to reach, just by using the method of acquaintance, any inhabitant of our Planet."[1] Karinthy and his friends had discovered that even if they themselves knew no one famous, *they all knew someone who knew someone famous*, and from there it was easy.

The question of how many steps are necessary to connect any two people in the world came to be understood as the *small world problem*. It was taken up by researchers from MIT and IBM who

DOI: 10.4324/9781003155119-4

attempted to calculate how long it would take for the chain of acquaintances to get to everyone in the world, based on the average number of acquaintances people have.[2] The problem with this approach is that such models fail to account for social stratification between classes of people who may be well-connected within their class, but poorly connected beyond it. So, the problem passed from mathematics to experimental sociology.

Social psychologist Stanley Milgram designed a small world experiment in which subjects were to send a package to a target individual, by forwarding it to an acquaintance that they thought would get it closer, who would forward it on in a similar way. Most of the chains failed to complete, but for those that did the number of links required ranged from 2 to 10, with an average of 5.[3] Interdisciplinary research followed, with replications as well as applications of the model within different domains. In the 21st century, Facebook provided an empirical answer to the small world problem based on an analysis of their users' friend networks; the average distance between every Facebook user on the planet with every other turns out to be only 3.57 links.[4]

During these decades of multidisciplinary research, the idea was also making its way into popular culture. An off-Broadway play entitled *Six Degrees of Separation*, by John Guare, which was followed by a 1993 film of the same name, introduced the term "degrees of separation." Shortly after its arrival in Hollywood, the concept made its leap to actor Kevin Bacon. As the story goes, one snowy January night in 1994 three college students were drinking beer and watching the movie *Footloose* on television, when an advertisement for the film *The Air Up There* came on—a coincidence it seemed, since Kevin Bacon was in both films. They wondered how many films the actor had been in, and how many other actors he had worked with. From this conversation they came up with a trivia game in which players try to link any actor to Kevin Bacon, in a maximum of six steps, through films in which they appeared together. They called their game "Six Degrees of Kevin Bacon.[5] The students appeared twice on MTV's first talk show, *The John Stewart Show* (the second time with Bacon as a guest), launching the game into popular culture.

Social scientists interested in the small world problem took notice of the *Oracle of Bacon*, a website created by then graduate student Brett Tjaden, based on the Six Degrees game, which calculates an actor's "Bacon Number," the number of steps needed to connect with Bacon. Scraping data from Wikipedia, it initially included 358 actors who collectively appeared in 128,000 films.[6] The Wikipedia dataset used for the Oracle of Bacon became key to a model used by scientists sociologist Duncan Watts and mathematician Steven Strogatz to demonstrate that many human and non-human networks, from power grids to cricket chirps, are *small-world networks* in which every node in a network is connected to every other in only a few steps.[7] Small world studies provided empirical grounding for an idea known as the "strength of weak ties," introduced by sociologist Mark Granovetter, who demonstrated the unexpected influence of social acquaintances on our lives.[8]

Karinthy died in 1938; we can easily imagine that the Kevin Bacon game would have pleased him, but that he would have felt vindicated by Wikipedia games in which players must get from one randomly assigned page to another using the fewest possible clicks.[9] He had admitted to playing his parlor game with objects as well as people, as he considered the networked nature of the world:

> The strange mind-game that clatters in me all the time goes like this: how can I link, with three, four, or at most five links of the chain, trivial, everyday things of life. How can I link one phenomenon to another? How can I join the relative and the ephemeral with steady, permanent things—how can I tie up the part with the whole?[10]

This chapter explores the networked nature of information. It begins with the prehistory of the Internet, when visionary thinkers imagined better ways to organize information so that it could be most effectively searched. It provides an overview of basic concepts associated with information search, retrieval, and evaluation across networks, before briefly considering citation analysis, a bibliometric method that maps the network of influence that scholarly work may have on the work of others. The chapter ends with a consideration of bias in internet searches.

## IMAGINING THE INTERNET

The principles underlying information retrieval on the Internet can be traced to Gabriel Naudé's checklist for information management: is a collection complete, is it searchable, and is it accessible? Optimizing the search and retrieval of information necessitates attention to all three. For library collections in the late 19th and early 20th centuries, this optimization centered around the creation and improvement of bibliographic catalogs and indexes, the professionalization of the work of cataloging, and the development of knowledge organization as a field, as discussed in the previous chapters.

Even before the digital age transformed the technologies used for information retrieval, people were thinking about how to automate the processes to make them more accurate and efficient. They did what they could do with the technologies they had: telephone, telegraph, and microfilm.

The Belgian documentarian, Paul Otlet, developed Universal Decimal Classification as an improvement on DDC because it could handle non-text documents. But he also wanted to create a system in which the *content* of information, not just the *containers* of information, could be retrieved. He envisioned a world in which texts, images, and sound could be streamed to users across a network. He imagined these "radiated libraries" as being made up of "electric telescopes" which would allow people to get answers to their questions, wherever they were located in the world, far from where the information was stored in repositories:

> From a distance, everyone will be able to read text, enlarged and limited to the desired subject, projected on an individual screen. In this way, everyone from his armchair will be able to contemplate the whole of creation, in whole or in certain parts.[11]

Otlet called this imagined system a *reseau*, which means both net and web, and translates gracefully into the English word "network." He imagined a social media–like component to his system as well, so that people could work together, creating and updating metadata collaboratively, to make searching more effective.[12] In the absence of the technologies he imagined, he prototyped his system using what was available. He invited the public to query his collection via telegraph or postal service, and his team, a human search engine, would provide the answers by consulting their astonishing card catalog. Before his project was abruptly terminated in World War II, Otlet's team had produced more than 16 million cards containing descriptive metadata from the works in their collections.[13] For many queries, they would not need to consult the original works in order to retrieve the answer.

Another early 20th-century futurist who was thinking about information retrieval was English writer and social activist, H.G. Wells (1866–1946), best known for his science fiction novels *The War of the Worlds* and *The Time Machine*. Wells imagined a world-wide encyclopedia through which universities and research centers around the globe could be connected. In such a system, research results could be communicated immediately and directly to other scholars in its field. Wells's vision of a decentralized, collaborative Wikipedia-like encyclopedia was connected to his belief that such a networked system could function as a *World Brain*."[14]

Nobel Prize-winning German chemist Friedrich Wilhelm Ostwald (1853–1932) also used the term *Gehirn der Welt* (World Brain) to describe his ambitions. With his prize money, he created an organization called *Die Brücke* (the Bridge), which he imagined as a station between information islands (libraries, museums, research centers, and individuals): "Any question which may be raised with respect to any field of intellectual work whatever finds either direct answer or else indirect, in the sense that the inquirer is advised as to the place where he can obtain sufficient information."[15]

Like Wells, Ostwald was not interested in the task of collecting information. His ambition was institutional; he wanted to build an infrastructure that could support and improve scholarly communication. Towards this end he promoted the internationalization and standardization of classification tools and technologies, which is his lasting legacy. The Bridge folded as a project when the money from his Nobel Prize in Chemistry ran out, but it is Ostwald we must thank for the standard paper sizes we still use today.[16]

As Otlet's physical collections grew, it became clear that improving information storage would be key to effective information retrieval. For much of the 20th century, microfilm technologies were the state of the art in information storage. Phyllis Mander-Jones (1896–1984), an Australian librarian and bibliographer, is noted for completing the largest and longest-running microfilming project in history. The Australian Joint Copying Project (AJCP) microfilmed available records held in public records offices, libraries, museums, churches, businesses, and personal collections in the United Kingdom that were of interest to scholars and the public in Australia and the Pacific. More than 10,000 reels of microfilm were produced by the AJCP under Mander-Jones' direction.[17]

As an information-storage technology, microfilm saved space, but reaching the image of a particular page in a microfilmed reel was slow, even with an index that identified where on the reel the image was located. Mechanizing this retrieval process became an engineering goal, a pursuit funded by the photographic industry. Within the same intellectual community to which Wells, Ostwald, and Otlet belonged was Emanuel Goldberg (1881–1970), the founding Director of the German company Zeiss Ikon. He had been born in Moscow, but received his PhD for his work on the kinetics of photochemical reactions from the Institute of Physical Chemistry at the University of Leipzig, which was led by Ostwald.

Goldberg acquired international patents for the first automated microfilm document retrieval system. His prototyped invention, the *Statistical Machine*, used coded search cards and light to move quickly to particular images in a microfilm reel. Goldberg also pioneered microdot photography, which would allow 64,500 book pages (legibly photographed on a surface of only 0.01 millimeter), to fit in the space of one square inch.[18]

Development of these inventions was interrupted by the rise of Nazism in Germany prior to World War II. Because Goldberg was Jewish, his work was purged from German scientific records. He fled with his family, first to Paris and then to Palestine. He could not pick up his early work after the war, because his records were lost when Zeiss was destroyed in the 1945 bombing of Dresden. Things were going no better for Goldberg on the other side of the Atlantic. The director of the U.S. Federal Bureau of Investigation, J. Edgar Hoover, wrote a report about the intelligence potentials of Goldberg's microdot camera, citing as its inventor a fictional person at Zeiss named Walter Zapp; it was the imaginary Professor Zapp rather than Goldberg who received credit in espionage literature, over the next few decades, for microdot technology.[19]

American engineer Vannevar Bush (1890–1974) was also working on a microfilm document retrieval system. Bush was Vice-President and Dean at MIT, and director of the federal Office of Scientific Research and Development that oversaw the Manhattan Project and guided the development of the atomic bomb. He is sometimes credited as the inventor of the first microfilm retrieval system, but Goldberg's earlier patent for the Statistical Machine prevented Bush from attaining one for his "Rapid Selection" technology. Both systems indexed microfilm using light. Working at MIT with the financial support of Kodak, Bush was able to take his prototype, the *Memex*, several stages further than Goldberg had done at Zeiss. It was not quite a fully-working model when the development of digital storage and document retrieval rendered microfilm retrieval systems redundant.[20]

The transition within libraries from card catalogs and microfilm to digital databases and computers would soon change how research services operated. "Ready Reference" desks had appeared in libraries as early as the late 19th century; by the middle of the 20th century, reference librarians were sitting in front of shelves of encyclopedias and microfilm readers, taking calls, and walk-up searchers, though without the benefit of Otlet's classification system.[21] By the 1970s, reference service was beginning to be automated, a process that accelerated with the availability of searchable databases like Medline, a bibliographic finding aid for health information.[22]

In 1962 Joseph "Lick" Licklider (1915–1990) was working for the U.S. Defense Department as director of the Information Processing Techniques Office (IPTO) at the Advanced Research Projects Agency (ARPA). He wrote a series of memos to his ARPA colleagues, whimsically referring to them as "Members and Affiliates of the Intergalactic Computer Network." His memo concerned problems of interoperability and communication between computers. He was fascinated by the possibility of a network through which all human knowledge could flow, available freely to all.[23] Two years earlier he had published a paper on "man–computer symbiosis" in which he described the future of "cooperative interaction between men and electronic computers."[24]

Licklider had a large discretionary budget at ARPA. Among other projects, he helped fund the work of Douglas Engelbart (1925–2014) in his Augmented Research Center, at the Stanford Research Institute (SRI) where the computer mouse and the graphical user interface were born. Engelbart and his 17-person team developed the oN-Line System, a proto-hypertext tool that they demonstrated in San Francisco in 1968. That event has been remembered as the "Mother of All Demos." Engelbart used video projection to enlarge his bit-mapped computer screen to fit the wall and showed off his system for connecting digital documents to one another through hyperlinks, using a keyboard and a mouse.[25]

Engelbart's interest in the idea of hyperlinks had been inspired by an essay written by Vannevar Bush entitled "As We May Think." In it, Bush discussed the Memex of the future: a stand-alone desktop device containing a microfilmed encyclopedia that was navigated idiosyncratically, the user traversing the content and creating trails of personal association.[26] Bush's essay was also credited as inspiration by Ted Nelson who coined the terms *hypertext* and *hypermedia* in the early 1960s to describe the links that make navigation between documents possible. Nelson's idealistic but ill-fated hypertext publishing tool, Project Xanadu, sought to revolutionize collaboration, and to provide advanced version control of documents. It was briefly implemented by a company wanting to create record-keeping software for insurance companies: the company called itself Memex.[27]

Licklider too declared himself inspired by Bush's essay, but, like Engelbart, he was more personally energized by the challenges of information storage and retrieval across networked computers than he was by the idea of developing personal computing systems. He encouraged Robert Taylor (1932–2017) in the creation of the Advanced Research Projects Agency Network (ARPANET), a predecessor of the Internet. Taylor and Licklider are credited with changing the perception of computers from computational devices to machines for communication: "In a few years," they proclaimed, "men will be able to communicate more effectively through a machine than face to face."[28]

Twenty years later, Tim Berners-Lee would introduce the World Wide Web, building upon the work of those who came before him to transform the way the Internet was accessed, making it available to a much wider public. He developed *HTML markup language* which was similar to existing tagging systems for marking up text to distinguish headings, paragraphs, and lists, for example, but it introduced a new kind of markup tag for hyperlinks. He created the first web browser, the first web server, and specifications for a new internet protocol for transferring web content as well.

## SEARCH AND RETRIEVAL

It is common to compare the Internet to the ancient libraries of Alexandria and Assyria, but in fact, the Internet is not a collection. The Internet supplies the networked connections and the signals that link the web pages of the World Wide Web together. The World Wide Web is not a collection either. Web pages and web applications provide the content and interactivity that get delivered through the Internet. The files themselves are located on servers and in repositories distributed all across the planet.

We say we are "searching the web," but what we are actually querying is an index, in its essential functioning not so different from a card catalog. When we query the index in the back of a book, we get a page number. An internet search engine compares users' queries to continuously updated indexes and return lists of links to websites. All the big browsers of the Internet—Google, Microsoft's Bing, Baidu (serving 75% of China's market), and Yahoo—work essentially the same way.

This process is formally referred to as *information retrieval* (IR), or more prosaically as "search and fetch." A third process, occurring between *querying* a finding aid and *receiving* an answer, is the *selection* of a match. By running your finger down a list of words in an alphabetized index, and then stopping at the word you are looking for you are doing the job of matching your query to the index.

For online search engines, the selection process uses an algorithm to decide what links will be most relevant for your query. For large or networked collections, the matching process requires increasingly complex and proprietary algorithms under constant revision. They may also become a flashpoint for critique because the process of selection is vulnerable to bias.

In their core functions, neither a physical index nor a search engine provides the content of queried information, but only metadata regarding its location. Knowing the shelf location of a book does not by itself retrieve the book. Likewise, online search only provides hypertext links; clicking on them is up to us. The process of information retrieval thus technically requires three discrete steps: searching, selecting, and fetching, though search engines are evolving in ways that bring these steps closer together. Search engines increasingly aspire to give us information *before* we ask for it; they do this now by offering us advertisements they think we would like to see, based on data about our previous clicks they have collected and analyzed.

Like any other finding aid, online search engines match user queries to entries in an index which are created from what they glean from scouring the World Wide Web, as well as from data sources not available on the web. Google's index, for example, is over 100,000,000 gigabytes in size.[29] It is continuously updated and is *mirrored* (full working copies made) in multiple sites across the planet, so that information can be delivered at the highest speed that local infrastructure and technology allow.

Web pages typically include *meta tags*—lines of HTML dedicated to providing search engines with information about such things as the purpose of a web page and what kind of content it contains. Automated *web crawlers* are programs that continuously scan websites and follow links across the Internet, copying metadata and adding new websites to their regular ports of call. This is a quick and reliable process in the case of grabbing the metadata, which is designed for this purpose. Extracting meaning from other website content is more challenging, but advances in image recognition and *natural language processing* (NLP) technology are making it possible to index more complex or abstract features of a page as well.

In determining the likely relevance or importance of a page to a search query, a search engine may also factor in its own calculated measures. One early innovation at Google was *page ranking*: a page-rank algorithm takes into account how many other sites link to a particular page, as well as how many links point to those sites, and so on. This network-analysis approach led to other refinements in the algorithms that determine whether a website should appear at the top of a list of search results, or farther down. Google's overall ranking strategy now balances many factors, including indicators of a website's "expertise, authority, and trustworthiness" (E-A-T).

Expert medical advice found on a physician's website will be preferred to advice from a random blogger; having many links from articles by well-known experts could indicate that a web page is authoritative; and the presence of outbound links to high-quality pages could suggest that a site is trustworthy. Purely technical indicators are factored in as well, such as how quickly a page loads and displays in the browser, or how well it adapts to being displayed on a smartphone.

A final step in the process of information is the *evaluation* of search results. The first question asked is whether the retrieved results are relevant to the user's query. This requires more than a simple yes or no, since what is relevant to one person may not be to another. Relevance is often analyzed by focusing on the tension between two more specific questions: first, did the searcher get *all* the relevant information? This question measures the completeness of the information retrieved; a measure also called *recall*. The second question is: did the searcher get *only* relevant information? This question measures the accuracy of the information retrieved; a measure called *precision*.

*Recall* (completeness) is usually expressed as a percentage of all possible relevant responses to a search. Suppose you are searching for information on the "Babel Fish," an imaginary creature that when placed in the ear allows the host to understand every language ever spoken anywhere. The Babel Fish appears in Douglas Adams' novel, *The Hitchhiker's Guide to the Galaxy*, a story about a handheld book that provides helpful information about every destination in the universe.[30] If one search engine fetches 60% of all possible matches, and another returns 80%, the second one is said to have had better recall because the results were more complete.

*Precision* (accuracy) refers to the percentage of the responses that are relevant to a particular search. Imagine that one search engine provides 100,000 hits, and the other retrieves only 1,000. If only

10% in the first search were actually about the novel, while 100% of the second set were, then the second search, though less complete, is more precise. In an ideal world of search, we would want to retrieve 100% of only the most precise hits. But complete and completely relevant search results are hard to get, because any increase in recall reduces precision, and increasing precision reduces recall.

A meme that has traveled widely across social media displays a picture of a borrower's record, the card found inside a library book, with a quote written across it attributed to Neil Gaiman: "Google can bring you back 100,000 answers, a librarian can bring you back the right one." This meme elevates precision over recall. We want our finding aids to find exactly what we are looking for on the first try. Librarians are exceptionally good at this, not because they know where the information is, but because they know where to find the indexes, and how to use them.

## INFORMATION NETWORKS

Social network theorist Albert-László Barabási determined that the number of clicks that it takes to get from any page to any other across the billions of webpages on the Internet is, astonishingly, only 19.[31] That this is mathematically possible is only because, among the billions of nodes in the network, there are significantly fewer *hubs*—pages that are densely connected, with thousands of other websites pointing towards them.

It turns out that Kevin Bacon is not actually the center of Hollywood. He *became a hub* because of the virality of the Kevin Bacon game. The game connected the network of scientists who were studying the very phenomenon that was connecting them.

Some information scientists are interested in the networked connections between scholars in order to understand how knowledge is made. *Citation analysis* is one research methodology that provides an assessment of a work's influence by measuring how often it is cited by others. Citation analysis falls within the broader field of *bibliometrics*, which applies computational and statistical methods to bibliographic information. The related terms "scientometrics" and "informetrics" overlap in usage: scientometrics applies quantitative methods to the products of scientific research more narrowly; informetrics positions itself as inclusive of the other two terms.

Citations are a productive source of data because they are quantifiable, and at scale can be used to visualize networks that would be otherwise difficult to identify. But they are also a challenging data source. After a once startling idea has become widespread, for example, no one cites it anymore. That doesn't indicate its lack of influence, but the opposite. People often cite the same works that others do without ever reading them. And how should credit be mapped when a work has been co-authored, or when authors cite themselves?[32] When citation analysis is paired with *content analysis*, a set of methodologies for analyzing text, it is possible to find out the exact reason for the citation, and the context in which it is referenced.

Citation analysis can identify highly cited works which function as hubs within a scholarly network; these are works (nodes in a network graph) that are cited (linked to) by other works far more often than average. Mark Granovetter's article, "The Strength of Weak Ties" has been cited almost 66,000 times, one of the highest citation counts in social science literature. The work functions as a hub for people who study or use social network analysis. The paths that connect them are radically shortened because they are part of Granovetter's small world citation network.

Paul Otlet's Mundaneum (he used this name to refer to all of his projects collectively) can be understood as a knowledge hub that connected several different networks: members of the documentation movement, colleagues in other disciplines interested in information search and retrieval, peace activists, participants in the League of Nations, futurists, social activists, writers, artists, architects, scientists, and international organizations trying to change the world by sharing information.

After the republication of his essay "As We May Think" in *Life* magazine, Vannevar Bush became a hub in the network of people who were creating the digital networks and tools that would eventually become the Internet. Engelbart, Licklider, Nelson, and later even Berners-Lee all credited Bush's essay as inspiration for their work, and through this recognition turned it into a hub.[33] In 1980 a content analysis of the citation record for "As We May Think" revealed clusters of topics that had triggered its citation: history, hardware, information storage, software, and personal information systems.[34] In a follow-up study a decade later, after the launch of the World Wide Web, the same categories were seen, though there was an increase of publications that cited its contributions to the development of hypertext (in addition to a significant number of perfunctory citations from people who apparently did not read the essay). Arguably the most interesting result was that the citing works frequently employed words like "founder," "father," "seminal," "first," "beginning," and "earliest," to characterize Bush's place in the history of the Internet.[35]

Engelbart, Nelson, and Licklider all seem to have felt this way about him. What might appear strange about this, retrospectively, is that Otlet's radiated library with its proto-hypertext system, which functioned across a collaborative network, was much closer to their technological and philosophical inclinations than was Bush's Memex. All three were heavily invested in the communication possibilities inherent in networked communication; for Engelbart, even to the detriment of his career.[36]

The situation is more explicable in network terms. These men could not have found their way to the work of Otlet *through Bush* because Bush's publications never cited them. It has been suggested that Bush's failure to connect his ideas to the European scholars of Otlet's circle was not because he was unaware of them, but because he wanted his work to be distinguished from the classification and indexing work of the documentation movement.[37] By severing himself from Otlet's network, Bush succeeded in creating his own foundational lineage, providing Engelbart, Licklider, and other men in that period a father from which to spring, and a small-world network to which they could belong.

Otlet died before Bush's essay was written. One of the leaders in documentation after World War II was Susanne Briet, founding director of the *Union Française des Organismes de Documentation*. She became known as "Madame Documentation" after becoming Vice President of the International Federation for Documentation (FID). She was concerned with establishing standards to support interoperability and collaboration. Her understanding of how specialized scientific networks continuously produce and refine knowledge arguably anticipated the distributed, networked organization of information as it flows across the Internet.[38] It is interesting to speculate what might have been stirred up by an intellectual collaboration between Briet and Engelbart, Nelson, or Licklider as they imagined the future of information during the 1960s.

In 1965 Licklider dedicated a report to Vannevar Bush entitled, "Libraries of the Future." The report, which summed up research Licklider had supported over a five-year period was prescient in many ways, anticipating developments in 21st-century digital libraries. It reported new research on information retrieval, information storage, computer art, computer analysis of English syntax, and computational literature searching. But it was criticized at its release for focusing too narrowly on the information needs of scientists, and for being disconnected from the professional work of librarianship: notably, it only contained the word "librarian" once.[39]

The separation of American computer science from the European documentation movement, and from the foundational history of library science, may have been a factor in the complicated boundary work that went on during the Cold War, between information science, computer science, and cybernetics (a field that explores purposeful self-regulating systems).[40] Significant efforts have been made in the last few decades to reconnect long-sundered networks, bringing belated recognition and renewed attention to the work of Otlet, Ostwald, Wells, Goldberg, and Briet.[41] In 2014, Google recognized Otlet on the 70th anniversary of his death on a web page titled "Towards the Information Age." It includes a long list of people who collaborated with him in his quixotic attempt to unite the whole world—across national, political, and racial boundaries—into a single information network.[42]

This remembering process has been well-received in France. The reactions of information scientists there, reflecting their own history of the field, see something more interesting going on than a conflict over who invented hypertext. They suggest that the time has come to recognize the contributions of multiple intellectual lineages in the history of the Internet. These include "computing and documentation," certainly, but also "printing, utopias of universal knowledge, and social memory."[43]

## RETRIEVING INFORMATION IN CONTEXT

*Net neutrality* is a political movement and an information worldview that maintains that internet providers should function without discrimination—without blocking, slowing down, or charging money for access to content. *Search neutrality* is a related idea, though its proponents are chiefly concerned about the processes through which information is indexed, ranked, and retrieved; they target biases in editorial processes which manipulate the order in which links are viewed, or which exclude some of the results for reasons that are not transparent.

Google tells us that their algorithms employ data they have collected from us to provide us with what they calculate we most want to see. Among the things that they want us to see are advertisements that are tailored for us, based on data they have collected from our previous searches. Critics note that the number of ads and their prominent placement have steadily increased.[44] The algorithms that Bing, Yahoo, Google, Baidu, and other search engines employ are proprietary. It is not possible to know exactly why we are seeing what we are being given to see.

*Algorithmic bias* is said to occur when systematic errors in a computer program, at any stage, create or support existing patterns of social inequality. Complicated historical, social, technological, and economic circumstances lead search algorithms to discriminate against women and to privilege whiteness—a combination that produces dramatic bias against women of color.[45] In a study of search results conducted from 2009 to 2015, patterns of bias were found in the stark differences between Google search results for the key phrases "black girl" and "white girl." The study discovered that Google's algorithm associated black girls and women with negative stereotypes and porn, perpetuating racist stereotypes, and creating substantive negative consequences for people from minority and marginalized groups. These circumstances have been described as "algorithmic oppression."[46]

Internet searches often lead us to *Wikipedia*, a collaboratively created free encyclopedia launched in 2001 by the *Wikimedia Foundation*. Two decades later it is (according to Wikipedia) the 15th most popular site on the Internet.[47] It functions as an extremely powerful network hub. It is not coincidental that the Oracle of Bacon dataset, scraped from Wikipedia, became so useful for modeling small-world networks in nature as well as human society. Wikipedia is a small-world network made up of small-world networks. It fulfills the visions of Wells and Ostwald for a networked information system that functions as a continually updating "world brain." Otlet would also have loved the crowdsourced nature of the information gathering, which is centralized as the Internet is not. Bush would find on Wikipedia the freedom to travel, via his own idiosyncratic associations, from idea to idea, and Licklider might have seen in the ordinary, everyday use of Wikipedia in the 21st century, evidence of rather banal (thus deeply entangled) human-computer symbiosis.

Wikipedia editors operate in a community of practice that thrives on a subterranean level beneath the public facing Wikipedia, which anyone is free to join by becoming an editor themselves. There is an editorial hierarchy within that community, which gives some people more power than others to make critical changes, deleting, for example, a biographical page for an individual not judged to have sufficient "significance." Judgments about who is significant (or not) turn out to be susceptible to the same sorts of biases that affect social stratification elsewhere in human society. Inclusion matters. Someone with a Wikipedia page is a node in the small world Wikipedia network, just a few clicks away from everyone else with a page. Being excluded from the network makes it more difficult to be connected to the people who are inside of it.

Wikipedia is aware that it has a gender problem. Wikipedia's page "Gender Bias on Wikipedia" provides the history of what is usually called the Wikipedia gender gap: in a 2018 study, 90% of Wikipedia's contributors worldwide were men; this fell to 84% in English-speaking countries. Only 17% of biographical pages are about women, though 41% of all pages nominated for deletion are. When Donna Strickland won the Nobel Prize for Physics in 2018 for her work on pulsed lasers, there was surprise among journalists that she had no Wikipedia page providing background information about her life and accomplishments. Actually, she *had* had a page—for six minutes in 2014. It was deleted almost immediately after creation because a Wikipedia editor had felt that Strickland's biography didn't meet the bar for significance.[48]

Wikipedia continues to have trouble reaching their goal of having 25% of the site's editors be female.[49] In 2011, *The New York Times* ran an article, "Where are the Women in Wikipedia?" which sparked an active conversation on social media.[50] Sue Gardner, executive director of the Wikimedia Foundation from 2007 to 2014, assembled a summary of the online conversations in a blog entitled "Nine Reasons Women Don't Edit Wikipedia (in their own words)."[51] The reasons coalesced around a few key issues: Wikipedia's conflictual, unwelcoming, and misogynistic atmosphere, the prevalence of sexual harassment, and the fact that women were unhappy that what they added to Wikipedia was so often deleted or reversed by men.

There has been substantial research on the social and informational dynamics of deletion within Wikipedia's editorial community.[52] Women who choose to stay have developed ways to deal with the atmosphere. In one study, the researchers found that in order to make it safe for themselves, women engage in "identity management, boundary management, and emotion work."[53] These are similar experiences to those of women who remain in other male-dominated professional networks. The issues on Wikipedia are systemic and structural and can't be fixed just by adding more women.[54] Wikipedia has a race problem too, which you can read about on Wikipedia.[55]

Information retrieved from Wikipedia is susceptible to the bias that arises from the lack of diversity of its editors, a vulnerability that may not be understood by the millions of students who crib from Wikipedia to complete their homework every night, assuming that everything they read there is true.

Wikipedia's core mission is to provide accurate information, which it does in a crowd-sourced way, supported by the expertise of some of its contributors and the dedicated labor of others. The information it provides, supported by extensive citations, is more trustworthy by far than what can be found on the random websites that come up when students search for the quickest answers. Search engine algorithms attempt to distinguish credible sites from bot-produced content, and prioritize them within returns results, which is why we are sent so frequently to Wikipedia.

Information retrieval always occurs within a context that defines what can be searched, and the quality of what will be retrieved. It is up to us to evaluate the quality of the results that we receive. If we don't notice that the stereotypes and biases of our societies are also reflected there, then information retrieval functions as an engine of their replication.

## NOTES

1 Frigyes Karinthy, "Chain-Links," in *Everything is Different*, trans. Adam Makkai, ed. Enikö Jankó, Public Domain, http://vadeker.net/arti-cles/Karinthy-Chain-Links_1929.pdf. Retrieved 22 September 2022. Figyes Karinthy, "Láncszemek," in Minden másképpen van" (Budapest: Atheneum Irodalmi és Nyomdai R.-T, 1929): 85–91.

2 Manfred Kochen and Ithiel da Sola Pool, "Contacts and Influences," *Social Networks* 1 (1978): 5–51.

3 Stanley Milgram, "The Small World Problem," *Psychology Today* 2, no. 1 (1967): 60–67.

4 Sergey Edunov, Carlos Diuk, Ismail Onur Filiz, Smriti Bhagat, and Moira Burke, "Three and a Half Degrees of Separation," *Research at Facebook* (blog) 694, 4 February 2016. https://research.fb.com/three-and-a-half -degrees-of-separation/. Retrieved 9 September 2022.

5 Craig Fass, Mike Ginelli, and Brian Turtle, *Six Degrees of Kevin Bacon* (New York, NY: Plume Books, 1996).

6 "The Oracle of Bacon," http://oracleofbacon.org/. Retrieved 26 May 2022.

7 Duncan Watts and Steven H. Strogatz, "Collective Dynamics of 'Small-World' Networks," *Nature* 393, no. 6684 (1998): 440–442.

8 Mark S. Granovetter, "The Strength of Weak Ties," *American Journal of Sociology* 78, no. 6 (1973): 1360–1380.

9 "Wikipedia: Wiki Game," https://en.wikipedia.org/wiki/Wikipedia :Wiki_Game. Retrieved 29 May 2022.

10 Karinthy, "Chain-Links," 26.

11 Paul Otlet, *Monde: Essai d'universalisme: Connaissances du monde. Sentiments du monde, Action organiste et plan du monde (Editiones Mundaneum)* (Bruxelles: D. Van Keerberghen et fils., 1935): 390–391.

12 Alex Wright, "The Web Time Forgot," *The New York Times*, 17 June 2008.

13 Alex Wright, "The Secret History of Hypertext," *The Atlantic*, 22 May 2014.
14 Herbert George Wells, *World Brain* (Cambridge, MA: MIT Press, 2021).
15 Ostwald, "Scientific Management for Scientists," *Scientific American* 108 (1913): 5–6.
16 Thomas Hapke and Wilhelm Ostwald, "The 'Brücke' (Bridge), and Connections to Other Bibliographic Activities at the Beginning of the Twentieth Century," *Information Today* 29, no. 4 (1999): 142.
17 Mary-Ann Pattison, "The Australian Joint Copying Project," *Government Publications Review* 13, no. 3 (1986): 349–353.
18 Michael K. Buckland, "Histories, Heritages, and the Past: The Case of Emanuel Goldberg," in *The History and Heritage of Scientific and Technical Information Systems*, eds W. B. Rayward and M. E. Bowden (Medford, NJ: Information Today, 2004): 39–45.
19 Ibid., 6.
20 Michael K. Buckland, "Emanuel Goldberg, Electronic Document Retrieval, and Vannevar Bush's Memex," *Journal of the American Society for Information Science* 43, no. 4 (1992): 284–294.
21 Carol A. Singer, "Ready Reference Collections: A History," *Reference & User Services Quarterly* 49, no. 3 (2010): 253–264.
22 Steve J. Pritchard and Alison L. Weightman, "Medline in the UK: Pioneering the Past, Present and Future," *Health Information & Libraries Journal* 22 (2005): 38–44.
23 "Internet Hall of Fame Pioneer: J.C.R. Licklider," *Internet Hall of Fame,* https://www.internethalloffame.org/inductees/jcr-licklider. Retrieved 14 June 2022.
24 Linda C. Smith, "Procognitive Systems: J.C.R. Licklider's Vision for Library Systems of the Future," University of Illinois, 2015.
25 Alex Wright, "The Future of the Web Is 100 Years Old," *Nautilus*, 29 January 2015.
26 Vannevar Bush, "As We May Think," *The Atlantic Monthly* 176, no. 1 (1945): 101–108.
27 Gary Wolf, "The Curse of Xanadu," *Wired*, 1 June 1995.
28 Joseph C. R. Licklider and Robert W. Taylor, "The Computer as a Communication Device," *Science and Technology* 76, no. 2 (1968): 1–3.
29 See "How Google Search Organizes Information," *Google Search*, https://www.google.com/search/howsearchworks/how-search-works/organizing-information/. Retrieved 28 May 2022.
30 Douglas Adams, *The Hitchiker's Guide to the Galaxy* (London: Pan Books, 1979).
31 Albert-László Barabási, "Network Science," *Philosophical Transactions of the Royal Society A: Mathematical, Physical and Engineering Sciences* 371, 1987 (2013): 20120375.
32 Linda C. Smith, "Citation Analysis," *Library Trends* Summer (1981): 93.

33  Rosemary Simpson, Allen Renear, Elli Mylonas, and Andries van Dam, "50 Years after 'As We May Think': The Brown/MIT Vannevar Bush Symposium," *Interactions* 3, no. 2 (1996): 47–67.

34  See Linda C. Smith, "Memex as an Image of Potentiality in Information Retrieval Research and Development," in *Proceedings of the 3rd Annual ACM Conference on Research and Development in Information Retrieval* (Kent, UK: Butterworth, 1981): 345–369.

35  Linda C. Smith, "Memex as an Image of Potentiality Revisited," in *From Memex to Hypertext: Vannevar Bush and the Mind's Machine*, eds. James Nyce and Paul Kahn (London: Academic Press, 1991): 265.

36  Tia O'Brien, "From the Archives: Douglas Engelbart's Lasting Legacy, 1999," *Silicon Valley.com/The Mercury News*, 3 July 2013.

37  Bush, "As We May Think," cited by Wright, "100 Years." See also Vannevar Bush, "We Are in Danger of Building a Tower of Babel," *Public Health Reports* 68, no. 2 (1953): 149.

38  Michael K. Buckland, "What Is a 'Document'?" *Journal of the American Society for Information Science* 48, no. 9 (1997): 805.

39  Smith, "Prognitive," 12–14.

40  Ronald R. Kline, "What Is Information Theory a Theory of? Boundary Work among Information Theorists and Information Scientists in the United States and Britain during the Cold War," in *The History and Heritage of Scientific and Technological Information Systems*, eds. W. B. Rayward and M. E. Bowden (Medford, NJ: American Society of Information Science and Technology and the Chemical Heritage Foundation, 2004): 15–28.

41  Buckland, "Histories." See also Ronald D. Houston and Glynn Harmon, "Vannevar Bush and Memex," *Annual Review of Information Science and Technology* 41, no. 1 (2007): 55–92.

42  See "Towards the Information Age: Paul Otlet (1868–1944) Founder of the Mundaneum," *Google Arts & Culture*, https://artsandculture.google .com/story/awXRg4ha0wAA8A?hl=en. Retrieved 31 May 2022.

43  Alexandre Serres, "Hypertexte: une histoire à revisiter. Documentaliste— Sciences de l'Information," 32, no. 2 (1995): 2. Cited by Le Deuff, Olivier, and Arthur Perret, "Hyperdocumentation: Origin and Evolution of a Concept," *Journal of Documentation* 75, no. 6 (2019): 6.

44  Geoffrey Fowler, "How Does Google's Monopoly Hurt You?" *The Washington Post*, 20 October 2020.

45  See Helen Nissenbaum, "Shaping the Web: Why the Politics of Search Engines Matters," *The Information Society* 16, no. 3 (2000): 169–185.

46  Safiya Umoja Noble, *Algorithms of Oppression: How Search Engines Reinforce Racism* (New York, NY: New York University Press, 2018): 6.

47  "Wikipedia," *Wikipedia*, https://en.wikipedia.org/wiki/Wikipedia. Retrieved 29 May 2022.

48  Francesca Tripodi, "Ms. Categorized: Gender, Notability, and Inequality on Wikipedia," *New Media & Society* (June 2021): 1–21. http://doi.org/10 .1177/14614448211023772

49  "Gender Bias on Wikipedia," *Wikipedia*, https://en.wikipedia.org/wiki/
Gender_bias_on_Wikipedia. Retrieved 29 May 2022.
50  Susan C. Herring, J. Reagle, Justine Cassell, Terri Oda, Anna North,
J. West, and M. Ranga. "Where Are the Women in Wikipedia," *The
New York Times* (2 February 2011). https://www.nytimes.com/room-
fordebate/2011/02/02/where-are-the-women-in-wikipedia. Retrieved
22 September 2022.
51  Sue Gardner, "Nine Reasons Women Don't Edit Wikipedia (in Their
Own Words)," *Sue Gardner's Blog*, https://suegardner.org/2011/02/19/
nine-reasons-why-women-dont-edit-wikipedia-in-their-own-words/.
Retrieved 29 May 2022.
52  Jodi Schneider, Alexandre Passant, and Stefan Decker, "Deletion
Discussions in Wikipedia: Decision Factors and Outcomes," in *Proceedings
of the Eighth Annual International Symposium on Wikis and Open Collaboration*,
ed. Cliff Lampe (Linz, Austria: Wikisym, 2012): 17.
53  Amanda Menking, Ingrid Erickson, and Wanda Pratt, "People Who
Can Take It: How Women Wikipedians Negotiate and Navigate Safety,"
in *Proceedings of the 2019 CHI Conference on Human Factors in Computing
Systems*. Paper No.: 472 (Glasgow, Scotland: SIGCHI 2019): 1–14.
https://doi.org/10.1145/3290605.3300702.
54  Ibid, 14.
55  "Racial Bias on Wikipedia," *Wikipedia*, https://en.wikipedia.org/wiki/
Racial_bias_on_Wikipedia. Retrieved 19 June 2022.

# UTILIZING INFORMATION

A crust-covered lump of metal resting in the remains of a wooden box was brought up from the depths of the Mediterranean Sea near the Greek Island of Antikythera in 1901 where it had lain for 2000 years. The wreck of a Roman cargo ship had been discovered the year before by sponge divers. One of the divers who discovered the wreck described what looked to him like a "heap of dead naked people."[1] These turned out to be statues of marble and bronze, found among other high-end items produced in ancient Greece: pottery, glassware, and jewelry. Archeologists speculated that the items had been the inventory of a merchant ship traveling from the island of Rhodes to elite buyers in Rome, perhaps even to Julius Caesar himself. Among the treasures was one indeterminate thing, heavy and unlovely.[2]

The items were taken to the National Museum of Archeology in Athens to be cleaned and analyzed. The following year the museum's director announced the discovery to the press, revealing that the mysterious artifact had *gears*. The claim was met with skepticism.[3] The wreck was estimated to have occurred in the first or second centuries BCE, predating the appearance of precision gear clockwork by a millennium.

As it was being cleaned, the artifact broke into three pieces. Newly visible inscriptions allowed a philologist to recognize the device as an astronomical calculator of some kind.[4] Preservationists carefully separated the fragments into 82 pieces, of which seven

DOI: 10.4324/9781003155119-5

contain most of the surviving gear mechanisms and inscriptions. In the 1950s, the artifact was identified as a calendrical computer.[5] Many of the 30 interlocking bronze gears had teeth that were still intact enough to count, a crucial detail for analyzing their mathematical functioning. Visible inscriptions gave additional clues, confirming that the device had been built to calculate and predict the movement of heavenly bodies, based on mathematical and astronomical theories of its day. X-ray images provided even greater accuracy in gear teeth counts and led to the creation of the first working prototype of the mechanism.[6]

During the first decade of the 21st century, imaging technologies were evolving, and even higher resolution scanning of the surface of the Antikythera mechanism became possible using Microfocus X-Ray Computed Tomography, a process in which 2D X-ray projection images are translated by specialized software into 3D images. The device provided by the U.K. based X-Tek Systems Ltd, was dubbed "Blade-runner."[7] The Antikythera Mechanism Research Project (AMRP) team used this process to achieve greater spatial resolution than a CT medical scanner can accomplish, identifying seven previously undetected gears and 2000 new text characters.[8]

The new information confirmed the calendrical functions of the device; it was calibrated for a particular geographical place with its pointers and gears set for local use. On the front face of the mechanism, the twelve zodiac signs were displayed in equal 30-degree sectors, following the Babylonian approach. A rotating ring outside the dial marked off months and days using Egyptian month names but written in Greek letters. The inscriptions indicated that the device once had a mechanical display. A missing hand crank would have allowed the user of the device to set the date pointer, an action that caused the interlocking gears to move, calculating the positions of sun, moon, and planets.

At the back of the mechanism was an "Olympiad Dial," which could calculate the dates and locations of the Panhellenic Games, a series of athletic events held at different locations in two- and four-year cycles. When Roman Emperor Theodosius ordered the games to cease in 393 CE it was the end of a millennium-long tradition; the athletic festival had been held 293 times. The Antikythera device confirms their significance in the ancient

world.[9] Astonishingly, one group of gears provided an adjust-
ment for the calculations regarding the moon, based on a mathematical theory by Hipparchus in the second century BCE that
accounted for the effect of the moon's elliptic orbit on the irreg-
ularity of its motion.[10] Hipparchus has been suggested as a possible creator of the mechanism. Another possibility is Archimedes
who was credited by Cicero with having invented a mechanism
which displayed the planets moving around the earth at different
speeds.[11]

The Antikythera mechanism is considered the first analog computer; its computational algorithms were programmed into the
mechanics of the gears. As an information technology it also functioned as a finding aid which its users could "query" and retrieve
answers to narrowly focused questions: when will the next eclipse
occur? Where will future Panhellenic Games be held?

The story of the unraveling of the mystery of the Antikythera
mechanism sheds light on how data becomes information. From
the 82 fragments of the "primary document" secondary documents
of every kind have sprung: photographs, charts, diagrams, sche-
mata, models, calculations, algorithms, data sets, X-ray images,
computer-generated renderings, animations, books, articles, documentary films, simulations, and prototypes (one made out of
Legos). Inquiry into the history of the deciphering of the mechanism, and how so much information could be found inside a mute
lump of metal, produced more documents: interviews, records, letters, emails, and websites.

Scientific knowledge is created within networks that include
people, material objects of study, the practices, places, and technologies that allow those objects to speak, and the flood of data
that is created as a result. Data was collected or produced in waves
of observation, followed by cleaning, analysis, interpretation, and
sharing. Information about the mechanism gleaned by one group
was passed on to the next. New technologies revealed additional
data to analyze. Over the past 120 years, there have been archeologists, engineers, mathematicians, physicists, computer scientists,
imaging specialists, preservationists, philologists, linguists, and historians, among others, working to solve each new puzzle—often
on interdisciplinary teams. We know what we know about the

Antikythera mechanism because the data, and the information derived from the data, were shared.

This chapter surveys the methods and practices through which collected data becomes actionable information. It explores the potentials of linked data and machine learning to support data sharing, and collaborative knowledge creation. The chapter ends by examining the context that surrounds these practices.

## DATA ANALYTICS

Our present-day academic landscape emerged from a seemingly natural but socially constructed separation of the natural sciences from the arts and humanities.[12] This historical separation informs differences in the perceived validity of quantitative versus qualitative evidence, the utility of computational versus narrative reasoning, and the authority of numbers versus words. As our ontologies were forming over the centuries, one area of difference centered around the question of *precision* in scholarly inquiry. Scientific and economic scholarship simplified the messy complexity of the social world into models, judging spare numerical expressions to be more precise. At the same time, scholars in the humanities addressed that complexity by adding detail, and pursuing precision through explanation, example, and verbose linguistic expression.[13]

Qualitative data doesn't lend itself to computation, but it provides detailed information, rich with the context surrounding what has been collected; ethnographers refer to these sources as "thick descriptions." Information derived from qualitative research is less generalizable outside its domain, but more accurate within. Quantitative data collection and analysis makes the opposite choice. It applies traditional statistical techniques and, increasingly, machine learning models within artificial intelligence (AI) systems and applications, stripping out context to look for patterns in populations that become observable only in large data sets. The term "Big Data" refers not only to the size of datasets, but to the significance and potential of information that can be gleaned through analysis of them.

The processes through which quantitative data (as a single data set, or aggregated from multiple data sets) is compiled, translated, cleaned, and analyzed is referred to as *data analytics*. An associated term, *data mining*, refers more specifically to the data analytic techniques which identify the patterns in data that might be actionable in some way. Data science is an interdisciplinary field centered around methods of data analytics, in which information science, computer science, statistics, sociology, geography, bioinformatics, and business, among many other fields that seek to derive insights from quantitative data, all have a stake.[14]

Data analytics typically begins with a data set and a general area of interest or inquiry. Without necessarily articulating a specific hypothesis, analysis is conducted which may turn up expected (or unexpected) patterns in large data sets. Data mining techniques applied to biomedical data, for example, use machine learning algorithms to identify unanticipated relationships between genetic markers and disease which smaller samples would not have been able to flag.[15] In business settings, data analytics may inform decisions on marketing, customer service, or product development, so that choices made on a new line, are based on empirical evidence rather than on what the CEO wishes were true.

The process of turning data sets into information that can be utilized in the world, begins with acquiring and processing data. Because the accuracy of analysis increases as data sets get larger, multiple sets are often combined. It happens frequently that the data sets are structured differently because their sources were different, one data set acquired from an open access repository, another from a university-sponsored project, and a third from a non-scientific survey conducted by a non-profit organization, all with different initial goals that guided the collections, as well as varying levels of sophistication in their metadata.

Before such heterogeneous data can be combined into a single data set, a process called *data cleansing* (or data cleaning) will take each data set through a series of technical transformations. Strings of text will have white spaces, punctuation, and unwanted characters stripped away. Misspellings will be corrected, and synonyms detected. Dates will be converted to a standard numerical format. More complicated processes help to determine the quality and accuracy of the data by identifying and correcting data errors and removing "bad data" (which might be fabricated, nonsensical, or mistakenly included). Missing data can be filled through a variety of techniques which extrapolate based on the available data. When a data sets are found to have missing or *incompatible metadata*, new data structures have to be developed, transforming incommensurate fields into commensurate ones that fit within the new structures. These processes are notoriously time-consuming, but also essential. Evolving tools and technologies are making this work easier.

Data cleansing processes may also add error or bias to combined data sets, if by restructuring them, distinctions are lost. When comparing rates of global literacy, for example, a researcher may discover that literacy can be measured in different ways. One country might collect data on the average years of schooling that its citizens receive, while another country has produced data sets that are compiled from standardized reading tests. Can these two data sets be combined, to arrive at a measure called "literacy"?[16] They can, and often are, but there are dangers in combining data sets without taking into account the full context behind the collection of the data.

If the results of the analysis, in this hypothetical case, indicate a low level of regional literacy, the finding won't be able to guide an effective policy intervention, because it's no longer possible to say if what is most needed is to improve access to education for girls (which caused the average years of education count to be low), or to improve the quality of teacher training (which caused the test scores to be low). The analysis is accurate as far as it goes, but the information produced by the data cannot be productively utilized.

When a data set has been prepared, the next step is to choose what kind of analysis to conduct. Statistical techniques, like *regression analysis*, identify correlations between different variables; *multiple regression* can detect correlations between several variables simultaneously. If there is a need to identify patterns in the data, *association analysis* could be employed, because it can identify co-occurrences of items within a data set. A company might want to know, for example, that people who purchase a certain expensive fashion item also prefer an unrelated brand of furniture. This information could guide a marketing campaign or suggest a new product line.

Direct marketing strategies, which target particular customers based on predictions of what they are likely to buy in the future, often use *classification analysis*, which identifies and creates classes of items (or customers) and their commonly occurring attributes, providing a basis for predicting their behavior. A related technique, *clustering analysis*, looks at similarities and differences between data points, finding "clusters" of customers who seem to purchase the same sorts of things, or "clusters" of items another group of customers appears to be avoiding. A cluster is different from a class of items because the cluster can include items across multiple classes.

Clustering analysis has proven to be valuable in medical research as well. An analysis of 58 million patient visits in Finland over a period of three years discovered an expectable cluster between hypertensive and cardiovascular disease, but also an unexpected cluster of lower respiratory tract diseases with connective tissue disorders.[17] With this data in hand, the researchers' next step was to try to explain the appearance of the unexpected cluster in the data. This created a whole new direction of research that would never have been initiated without the study.

## WORKING WITH DATA

If the intent of a data analytic project is to explain social behavior or to guide policy, care has to be taken that *statistical correlations* are not mistaken for *causation*, and that no factors have been left out of the analysis that might help to explain the phenomenon or process being studied.

A study which set out to understand why some people prefer to read using a digital device (via audio or e-book) and others reach for a physical book, researchers discovered a correlation between the use of electronic devices and interest in the arts.[18] The collected data showed that those who did more reading electronically also had higher levels of engagement with the arts (which was measured by attendance at art exhibits, visits to museums, and financial contributions to arts organizations). Should they have concluded that this result was evidence that going to museums leads to digital reading, or that, perhaps, digital reading causes people to give money to art-related causes?

The researchers don't assert this, understanding that such an interpretation would be a *spurious correlation*—a term that is used to describe a data model in which some third "confounding" factor may be causing both observed effects. A good candidate for missing factor in this case comes from another finding in the data: digital reading correlated with an individual's level of education. While the rate of print reading was about the same for High School graduates and individuals with PhDs, the practice of digital reading rose steeply for each additional level of educational attainment.[19] So, is that the end of this data story? Should the researchers conclude that higher education causes people to read eBooks and contribute to arts organizations? Or could there be another factor that might explain both of those things?

Research on educational attainment finds that social stratifications (based on race, religion, language, culture, caste, economic class, gender, skin color, etc.) can explain differences in access to and quality of early education, as well as opportunities to pursue higher education.[20]

Returning to the hypothetical study referenced earlier (which combined the two data sets, one that measured literacy through years of education, and one through standardized reading tests), this e-book study seems to support the idea that the data sets can be safely combined. People with the lowest level of education were found to read the least—many of them reporting that they don't read at all (though the study didn't ask if they were *able* to read). It does seem safe to assume that years of education can be combined with test scores to create a data type called "literacy level." So, let's imagine that the researchers decide to go ahead with combining the data sets and do the data analysis and they find that a certain region has a high level of literacy. They use this data to make a comparison with other regions, with policy implications for educational funding.

Before the results are published, a colleague looks at the draft report and asks if they took into account the large refugee and migrant population in the region; the migrant children all go to school, but the lack of teaching resources for bilingual instruction (or any materials in their native languages at all) in addition to widespread discrimination amid the failure to integrate them into the larger society, has led to very low literacy in those communities. The data set containing data about years of schooling does not, in this part of their region of study, provide an accurate measure for literacy.

Lack of familiarity with the cultural context of the data (sometimes referred to as its "knowledge domain") undermined the validity of their conclusions. Even worse, by combining the data sets, the experience of the refugee children was erased. Let's end the story more happily by imagining that the researchers choose to go back, disaggregating (separating) the data that related to the refugee population, and analyzing it as a separate case, collaborating with their colleague, incorporating qualitative sources of data from their field research that sheds light on the circumstances that affect education in migrant and refugee communities in that part of the world. Their *multi-method* research now combines the benefit of Big Data analytics with the deeper exploration of the cultural context surrounding an outlying case.

A different kind of challenge faces researchers if all goes well with the data collection, preparation, and analysis, but the results are not what they (or their client) were hoping for. The term *data massaging* refers to the use of analysis, visualization, and communication that foreground results that are most desirable, and deemphasizes those that are not. Data analysts use *structured query language* (SQL) to retrieve data from a database, and can repeat their queries, changing parameters in small ways, until the answers they get back provide a response that better suits the questions they are tasked with investigating.

There is an important line to be drawn between the perfectly appropriate tailoring of the communication of data when not everything in a study is relevant to the problem at hand, and what would be considered unethical "cherry picking" of data, which ignores findings that contradict preferred interpretations. At the extreme end of unethical behavior is the deliberate falsification of data or its analyzed results.

Data is considered "good" when it represents the population from which it has been taken, when it has been collected in an ethical manner, when its context has been sufficiently and accurately reflected in the metadata, and when the researcher understands the domain from which the data has been taken.[21] When data is biased or inaccurate, or when combined data sets are incommensurate, then the information that is derived from their analysis won't really be information at all.

## SHARING DATA

Among the most visionary aspects of the work of Paul Otlet was the idea that books and other documents should be linked to each other through the use of coded metadata, functioning somewhat (but not exactly) as hyperlinks do today.[22] Otlet wanted someone who was searching for information to be able to discover that two linked books were in agreement or disagreement with each other, for example, without having to go to all the trouble of acquiring both books in order to find that out. Otlet imagined information being directly linked to information, within a network that continuously updated its metadata.[23] He used auxiliary tables, separate from the regular index system, to store codes specifying links between topics.[24]

That is not how the Internet was designed to work; it was set up so that web *pages* would connect to one another through internet addresses. The content of pages was not originally machine-interpretable, although Tim Berners-Lee hoped that it would be eventually. In a famous speech given at the first International World Wide Web Conference in 1994, three years after he launched his web browser, he articulated the notion of a *Semantic Web*, in which the meaningful content on websites, and not just its metadata, could be read by a computer and understood "semantically." Analyzed and acted upon, such content would allow our computers to function as intelligent agents that could connect to all the sources of information in our lives and do more complicated tasks such as making medical appointments or reserving tables at our favorite restaurants.

What he was suggesting doesn't sound very radical in the era of Siri and Alexa. But he wanted something more than what we get from our personal assistants now. In a truly Semantic Web, our "agent" would deliver better answers to our queries because it would comprehend more about the nature of what we are asking for and what it is retrieving.[25] By 2010 Berners-Lee had narrowed his rhetoric regarding the Semantic Web idea towards a somewhat simpler vision: transforming the Web from a network of *linked documents* to a web of *linked data*.

If computers could learn about the relationships between different kinds of data on web pages, he argued, they would be able to parse the meaning, and not just the form, of what they found. Computers would then use the Internet more like people do, surfing the Web on their own, moving from data to linked data rather than from page to linked page. Pieces of information would have web addresses, just as webpages do now.[26]

For different systems such as databases and applications to communicate with one another, semantic ontologies must first be created and implemented. These provide a shared understanding of the nature of things in the world and the relationships between them. The computer learns that a person *has* an occupation, that being an author *is* an occupation, that an author *creates* published works, that a journal article *is* a published work. A personal assistant that has incorporated a semantic ontology could put these understandings together in more complex ways. It would know that a restaurant is a place, that hunger is a feeling, and so is pain, but hunger requires a restaurant, and pain requires a doctor (a person, who is found in a place). The semantic web uses a *Resource Description Framework* (RDF) to organize these relationships, much as Otlet's auxiliary tables held coded links between topics.[27]

From the point of view of scientists, the ability to access and link distributed data more efficiently may provide researchers with answers to old questions, now currently locked in inaccessible data sets. It may lead them to ask new questions based on detected patterns, semantically understood by increasingly intelligent programs. Most practically, data will become reusable. Studies can be replicated, increasing the reliability of findings, and the data can also be deployed in new contexts. Semantically-aware algorithms would be able to recognize unexpected patterns as well as their potential value and bring these to the attention of researchers.

For government administrators, a more semantic web promises a solution to the chronic information challenge experienced by government bureaucracies worldwide: data is typically distributed across agencies, and even when it is shared, it may be organized so heterogeneously that it is difficult or impossible to merge it into larger data set to be most productively analyzed. Human processing of data is slow and expensive. For governments, non-profit organizations, and corporations, linked-data promises to improve efficiency, and to save money. The hope is also that linked data may also lead to creativity and innovation as massive amounts of currently inaccessible data in unlinked databases start to become available. This is already happening, through Open Government and other Open Access repositories. The problem is, as always, in the implementation.

Search engines have been stymied in incorporating semantic techniques by the way that metadata is currently organized and created. This is not a new problem. Otlet couldn't figure out how to keep his classification system accurate without involving an army of trained people occupied in the continuous process of updating the metadata (recorded on the millions of index cards they eventually created) as well as maintaining the auxiliary tables that held the densely coded links between cards.

It is not so surprising that using sophisticated machine learning to transform the Internet into a semantic web still requires a significant amount of human labor. The term *folksonomy*, also known as collaborative tagging, group tagging, or social tagging, refers to the creation of a semantic ontology developed from the bottom up—where users in a public forum connected to a particular knowledge domain classify information without vocabulary control limiting the categories that can be used. On the positive side, folksonomies are flexible, easy to edit, and can get at critical knowledge within a community that only members fully understand, and that an external indexing system would be likely to miss. The downside of collaborative tagging is that it can be so individualistic and idiosyncratic that the ontology it produces does not enhance search and retrieval. These are essentially the same problems that vocabulary control in library cataloging was designed to deal with, to control for misspellings, synonyms, dialectical differences, and diverse cultural meanings. In practice, when folksonomies "work" they end up stabilizing into taxonomies, and vocabulary control is deployed after they get to that stage.[28]

Transforming the Internet from being a web of linked pages to a web of linked data also requires that website designers change the way in which they share and display data. First, data needs to be *open*, meaning that it is licensed to be freely available for downloading and use. The data also needs to be *structured*, presented within an actual table (rather than an image of a table), so that it is computer-readable. Ideally the table should be in a *non-proprietary format* such as CSV. Finally, to allow computers to link to the data directly, and not just to the page, the data needs its own *universal resource identifier* (URI).

Facebook, Google, and other websites have incorporated a proprietary AI-driven system called the *Knowledge Graph* into their products. This system was developed by *Yewno*, a company whose stated mission is "extracting knowledge from an overwhelming quantity of unstructured and structured data."[29] The Knowledge Graph creates semantic ontologies that allow it to understand something about the meaning of search queries and results, in order to retrieve with greater accuracy what it thinks you want to know.[30]

Google's Knowledge Graph is an encyclopedia-style database, used to populate its Knowledge Panel. This first manifested as a small box of information in the upper-right-hand corner of a page of search results, but over time it has expanded to take over more of the screen. The information provided in this box includes the kind of things most people querying on the same keywords might want to know; whether a restaurant is still open, for example. Pulling directly from Wikipedia's database, as well as other encyclopedic-type sources of information, the Knowledge Panel collapses the "selection" and the "fetch" steps of traditional information retrieval, displacing links, though still providing them in case the information provided is not all that is needed.

The goal of Google Search, according to Google, is "to organize the world's information and make it universally accessible and useful."[31] Linking data is one strategy for accomplishing that. But in order for the vision of linked data to make a significant difference, an enormous amount of data is required. The need is sometimes referred to as *the Three Vs*—Volume (a whole lot of data), Variety (of many different kinds), and Velocity (accessed quickly). Critics charge that linked data will make government censorship of internet content easier, more efficient, and more invasive. More of our private data will be available to people who want to sell us things legally, but also will make it easier to manipulate us fraudulently. The same processes that work towards universal access to information also include significant risks.

*Scientific data sharing* fits within a larger community of collaborative knowledge creation practices associated with *crowdsourcing*, a strategy in which large numbers of individuals contribute towards a common goal that individuals or small groups could not accomplish on their own.

One common type of crowdsourcing is *crowdfunding*, when large numbers of people contribute small amounts of money to support a person, project, or cause. Increasingly, creative projects like indie games or films use crowdfunding for capital investment.[32] Some prize contests, where the goal is to encourage innovation and experimentation on a particular scientific or social problem, is also a kind of crowdsourcing.[33]

The projects sponsored by Wikimedia, including Wikipedia, depend on volunteers to continuously update the information on their sites. This strategy has obvious advantages, since many more people can work on the task than a company can afford to hire. But there are disadvantages to crowdsourcing information collection as well. It is more difficult to ensure the integrity and good will of all the volunteering editors and the accuracy and objectivity of their contributions. It is challenging to prevent the introduction of bias (indvertantly or deliberately) into a crowdsourced knowledge system.

The term *citizen science* describes work done by amateur or non-professional scientists and volunteers towards a complicated, large-scale, or ongoing project or area of scientific research. There is a longstanding tradition for birdwatchers, for example, to provide their bird lists for ornithological studies.[34]

To ensure the quality of scientific data produced or analyzed by volunteers, scientists may set up a more formal *Citizen Cyberspace Project* (CCP). The most well-known CCP is Zooniverse, whose first project was the Galaxy Zoo, created in 2007 to recruit volunteers to help locate and classify the shape of galaxies in close to a million images. By 2022 two and a half million volunteers had made almost 700 million individual contributions scrutinizing, transcribing, classifying, or analyzing data.[35]

Since the creation of metadata often requires human intervention, even when machine learning algorithms are being used, many Zooniverse projects ask volunteers to transcribe and documents, or to scan photos of animals or plants, and to categorize what they see, or to help in the creation of metadata. There are challenges involved with relying on volunteers; there need to be enough people to accomplish the task and to ensure the quality of the work, and to maintain the credibility of data sets created in this way.[36] In addition to scientific integrity, a range of information policy issues have arisen related to the ethics of crowdsourcing and citizen science projects, including the protection of intellectual property and the privacy of its participants.[37]

There are many positive cultural outcomes from such collaborative projects, however, beyond their contributions to important research projects. Volunteers may form a community as a result of their participation in a project; retired people may achieve a new sense of purpose; children participating in these projects in school may acquire curiosities that propel them towards future careers. When a scientist engages a community to collaborate in the study of a question that is of particular concern to them, seeking a concrete solution through data collection and analysis, it may be referred to as *participatory action research*, or community science.[38]

Scientists increasingly work together through their communities of practice as well. It has been argued, for example, that the field of computational astrophysics is served by the sharing of data and open-source software through professional community networks, and that this shared work can be done without sacrificing individual success.[39]

During the Covid-19 pandemic, there were notable successes that resulted from cooperation between international teams. BioNTech, the company that contributed the RNA technology that led to the Pfizer Covid-19 vaccine, worked closely with InstaDeep, a British AI company. Through collective effort, they were successful in creating an early warning system that could identify new variants of the disease.[40]

The deluge of Covid-related data that was produced and shared around the world, during the pandemic was of uneven quality. Much of it was fragmented and incomplete. Because not all parts of the world, or all sectors of a society received the same amount of attention or resources, the data was not representative, a circumstance which can bias the results. Some datasets could not be combined effectively because of incompatible metadata. Another problem was dramatically different policies regarding content and confidentiality. Aggregated case counts protected privacy but did not provide enough of patients' histories to provide the needed context. [41]

One promising new approach called *federated learning* emerged during the pandemic. Employed by an international team from the University of Cambridge and the Huazhong University of Science and Technology, for example, the technique allowed hospitals to train AI models using data sets from other hospitals, without having to share the sensitive underlying data.[42] The OPEN Covid-19 working group and other collaborative initiatives that began during the pandemic explored new approaches to data sharing.[43] There is a need for collaborative infrastructures, including international conventions regarding data sharing, to encourage practices that enable ethical scientific study.

## UTILIZING INFORMATION IN CONTEXT

It matters what gets included in a data set and what does not. Bias can make its way into a data set without conscious intent and for this reason it can be difficult to identify. If we are not a member of a group being disadvantaged, we might be unaware (or unwilling to believe) that certain inequalities exist in our own communities. This can make it more difficult for us to recognize them in a dataset. Unconscious bias can sometimes reflect structural racism, in which race-based inequalities have become part of a society's institutions and norms. It becomes visible, of course, when the biased research is utilized in the world and something goes wrong as a result.

Historically, scientific research focused on the experiences of the majority population, or other high-status groups. Women were systematically left out of 20th-century biomedical research, for example, leading to less appropriate treatments and poorer outcomes for women suffering from heart disease.[44] Minority populations are still systematically undercounted, resulting in the failure of their communities to receive resources to which they may be entitled under the law.[45]

Imagine a research team studying the health needs of a community. It has to decide how the "needs" of different racial groups are going to be measured. They know they will need numerical data that a computer can understand, and they want a lot of data, but they don't have time for a qualitative study. They look around for available data sets that will serve the purpose and they find one that captured "money spent on health care," by race. They decide that this can serve as a *proxy variable* to stand in as a measure of the health needs of different racial groups, for which they have found no direct data.

This example is not hypothetical; it comes from an algorithm widely used to estimate health needs in the United States. In one study using this variable it was found that white people spend significantly more on average on health care than Black people. The data was transformed into the actionable information that Black communities need less care. That information was utilized in policy: less money was allocated for their follow-up health care. This proved to be a disaster for health outcomes in Black communities.

It turned out that money spent was a terrible proxy for actual healthcare needs, a fact that would have been obvious had the historical context surrounding the question been taken into account. In the United States, intractable economic inequalities, and a market-driven system of health insurance, have led to a situation in which it is difficult for non-white people to afford the health care that white people take for granted. Black people spend less because they have less money to spend. The study ended up contributing directly to the reproduction of a race-based health disparity in one community.[46] White communities received more resources even though they needed them less.

Working with data ethically requires more than simply avoiding bias in data collection. Issues of privacy, confidentiality, transparency, identity protection, security, and oversight are all ethical issues that fall into the larger area of information governance. Laws, policies, and regulations provide guidelines and outline expectations for ethical research practices, especially when human subjects are involved, as well as for ethical data handling in non-research settings, anywhere that data is collected, analyzed, shared, and utilized.

The public has a say in ethical debates as well; outcry followed the publication in 2014 of a study conducted by Facebook and researchers at Cornell University which manipulated Facebook algorithms to show users either more positive or negative content. They did this to study the emotional impact of social media comments upon users. The public was outraged to be experimented upon without consent. That the researchers who created this experiment were surprised about the level of anger that their experiment triggered underscores the need for effective data governance.[47]

*Critical information studies* (and critical data studies) focus on these, and other, ethical issues, situating the utilization of information within historical, social, and political contexts, and addressing issues of power, control, and social justice. In his book, *The Order of Things*, Michel Foucault suggested that every historical era embraces a social ontology that it believes to be natural.[48] What follows from such hierarchical convictions can be disastrous. In Nazi Germany, Hitler and his followers justified genocide through racial theories that classified peoples by physiological characteristics like skin color, religion, geographic origin and sexual orientation. The Nazis kept track of such data *on index cards.*

In retrospect it is obvious that racist classifications produced biased science, which helped to reproduce racial and gender-based oppressions; in that era racial theories, many originating in the United States, not long after the abolition of slavery, were accepted by mainstream society as unbiased scientific observations. Critical approaches to data help to bring into the light the unconscious biases and persistent inequities of *our* day, so that we can attempt to design information systems that do not inadvertently reproduce them.

One of the lessons to be taken from the story of the successful reconstruction of the Antikythera mechanism from a hunk of metal brought up from the bottom of the sea, is that sharing data, information, and knowledge of all kinds, across national borders, and across time, may be key to solving the world's most intractable problems. But diversifying teams and prioritizing their interdisciplinarity is increasingly understood to be necessary to make sure that data sets are ethically created, analyzed without bias, and utilized in ways that work for the good of all.

## NOTES

1 Tony Freeth, "An Ancient Greek Astronomical Calculation Machine Reveals New Secrets," *Scientific American*, 1 January 2022.

2 Derek De Solla Price, "Gears from the Greeks," *Journal for the History of Astronomy* 8 (1977): 143.

3 Konstantinos Prokopios Trimmis, "The Forgotten Pioneer: Valerios Stais and His Research in Kythera, Antikythera and Thessaly," *Bulletin of the History of Archaeology* 26, no. 1 (2016): 10.

4 Tony Freeth, "Building the Cosmos in the Antikythera Mechanism," *Proceedings of Science* 170 Antikythera and SKA (2013): 1–16. https://doi .org/10.22323/1.170.0018.

5 Derek J. De Solla Price, "An Ancient Greek Computer," *Scientific American* 200, no. 6 (1959): 60–67.

6 Lauren Poole, "Bromley's Model of the Antikythera Mechanism," *Powerhouse*, 1 November 2017. https://www.maas.museum/inside -the-collection/2017/11/01/bromleys-model-of-the-antikythera -mechanism/.=

7 Andrew Ramsey, "X-Ray Tomography of the Antikythera Mechanism," *Proceedings of Science* 170, Antikythera and SKA (2013): 1–12. https://doi .org/10.22323/1.170.0022.

8 Michael Edmunds and Tony Freeth, "Using Computation to Decode the First Known Computer," *Computer* 44, no. 7 (2011): 32.

9 Tony Freeth, Alexander Jones, John M. Steele, and Yanis Bitsakis, "Calendars with Olympiad Display and Eclipse Prediction on the Antikythera Mechanism," *Nature* 454, no. 7204 (2008): 614–617.

10 Tony Freeth et al., "Decoding the Ancient Greek Astronomical Calculator Known as the Antikythera Mechanism," *Nature* 444, no. 7119 (2006): 587.

11 Michael T. Wright, "Archimedes, Astronomy, and the Planetarium," in *Archimedes in the 21st Century*, ed. Chris Rorres (Cham: Birkhäuser, 2017): 125–141.

12 Gary W. Trompf, "The Classification of the Sciences and the Quest for Interdisciplinarity: A Brief History of Ideas from Ancient Philosophy to Contemporary Environmental Science," *Environmental Conservation* 38, no. 2 (2011): 113–126.

13  Bonnie Mak and Julia Pollack, "The Performance and Practice of Research in a Cabinet of Curiosity: The Library's Dead Time," *Art Documentation: Journal of the Art Libraries Society of North America* 32, no. 2 (2013): 202–221.

14  See Sirje Virkus, and Emmanouel Garoufallou, "Data Science and Its Relationship to Library and Information Science: A Content Analysis," *Data Technologies and Applications* 54, no. 5 (2020): 643–663.

15  For examples, see Anugrah Srivastava and Advait Naik, "Big Data Analysis in Bioinformatics," in *Advances in Bioinformatics*, eds. Vijai Singh and Ajay Kumar (Singapore: Springer, 2021): 405–429.

16  Max Roser and Esteban Ortiz-Ospina, "Literacy: Data Quality Challenges and Limitations," in *Our World in Data: Literacy*, https://ourworldindata.org/literacy. Retrieved 31 May 2022.

17  Pasi Fränti, Sami Sieranoja, Katja Wikström, and Tiina Laatikainen, "Clustering Diagnoses from 58 Million Patient Visits in Finland between 2015 and 2018," *JMIR Medical Informatics* 10, no. 5 (2022): e35422.

18  James Murdoch, Mark Bauerlein, Marie Halverson, Natalie Morrissey, and Esther Galadima, "How Do We Read? Let's Count the Ways: Comparing Digital, Audio, and Print-Only Readers," *National Endowment for the Arts Report* (2020): 16. https://www.arts.gov/sites/default/files/How%20Do%20We%20Read%20report%202020.pdf. Retrieved 23 September 2022.

19  Ibid., 21.

20  Shervin Assari, Cleopatra H. Caldwell, and Mohsen Bazargan, "Association between Parental Educational Attainment and Youth Outcomes and Role of Race/Ethnicity," *JAMA Network Open* 2, no. 11 (2019). https://doi.org/10.1001/jamanetworkopen.2019.16018

21  Jana Diesner, "Small Decisions with Big Impact on Data Analytics," *Big Data & Society* 2, no. 2 (2015): 6.

22  Olivier Le Deuff and Arthur Perret, "Hyperdocumentation: Origin and Evolution of a Concept," *Journal of Documentation* 75, no. 6 (2019).

23  Alex Wright, "The Future of the Web Is 100 Years Old," *Nautilus* (2015), https://nautil.us/the-future-of-the-web-is-100-years-old-2894/. Retrieved 2 June 2022.

24  Alex Wright, "The Web Time Forgot," *New York Times* 17 (2008).

25  Tim Berners-Lee, J. Hendler, and O. Lassila, "The Semantic Web," *Scientific American* 284, no. 5 (2001): 28–37.

26  Christian Bizer, Tom Heath, and Tim Berners-Lee, "Linked Data: The Story So Far," in *Semantic Services, Interoperability and Web Applications: Emerging Concepts*, ed. Amit P. Sheth (Hershey, PA: IGI Global, 2011): 205–227.

27  Charles Van den Heuvel, "Web 2.0 and the Semantic Web in Research from a Historical Perspective: The Designs of Paul Otlet (1868–1944) for Telecommunication and Machine Readable Documentation to Organize Research and Society," *Knowledge Organization* 36, no. 4 (2009): 214–226.

28  Mahdi Khademian and Morteza Kokabi, "Library Thing Social Tags versus Library of Congress Subject Headings: A Literature Review," *Library and Information Science Research* 8, no. 1 (2018): 313–335.

29  "Yewno," https://www.yewno.com/about. Retrieved 1 June 2022.

30  Amit Singhal, "Introducing the Knowledge Graph: Things, Not Strings," 16 May 2012, https://blog.google/products/search/introducing-knowledge-graph-things-not/. Retrieved 1 June 2022.

31  "Google Search | Overview," https://www.google.com/search/howsearchworks/. Retrieved 15 June 2022.

32  Johannes Wachs and Balázs Vedres, "Does Crowdfunding Really Foster Innovation? Evidence from the Board Game Industry," *Technological Forecasting and Social Change* 168 (2021): 120747.

33  For an infographic of historical examples of crowdsourcing see "A Brief History of Crowdsourcing [Infographic]," *Crowdsourcing.org*, 18 March 2012.

34  See, for example, the eBird project at the Cornell Lab of Ornithology, https://ebird.org/home. Retrieved 4 June 2022.

35  See Zooniverse.org, https://www.zooniverse.org/about. Retrieved 3 June 2022.

36  Peter T. Darch, "Managing the Public to Manage Data: Citizen Science and Astronomy," arXiv preprint arXiv:1703.00037 (2017): 27.

37  Christi J. Guerrini, Mary A. Majumder, Meaganne J. Lewellyn, and Amy L. McGuire. "Citizen Science, Public Policy," *Science* 361, no. 6398 (2018): 134–136.

38  Jessica M. Kramer, John C. Kramer, Edurne García-Iriarte, and Joy Hammel, "Following through to the End: The Use of Inclusive Strategies to Analyse and Interpret Data in Participatory Action Research with Individuals with Intellectual Disabilities," *Journal of Applied Research in Intellectual Disabilities* 24, no. 3 (2011): 263–273.

39  Matthew J. Turk, "Scaling a Code in the Human Dimension," in *Proceedings of the Conference on Extreme Science and Engineering Discovery Environment: Gateway to Discovery* (2013): 1–7. https://doi.org/10.1145/2484762.2484782

40  Qeis Kamran and Berit Schumann, "Towards an Effective Rapprochement between Artificial Intelligence and Medical and Pharmaceutical Research," *Modern Approaches in Drug Designing* 3, no. 4 (2022): 1–4.

41  Bhaskar Chakravorti, "Why AI Failed to Live Up to Its Potential during the Pandemic," *Harvard Business Review*, 27 March 2022.

42  Dong Yang, Ziyue Xu, Wenqi Li, Andriy Myronenko, Holger R. Roth, Stephanie Harmon, Sheng Xu et al., "Federated Semi-Supervised Learning for COVID Region Segmentation in Chest CT Using Multi-National Data from China, Italy, Japan," *Medical Image Analysis* 70 (2021): 101992.

43  Olga Kokshagina, "Open Covid-19: Organizing an Extreme Crowdsourcing Campaign to Tackle Grand Challenges," *R&D Management* 52, no. 2 (2022): 206–219.

44  Allison M. Whelan, "Unequal Representation: Women in Clinical Research," *Cornell Law Review Online* 106 (2020): 103–104.
45  See, for example Vasile Cernat, "Roma Undercount and the Issue of Undeclared Ethnicity in the 2011 Romanian Census," *International Journal of Social Research Methodology* 24, no. 6 (2021): 761–766.
46  Ziad Obermeyer, Brian Powers, Christine Vogeli, and Sendhil Mullainathan, "Dissecting Racial Bias in an Algorithm Used to Manage the Health of Populations," *Science* 366, no. 6464 (2019): 447–453.
47  Anita Chan, "Big Data Interfaces and the Problem of Inclusion," *Media, Culture & Society* 37, no. 7 (2015): 1078–1083.
48  Michel Foucault, *The Order of Things* (London: Routledge, 2005).

# 6

# GOVERNING INFORMATION

The 11th-century Bayeux Tapestry is not technically a tapestry, because it was embroidered, not woven. In its 70 panels, which stretch 230 feet (70 meters), it tells the story of the Battle of Hastings; within it one can count 623 men, 207 birds, 190 horses, 35 dogs—and three women.

The identification of two of the women is a matter of debate, but the third is Edith of Wessex, Queen of England. She is depicted weeping at the feet of her husband, King Edward "the Confessor" who had died, it is believed, of a stroke. Edith and Edward were childless, an unfortunate circumstance that set off a war of succession. On the tapestry Edith is pointing toward her brother, Harold Godwinson, who would soon take the throne.

Edith and her brother Harold were half Anglo-Saxon and half Danish. The fortunes of their powerful and ambitious father, Godwin, Earl of Wessex, had been significantly improved by King "Cnut the Great," who had ruled England, Denmark, and Norway in a Great North Sea Kingdom 30 years before. Harold was crowned King Harold II with unseemly rapidity after Edward's death. Arguably, William, Duke of Normandy had the better claim, being King Edward's maternal cousin (once-removed), and possibly his intended heir. As William saw it, this situation left him no choice but to cross the channel to fight for his crown.

The majority of the embroidered panels recount the bloody events of 14 October 1066. The Battle of Hastings ended with

DOI: 10.4324/9781003155119-6

William triumphant on a battlefield littered with the dead; altogether about 6,000 perished that day. Edith lost four brothers in the war including Harold, who would be remembered as "the last Anglo-Saxon King." William earned the sobriquet "the Norman Conqueror."

Twenty years later King William ordered a census. Possibly he suspected that the 250 new Norman overlords he had appointed were not reporting their full incomes. The *Anglo-Saxon Chronicle* provides a colorful account of William sending out his trusted representatives to do the data collecting. They were tasked with finding out:

> what, or how much, each man had, who was an occupier of land in England, either in land or in stock, and how much money it was worth. So very narrowly, indeed, did he commission them to trace it out, that there was not one single hide, nor a yard of land, nay, moreover (it is shameful to tell, though he thought it no shame to do it), not even an ox, nor a cow, nor a swine was there left, that was not set down in his writ. And all the recorded particulars were afterwards brought to him.[1]

The collection of data by a government always occurs within social relationships with varying configurations of rights, statuses, and legal obligations. Landowners had the right to appeal to the authority of William's census records to settle disputes, but not the right to withhold their own information from it.

In compiling what came to be known as the "Domesday Book," the census takers consulted existing records and held public inquests, surveying 268,984 households. Men's occupations were recorded, but (with the exception of nuns and thieves) women were almost always defined in relationship to men as widows, wives, sisters, daughters, or nieces. There were, however, a few notable outliers: a "female jester,"[2] and the former Queen, Edith of Wessex.

Not only was Edith, widow of Edward the Confessor, the wealthiest woman to be listed in the Domesday Book, she had been, while her husband was alive, the fourth-wealthiest person in the entire land. As one of the few Anglo-Saxon overlords to retain their holdings after the conquest, she had vowed fealty and paid tributes to William, and was allowed to live comfortably until her death in 1075. She commissioned a book about the life of her husband, and it has been suggested that she may have had a hand in the creation of the Bayeux Tapestry.[3]

Edith died before the census was taken, and was buried next to her husband, with honors. She appears in the Domesday Book only because its data collection was longitudinal: William wanted to be able to compare the value of land during the time of Edward the Confessor to its value in his present day, 20 years after the conquest.

But the Domesday Book had another purpose. It was also a public record. An account of the book written a century later emphasizes this aspect of its use.

> [The book] was written in plain words, so that everyone should be content with his own rights and not usurp the rights of others...The natives call this book "Domesday," that is, the day of judgment. This is a metaphor: for just as no judgment of that final severe and terrible trial can be evaded by any subterfuge, so when any controversy arises in the kingdom concerning the matters contained in the book, and recourse is made to the book, its word cannot be denied or set aside with impunity.[4]

The book was indexed to make its information more easily retrieved: "The king's name comes first, followed by the names of other nobles, namely those who hold from the king in chief, in order of rank. Furthermore, the list of names is numbered, so that what belongs to each person can easily be found by number below, in the same order, in the book itself."[5]

The Bayeux Tapestry and the Domesday Book tell authoritative, political tales about the events and consequences of the Conquest. Both documents were *governed*, meaning that they were ordered, created, managed, secured, and made available according to policies and practices that effectively provided oversight and protection for both documents for nearly a millennium. A key difference between them is the nature of the information they hold, and the kind of governance they require.

The embroidered Bayeux Tapestry, which lived most of its life in the Bayeux Cathedral in Normandy, stores *memories* that continue to have *narrative power*. Centuries after it was created the Tapestry would serve as a political tool by Napoleon and later the Nazis.

Today the French government provides access to it for scholars and the public as a matter of history and cultural heritage.

The Domesday Book stores *records* that continue to have *legal weight*. Making it available for public use has been the responsibility of the U.K. government for centuries. It was initially held in the Royal Treasury in Winchester and moved to the Palace of Westminster in the early 13th century, where it remained until the 19th century. It was rebound several times, eventually into two volumes. As a public document, it has long served in courts of law. It was cited as recently as 2019 in a civil court case in Leighton–Linslade, Bedfordshire, England to establish the longevity of a marketplace, in a dispute over rents.[6]

Because it is also a historically significant treasure (in addition to being a public record) it was never made readily available to the public at large. It was printed in 1783, but even then the Society of Antiquarians that had lobbied for the printing did not have easy access to it; the few printed copies were given to members of the Parliament.[7] In 1800 a report on the "shocking state" of most public records inspired the Parliament to call for the publication and distribution of indexes and original records, including the Domesday Book.[8] By the end of the 19th century, the government had published photographic facsimiles for each county, to facilitate access. During the 20th century many editions were released; in the early 21st century, the Domesday Book became digitally available and searchable online. In the history of the public use of government information, it is the longest continuously used public record in history.

This chapter surveys some of the information policies that fall into the area of information governance. After exploring freedom of information, we examine policies and practices related to copyright, fair use, open access, privacy, and consent. The chapter ends with a consideration of the challenges involved with the governance of surveillance technologies.

## FREEDOM OF INFORMATION

When is information free to be shared and when may it legally be withheld? Who has the right to demand it? Why do governments oppose the free flow of information and for what purpose? How has the digital era changed the way that organizations protect and govern information?

*Information policy* is a subfield of information science which is concerned with the *governance* of information. This is distinct from activities involved in *governing* a city or a nation. It refers to the protection and management of flows of information and stores of data within organizations, including government bodies. *Information governance frameworks* ensure the safety and appropriate use of information, at every stage in its lifecycle. These frameworks typically consist of guiding principles and procedures, as well as processes for enforcing compliance with regulations and laws.[9]

National constitutions include language that addresses the governance of information in several areas. One of these will always be guidance on how information is to be managed within the government, including rules that shape the communication of information between branches and agencies, and between the government and the public.

Levels of accountability and transparency in government reflect what information a particular government believes it owes to its people. *Financial accountability*, for example, involves recording and reporting how government branches, agencies, and employees are spending tax dollars. The degree to which government records are shared with the public can serve as a measure of the integrity of a political system, since a transparent system is more likely to reveal (and deter) mistakes, unethical behavior, and crimes by officials.[10]

Sweden was the first to enact, in 1766, a law establishing *press freedom* and the *right of access to information* held in government archives. The law was inspired by the Enlightenment-era writings of Anders Chydenius (1729–1803), a Swedish-Finnish politician, philosopher, and Lutheran priest. France followed in 1789, when the right of access to information regarding government expenditures from tax revenue was instituted as part of their declaration of human and civil rights. It wasn't until the 20th century, however, that these rights achieved wider acceptance globally. The UN's *Universal Declaration of Human Rights* includes a statement in Article 19 on *freedom of information* as an integral part of *freedom of expression*, defined as the right "to seek, receive and impart information and ideas through any media and regardless of frontiers."[11]

In 1947, the drafters of this declaration could not have imagined the Internet, but they understood in principle that new technologies would create new inequalities. *Universal access to information* is increasingly understood within a human rights framework; over 100 countries now have laws that grant citizens (and others) some degree of free access to government information. UNESCO named 28 September as "International Day for Universal Access to Information," reflecting this priority for governments worldwide.

In the U.S., the 1966 Freedom of Information Act (FOIA) followed two decades of national information secrecy, an essential feature of its Cold War policy.[12] In the United Kingdom, the Freedom of Information Act (FOIA) was passed in 2000, followed by the Freedom of Information (Scotland) Act (FOISA) in 2002, granting the right to request information directly from government agencies, local councils, schools, National Health Service hospitals and providers, and publicly owned companies, museums, galleries, and theaters.

Every nation has experienced struggles in implementing freedom of information laws. In some governments, apparent openness is more performative than actual; in Kazakhstan, accessing government information is stymied by bureaucratic obstruction, a situation described as "half-open government."[13] Nigeria passed a freedom of information law in 2011, but still faces the challenges of low rates of literacy, a tradition of government secrecy, and poor record-keeping—all exacerbated by a lack of adequate digital infrastructure.[14] In Ghana, libraries are stepping up to provide access to government information where infrastructure is lacking.[15]

Libraries have often facilitated access to government information. In 1813, the U.S. government began delivering document copies to designated libraries around the country; there are now over 1,100 *Federal depository libraries* where governmental information can be viewed. Often libraries will step up during emergency situations, helping governments to get information into communities.[16]

Threats to freedom of information may accompany erosions of other rights. The Afghan Taliban provide an extreme example, depriving girls of their right to education.[17] Freedom of the press has suffered in the 21st century, with a marked increase in physical and psychological threats to the well-being of journalists.[18] Media organizations are among the most active users of Freedom of Information laws. The International Press Institute (IPI), a network of journalists, editors, and media executives dedicated to protecting press freedom and independent journalism, set up a Covid-19 Press Freedom Tracker to bring attention to these threats. Another tracker set up during the Russian invasion of Ukraine produced hundreds of alerts related to the targeting, capture, detention, torture, and killing of journalists.[19]

Human rights and information freedom tend to rise and fall together, representing shifts toward democratic governance on one hand, and authoritarian governance on the other. Restrictions, intimidations, and violence inflicted upon the press, opposition figures, and social activists are endemic in countries where information freedom is endangered.[20] The digital age has expanded freedoms in some ways, but authoritarian governments have learned to use the new tools to their own ends as well.

## COPYRIGHT AND FAIR USE

Are the ideas in a book the same as the words used to express those ideas? When is it okay to use information someone else owns? What uses are permitted? Information policies span two opposing frames of reference, which are often in conflict. One sees information as a *commodity* (which can be owned and sold) while the other views information as a *resource* (to be managed and shared). Laws and regulations, which vary from country to country, must balance the rights of those asking for information with the rights of those who own and control it. Governments must deal with the question of what *parts* of a work can be owned, for example.

The English Parliament passed the first trademark legislation in 1266, and codified a copyright law in 1710, the *Statue of Anne*, named after the then reigning Queen Anne. It protected the legal rights of publishers, with more limited recognition of authors, a balance that shifted over time. Importantly, it viewed copyright as different from other property rights, and led to modern understandings of *fair use*, which lays out the ways that the public may legally use copyrighted material. Many nations borrowed, or were influenced by, the Statue of Anne in the development of their own copyright laws.[21]

The *World Intellectual Property Organization* (WIPO) *Copyright Treaty* was signed in 1996 by its participating nations. It was based on the *Berne Convention*, adopted in 1886, which established minimum protections for creators, as well as provisions for developing nations to gain access to information.[22] As a principle, the protection of the rights of ownership of information is regarded as more critical in wealthy countries (where content creators own most global copyrights and patents) than in poor nations with fewer patent holders and less money to pay for content. There is an inherent tension between the rights of content creators to own and make a living from their intellectual property, and the rights of the public to have access to information.

The idea that information can be owned at all is a value which some indigenous peoples reject. Indigenous artists may view their work to be the cultural heritage of their tribe, collectively held. A conflict in South Dakota between the Standing Rock Sioux Tribal Council, and the Lakota Language Consortium, a non-profit organization, for example, illustrates the difficulties involved in finding a common understanding. The Consortium spent years recording Lakota elders speaking their native language, in order to create language materials that could be used to teach it. The organization attained copyrights for these materials. The tribe must now pay for knowledge that their family and community members freely shared, not understanding that it was being commodified and that they would have to buy it back.[23]

The indigenous data sovereignty movement seeks to avoid situations like this, helping indigenous people to govern the collection, analysis, storage, and application of their own information.[24] The need to protect *Indigenous cultural and intellectual property* (ICIP) is addressed by the WIPO, which has attempted to account for diversity in understanding of the term "property."[25]

By itself, the WIPO has no power to implement or enforce its treaties. Countries must pass their own laws. In the United States, for example, the *Digital Millennium Copyright Act* (DMCA) was passed in 1998, implementing two WIPO treaties related to copyright protection. The DMCA established, for example, that streaming games are protected by the doctrine of *fair use*, with the caveat that music soundtracks are protected by their own copyright, which cannot be granted along with the games; the streamers of games where copyrighted music can be heard are therefore engaging in copyright infringement. The DMCA has proven to be controversial; many internet videos that are accused of copyright infringement actually turn out to meet the standards of fair use. Meritless accusations of copyright infringement on YouTube, Twitch, and other sites can have a significantly negative effect on content creators because of the time and expense required to appeal and resolve them.[26]

Fair use provisions as found in the U.S. Copyright Act allow the use of copyrighted materials for criticism, comment, news reporting, scholarship, and teaching. Copyright holders can sue for infringement in court, but the fair use doctrine limits this right and provides a defense to such suits. Fair use is decided in court on a case-by-case basis and takes into account the nature of the copyrighted work in question, the purpose and kind of use (such as commercial or non-profit), how much of the work is being used, and impact on the value of the work.

The doctrine of fair use is central to the practices of *open access* (OA) publishing. Open access can be understood as a world view, a set of practices, and a social movement—all based on the value that providing free access to information is a positive good. The term open access is related to but distinct from open-source software, which is shared with the understanding that the receiver may modify and redistribute it. The OA movement is mainly concerned with academic publications, especially when they involve research that is paid for by governments.

In traditional publishing, articles are locked behind paywalls, and libraries pay fees so that visitors can access them. Supporters of OA argue that this is a poor return on public investment. *Gold open access* is a strategy in which academic journals make articles accessible without a paywall; authors retain their copyright but may have to pay for their work to be published. In *green open access* authors make copies of their work available to the public through various means: academic libraries may curate works and make them available online, or authors may share pre-publication drafts of works, which are not owned by the publisher.

Sharing a copyrighted work without legal permission is termed *black open access* (also "rogue" or "Robin Hood" open access). That is what is happening when social network sites for academics encourage their members to upload their published papers regardless of copyright. Such sites are periodically challenged by publishers, but enforcement is uneven. A study of *Sci-Hub*, an online repository of 74 million science articles, showed that a significant number of people could have acquired what they downloaded legally; they just preferred, for whatever reason, to access it there. Only a minority identified that reason as belief in the values of OA. [27]

Information continues to move, despite copyright law and the existence of paywalls, and the long arc of this story seems to be bending towards increased, but perhaps more-regulated, information sharing. In the United States, the Biden administration has ordered that by 2026 all tax-payer funded research must be made available to the public without cost. But what about data? Recent *Open government* initiatives around the world have pushed the envelope on freedom of information laws and opened up their data repositories to the public. As a result, a tremendous amount of data is now available to researchers worldwide that has never been before. Unfortunately, much of it lacks coherent organization or consistent metadata, making its reuse value very low. [28]

Researchers, entrepreneurs, and organizations who work with Big Data and AI/machine learning are operating without the kind of information infrastructure enjoyed by other areas of information science. There is no comprehensive indexing infrastructure for data sets as there is for print media, for example. Specialized publishers, distribution channels, bibliographies, catalogs, indexes, and of course libraries, have been developing such infrastructure for more than a century. Unlike books, data sets have no traditional repository where they can be easily located and accessed. [29] The creation of infrastructure for data will have to develop in partnership with processes of data governance which are still evolving as well.

Information moves differently across national borders during times of war. During the Russian invasion of Ukraine, military intelligence was shared to an unprecedented degree between the nations of NATO and Ukraine.[30] There was also a marked increase in the gathering and sharing of *open-source intelligence* (OSINT), a term that refers to information derived from open sources such as print and online media, public government data, academic publications, websites, and other open-access sources. The non-profit online collective Bellingcat, first created through the support of a Kickstarter crowdfunding appeal, facilitates amateur crowdsourced OSINT gathering. Early in the war, the Bellingcat community was able to determine that a Malaysian passenger jet shot down over Ukraine had been hit by a Russian surface-to-air missile, through open data sources including Google Earth images and dashcam videos posted on social media by Russian soldiers.[31] The Center for Information Resilience, a non-profit organization in the United Kingdom, used information available through the Russian-Ukraine Monitor map (another crowdsourced data gathering project) to provide evidence of mass graves in the Yalivshchyna Forest outside the Ukrainian city of Chernihiv in February and March 2022.[32]

Twitter and other social media sites have also become an important source of information for cybersecurity amateurs and experts (and criminals as well). Online communities support a variety of OSINT practices with a variety of missions and motivations, sometimes leading to misguided online vigilantism, but also producing actionable intelligence regarding human trafficking and other human rights abuses.[33]

Data sharing falls on the resource side of the continuum between information as a resource and information as a commodity. Organizations may move back and forth along that continuum in response to national politics or global events. During the first years of the Covid-19 pandemic, for example, some news organizations removed the paywalls for their pandemic-related content. Though critics warn that data sharing comes with significant risks to personal privacy and security, the Covid-19 pandemic increased the urgency of calls for open data and data sharing, particularly of data sets used in clinical trials.

## PROTECTING PRIVACY

Privacy is an area of active research interest within information science from several different angles, It is sometimes approached through the lens of information behavior. People's feelings, attitudes, and actions towards their privacy, and the sharing of private information, are understood to be embedded in cultural and sociotechnical contexts.[34] To understand the privacy attitudes of young people who engage in sexting, for example, researchers have to look at the norms and expectations that define the situation. In what context is the sharing of intimate images viewed as acceptable behavior? When does it become a violation of privacy?[35]

Information privacy is also relevant to political and economic contexts surrounding the commodification of information. Online newspapers with a *paywall* may give away a few articles a month before they require a subscription to provide additional content. They sometimes allow access "for free" if contact information is provided to set up an account. This barrier to information access is called a *datawall*—the website may appear to be giving away content, but users in fact are paying for it with personal data, which may then be traded, sold, resold, and stolen.[36]

In the governance of information, privacy policies are increasingly understood within a human rights framework. Regulations dictate how private information may be collected and how it must be treated. For example, data acquisition in research that involves human subjects may require that *informed consent* be received from the subjects before any data collection occurs. What sorts of research require what sorts of consent disclosures and permissions can be different in different fields, and in different parts of the world. Consent has a legal as well as an ethical element. Consumers are asked to consent when they install a software application that collects private data. They are provided with a statement about the use and protection of their data, followed by a check box to say they have read the information and consent to the use. Many people click without reading; in that case they may have legally consented, but their choice isn't particularly informed. These consent rituals reflect laws and policies that were created as part of a governance process.

There are four common strategies commonly used for acquiring consent from customers or research subjects. The *compulsory approach* ties consent to the use of the application or service. If people want to use, it, they must give up their private data. This works if they are free to not use the product or receive its benefits. But what if they really need the service or are compelled? It can be hard to refuse to engage with a social media site if friends are trying hard to convince you not to worry about the risks.

A second strategy is the *opt-out approach*; here consent is assumed by default. People must take an action to refuse their consent. It may not be obvious how to perform that extra step. Unless risks are clearly explained, some users will not understand why they should opt out. Others may just do whatever their friends and families do, so it may not really function as a mechanism for ensuring that consent is informed.

The third strategy is the *opt-in approach*, where people must take an action (usually a click) to consent to have their information used. This assumes that the consent is wholly voluntary, not coerced, but without *some* attempt at persuasion, not enough people will choose to opt in. In the most privacy-protective opt-in scenario, those who choose not to share their private data would lose no privileges or functionality at all. But in that circumstance, why would anyone opt in? And if users *must* opt in to get any substantive benefit from the service, arguably it is no longer really opt in at that point, but functionally compulsory.

The fourth strategy is the *market-model approach*, in which people are paid for giving up their data. This strategy may appear to be the fairest of them all, but less wealthy people have a greater incentive to give up their private data—creating a system in which wealthy people benefit as a direct result of risks carried by the poor. An unregulated data market can lead to systematic exploitation of people who don't understand the risks involved, or the value of what they are giving away.

There is an inevitable conflict between the need for accuracy in scientific research and the need to honor the privacy rights of human subjects. The more data that is collected, the more likely it is that patterns can be found in that data that will lead to scientific breakthroughs. More data means greater treatment effectiveness and less medical error. But the risks of privacy loss grow at the same time.[37]

In 1988 the U.S. Federal Trade Commission (FTC) created the *Fair Information Practice Principles*. These are not laws but guidelines, detailing the requirements that must be met for an online enterprise to be judged to have fair information practices. The five principles address notice, consent, access, security, and enforcement. The *General Data Protection Regulation* (GDPR) governs data protection and privacy in the European Union (EU) and the European Economic Area (EEA). It also affects the rest of the world, because it dictates the terms under which personal data can be transferred into and out of the EU and EEA. The GDPR goes several steps further than the FTC guidelines to protect the rights of those who are sharing information, and it problematizes the needs of those who wish to collect private information, regardless of purpose.[38]

The goals of the GDPR are protective and preventative, rather than reactive and remedial. It calls for the full opt-in approach to consent, requiring that privacy protections be baked into the design of services, and that users who decline to opt in do not lose any functionality as a result. To be compliant with the GDPR, security must also be ensured in every stage of the data life cycle, and all policies relating to private data (including how the data will be used) must be transparent. The bottom line for the GDPR is that privacy policies are human-centered, meaning that they should work to protect the privacy of individuals rather than trying to convince people to give up their information.

In the U.S., the *Health Insurance Portability and Accountability Act* (HIPAA) is the most important U.S. federal law governing health data privacy. The GDPR provides special protection for "data concerning health"—a category which closely resembles HIPAA's "sensitive personal information." Other countries are now passing GDPR-like privacy laws, but development is uneven.

A *right to privacy* was included in the United Nations 1948 Universal Declaration of Human Rights, and reiterated in the 1966 International Covenant on Civil and Political Rights. Understanding that privacy rights were being challenged in unprecedented ways, the UN Human Rights Council adopted a resolution on "the right to privacy in the digital age." A committee was convened in 2019 to deliberate on how information technologies, particularly those involving machine learning algorithms, affect the right to privacy. Their report, released in 2021, called for a human rights–based approach to ameliorating AI-related privacy risks which emphasizes core principles of equality, non-discrimination, participation, and accountability.[39]

The privacy-related concerns of an organization are complex and multi-faceted, extending from its human relations department to its research and development lab. The job of securing information from passwords to documents to data sets (across their entire lifecycle), falls under the broad umbrella of *Information Management* (IM). Within an organization, IM is responsible for establishing a governance framework that will guide and protect all of its information systems including the identity management of employees, the handling of private information gathered from clients and customers, and cybersecurity measures taken to protect the organization from external (or internal) threats.

Organizational structures and processes for making decisions about adoption of software, preparatory research anticipating how the changes will impact the efficiency and usability of information systems, the assessment of new security vulnerabilities that may result, the development of necessary training materials for employees, and the effective communication of new policies and procedures, are also management tasks. As a professional area, IM shares concerns with a number of fields: Information Systems, Management Information Systems, Knowledge Management, and Information Technology (IT). The acronym IM/IT reflects an increasing overlap, and sometimes merging, of the responsibilities, titles, and job descriptions in the two professional fields.

## GOVERNING INFORMATION IN CONTEXT

All governments collect some personal data by compulsion, as William the Conqueror did in the 11th century, to raise revenue, or to organize a military draft. Citizens must also share personal data in return for legal rights when they get married, for example, or apply for government services. To varying degrees, governments also collect private information surreptitiously and without consent. It would not be possible to fight the spread of child pornography or terrorist attacks if law enforcement lacked the legal right to conduct physical and digital surveillance to some degree. The problem is that the same technologies that enable surveillance for the public good in one regime or political administration, can easily be employed as a tool of repression in the next.

The International Federation of Library Associations and Institutions (IFLA) has released a statement affirming privacy as a human right and recommending that libraries attempt to protect this right through advocacy and direct action including, for example, refusing to allow electronic surveillance, limiting the collection of personal data in libraries, or purging borrower records. The statement acknowledges the limits of the power of libraries to influence data collection by commercial vendors operating within them, or to negotiate the demands of law enforcement or other agencies for data about library users.[40]

Around the world the Covid-19 pandemic, like public health crises before it, caused local and national governments, organizations, and institutions to increase surveillance related to quarantines and social distancing regulations.[41] Even before the pandemic, college campuses had begun to install surveillance equipment for the purpose of student security (surveilling on behalf of students) and compliance in attendance and exams (surveilling of students). Under pandemic conditions, surveillance on campuses, of both kinds, increased.[42]

Studies have shown that people's expectations regarding their privacy can change during times of crisis.[43] A loosening of adherence to guidelines for privacy governance also seems to occur. A comparative study of disaster apps (websites or applications recommended to users for use during disasters) found multiple inconsistencies between the transparency of the apps' stated policies and their actual practices. Some third-party apps misrepresented themselves as government apps; some government apps, while transparent, shared data with nontrusted third parties; some apps were neither transparent nor compliant.[44] An important question following periods of quarantine is whether apps with problematic privacy habits will be retired, and crisis-level surveillance will be rolled back, when the crises that enabled them are over.[45]

Like privacy, surveillance must be understood within specific sociocultural and historical contexts that define norms and expectations. Attitudes towards the deployment of surveillance technologies differ between and within countries.[46] Surveillance is also fully embedded in racialized and gendered social systems. A study of Muslim travelers from the Middle East and South Asia, who experience hyper-surveillance by airport security and customs officials, found that the social context of the surveillance was different for Muslim men and women. Women who wear the hijab are subject to scrutiny because, in transgressing gender norms, they may be viewed, in both a sexist and racist frame, as a cultural danger to society. But Muslim men more often than women find their names on Secondary Security Screening Selection Lists, which causes them to be pulled out of line, because they are symbolically associated with violent terror.[47]

College students have become leaders in anti-surveillance activism, galvanized by revelations of bias in facial recognition software that misidentifies dark-skinned people, risking mistaken identifications and false arrests, and exacerbating systemic issues of racial profiling and bias.[48] The antecedents of modern surveillance technologies are the oppressive mechanisms of the Atlantic slave trade and of the corresponding colonial rule. It is no coincidence that biometric technologies such as face scanners still reflect 19th-century racial science, language, and rhetoric. Some of their algorithms were even found to use the discredited terms "Mongoloid, Negroid, and Caucasoid" in classifying the faces that they scan.[49]

Surveillance technologies are developing faster than researchers can study their social consequences—too fast for effective regulation to keep up with new capacities, or to slow their deployment or prevent misuse by authoritarian (or liberal democratic) governments. The 21st century has seen an expanding global use of AI-powered surveillance technologies in international conflicts, and as a tool for monitoring and controlling citizens. The Global Surveillance index, an initiative of the Carnegie Endowment for International Peace, concludes that the use of AI-based surveillance technology is spreading rapidly, especially in authoritarian countries with few protections regarding information freedom, access, and privacy. Investments in surveillance technologies tend to increase in direct proportion to military expenditures.[50] Profit is a major factor in the growth as well: it has been projected that the global video surveillance market may exceed $64 billion by 2031.[51]

In 2014 the UN Human Rights Council released a document entitled "International Principles on the Application of Human Rights to Communications Surveillance," which provides guidelines by which to measure whether a state's use of surveillance complies with international standards. The principles mandate that surveillance be legal, be necessary, have a legitimate aim, be adequate to the aim, be transparent, and have public oversight through an independent judicial authority that offers due process to all parties.[52] The principle of *proportionality* qualifies all the other principles: is the reason for surveilling a serious one? Is there a high probability that relevant evidence will be obtained? Have less-invasive approaches been exhausted? Will excessive information be destroyed? Will the surveillance activity be limited to its stated aim? Does the use of surveillance respect the underlying purpose of privacy protections?

There is no international agreement, much less compliance, on such shared principles. The resulting report, released in 2021, regarding the right to privacy in the digital age calls for every nation to practice transparent governance where it regards procedures, practices, and legislation involving the surveillance of private communications or biometric data.[53] The report addresses, in particular, the use of surveilled data within information systems that use algorithms to automate decision making, or that target or profile populations, even if the point of the technologies is to provide security for its citizens, or to manipulate users to make a profit.

Greater transparency from governments and corporations, and renewed commitments to freedom of information at the global, national, and local levels, would allow for a more vigorous public debate on surveillance technologies, and a more participatory and democratic consensus about where the lines between privacy and security should be drawn.

## NOTES

1  "The Anglo-Saxon Chronicle: Eleventh Century," *The Avalon Project: Documents in Law, History & Diplomacy.* Yale Law School, https://avalon.law.yale.edu/medieval/ang11.asp. Retrieved 30 May 2022.
2  "Adelina the Jester," *Open Domesday*, https://opendomesday.org/name/adelina-the-jester/. Retrieved 30 May 2022.

3  Pauline Stafford, "Edith, Edward's Wife and Queen," in *Edward the Confessor: The Man and the Legend*, ed. Richard Mortimer (Woodbridge: The Boydell Press, 2009): 126–128.

4  Richard fitzNigel, "Dialogus de Scaccario," in *The Dialogue of the Exchequer*, eds. Emilie Amt and S. D. Church (Oxford: Oxford University Press, 2007): 96–99.

5  Ibid., 272.

6  R. Harvey, (on the application of) *Leighton Linslade Town Council EWHC 760 (Admin)*, 15 February 2019, http://www.bailii.org/ew/cases/EWHC /Admin/2019/760.html.

7  Margarte M. Condon and Elizabeth M. Hallam, "Government Printing of the Public Records in the Eighteenth Century," *Journal of the Society of Archivists* 7, no. 6 (1984): 348–388.

8  Michael Riordan, "Materials for History? Publishing Records as a Historical Practice in Eighteenth-and Nineteenth-Century England," *History of Humanities* 2, no. 1 (2017): 63.

9  P. Hermon and H. C. Relyea, "Information Policy," in *Encyclopedia of Library and Information Science*, 2nd ed., ed. Miriam A. Drake (New York: Marcel Dekker, Inc, 2003): 1300.

10 Can Chen and Sukumar Ganapati, "Do Transparency Mechanisms Reduce Government Corruption? A Meta-Analysis," *International Review of Administrative Sciences* (2021): https://doi.org/10.1177 /00208523211033236.

11 Universal Declaration of Human Rights, United Nations (1948). https:// www.un.org/en/about-us/universal-declaration-of-human-rights.

12 Michael R. Lemov and Nate Jones, "John Moss and the Roots of the Freedom of Information Act: Worldwide Implications," *Southwestern Journal of International Law* 24 (2018): 1.

13 Karl O'Connor, Saltanat Janenova, and Colin Knox, "Open Government in Authoritarian Regimes," *International Review of Public Policy* 1, no. 1 (2019): 65–82.

14 N. J. Madubuike-Ekwe and Joseph N. Mbadugha, "Obstacles to the Implementation of the Freedom of Information Act, 2011 in Nigeria," *Nnamdi Azikiwe University Journal of International Law and Jurisprudence* 9, no. 2 (2018): 96–109.

15 Kofi Koranteng Adu and Patrick Ngulube, "Key Threats and Challenges to the Preservation of Digital Records of Public Institutions in Ghana," *Information, Communication & Society* 20, no. 8 (2017): 1127–1145.

16 John Carlo Bertot, Paul T. Jaeger, Lesley A. Langa, and Charles R. McClure, "Public Access Computing and Internet Access in Public Libraries: The Role of Public Libraries in E-government and Emergency Situations," *First Monday* 11, no. 9 (2006), http://firstmonday.org/issues/ issue11_9/bertot/index.html. Retrieved 23 September 2022.

17 Hannah Bogaert, "History Repeating Itself: The Resurgence of the Taliban and the Abandonment of Afghan Women," *Immigration and Human Rights Law Review* 4, no. 1 (2022): 3.

18  Lambrini Papadopoulou and Theodora A. Maniou, "'Lockdown' on Digital Journalism? Mapping Threats to Press Freedom during the COVID-19 Pandemic Crisis," *Digital Journalism* 9, no. 9 (2021): 1344–1366.

19  International Press Institute, https://ipi.media/. Retrieved 3 June 2022.

20  Sallie Hughes and Yulia Vorobyeva, "Explaining the Killing of Journalists in the Contemporary Era: The Importance of Hybrid Regimes and Subnational Variations," *Journalism* 22, no. 8 (2021): 1873–1891.

21  Joris Deene, "The Influence of the Statute of Anne on Belgian Copyright Law," in *Global Copyright: Three Hundred Years since the Statute of Anne, from 1709 to Cyberspace*, eds. Lionel Bently, Uma Suthersanen, and Paul Torremans (Cheltenham: Edward Elgar, 2010): 136–143.

22  "Policy," *World Intellectual Property Organization*, https://www.wipo.int/policy/en/. Retrieved 2 June 2022.

23  Graham Lee Brewer, "Lakota Elders Helped a White Man Preserve Their Language: Then He Tried to Sell It Back to Them," *NBC News*, 3 June 2022.

24  "About Us," United States Indigenous Data Sovereignty Network, https://usindigenousdata.org/about-us. Retrieved 22 June 2022; "Our Charter," Te Mana Raraunga Maori Data Sovereignty Network, https://www.temanararaunga.maori.nz/tutohinga. Retrieved 22 June 2022.

25  "Indigenous Peoples and Local Communities Portal," *WIPO*, https://www.wipo.int/tk/en/indigenous/. Retrieved 2 June 2022. See also Nicole Martin, "Indigenous Rights: An Analysis of Intellectual Property Protections," *American University Intellectual Property Brief* 13 (2021): 33.

26  Jessica Vogele, "Where's the Fair Use: The Takedown of Let's Play and Reaction Videos on YouTube and the Need for Comprehensive DMCA Reform," *Touro Law Review* 33 (2017): 589.

27  J. Bohannon and A. Elbakyan, "Data from: Who's Downloading Pirated Papers? Everyone," *Dryad Digital Repository* (2016). https://doi.org/10.5061/dryad.q447c.

28  See, for fun, Auriane Marmier, "The Publication of Open Government Data," *Dance Your PhD 2022*, https://www.youtube.com/watch?v=g0pK0TZ61bY. Retrieved 4 June 2022.

29  Maggie Puniewska, "Science Has a Sharing Problem," *The Atlantic*, 15 December 2014. https://www.theatlantic.com/health/archive/2014/12/scientists-have-a-sharing-problem/383061/. Retrieved 6 June 2022. See also Patricia A. Soranno, Kendra S. Cheruvelil, Kevin C. Elliott, and Georgina M. Montgomery, "It's Good to Share: Why Environmental Scientists' Ethics are Out of Date," *BioScience* 65, no. 1 (2015): 69–73.

30  Shane Harris and Dan Lamothe, "Intelligence-Sharing with Ukraine Designed to Prevent Wider War," *Washington Post*, 11 May 2022.

31  Karl Vick, "Bellingcat's Eliot Higgins Explains Why Ukraine Is Winning the Information War," *Time*, 9 March 2022. https://time.com/6155869/bellingcat-eliot-higgins-ukraine-open-source-intelligence/. Retrieved 4 June 2022.

32  Ross Burley, "The Yalivshchyna Burial Site: Mass Graves after Russian Invasion," Centre for Information Resilience, 10 April 2022. https://www.info-res.org/post/the-yalivshchyna-burial-site-mass-graves-after-russian-invasion. Retrieved 4 June 2022.

33  Yasmine Belghith, Sukrit Venkatagiri, and Kurt Luther, "Compete, Collaborate, Investigate: Exploring the Social Structures of Open Source Intelligence Investigations," in *Proceedings of the 2022 CHI Conference on Human Factors in Computing Systems* (2022): 1–18. https://doi.org/10.1145/3491102.3517526.

34  Helen Nissenbaum, "A Contextual Approach to Privacy Online," *Daedalus* 140, no. 4 (2011): 32–48.

35  Amy Adele Hasinoff and Tamara Shepherd, "Sexting in Context: Privacy Norms and Expectations," *International Journal of Communication* 8 (2014): 24.

36  L. J. Hinchcliffe, "From Paywall to Datawall," *The Scholarly Kitchen* (2018), https://scholarlykitchen.sspnet.org/2018/10/11/from-paywall-to-datawall/. Retrieved 31 May 2022.

37  W. Nicholson Price and I. Glenn Cohen, "Privacy in the Age of Medical Big Data," *Nature Medicine* 25, no. 1 (2019): 37–43.

38  "What is GDPR, the EU's New Data Protection Law?" *GDPR.EU*, https://gdpr.eu/what-is-gdpr/. Retrieved 6 June 2022.

39  "The Right to Privacy in the Digital Age," *United Nations Digital Library* 2019, https://digitallibrary.un.org/record/3837297?ln=en. Retrieved 22 June 2022.

40  "IFLA Statement on Privacy in the Library Environment," International Federation of Library Associations and Institutions. https://www.ifla.org/publications/ifla-statement-on-privacy-in-the-library-environment/. Retrieved 4 June 2022; See also Trina J. Magi, "Confidentiality: Best Practices Protecting Library Patron Confidentiality: Checklist of Best Practices," https://www.ila.org/advocacy/making-your-case/privacy/confidentiality-best-practices. Retrieved 22 June 2022.

41  Jessie Miller, "Tracking the Tracing: A Global Investigation of Privacy Issues in the Age of COVID-19," *Dartmouth Undergraduate Journal of Politics, Economics and World Affairs* 1, no. 3 (2021): 2.

42  See Tian Wang, Lin Guo, and Masooda Bashir, "COVID-19 Apps and Privacy Protections from Users' Perspective," *Proceedings of the Association for Information Science and Technology* 58, no. 1 (2021): 357–365.

43  Shin Bin Tan, Colleen Chiu-Shee, and Fábio Duarte, "From SARS to COVID-19: Digital Infrastructures of Surveillance and Segregation in Exceptional Times," *Cities* 120 (2022). https://doi.org/10.1016/j.cities.2021.103486.

44  Madelyn R. Sanfilippo et al., "Disaster Privacy/Privacy Disaster," *Journal of the Association for Information Science and Technology* 71, no. 9 (2020): 1002–1014.

45 Frederic Gerdon et al., "Individual Acceptance of Using Health Data for Private and Public Benefit: Changes during the COVID-19 Pandemic," *Harvard Data Science Review*, Special Issue 1: COVID-19: Unprecedented Challenges and Chances (2021): 22.

46 Genia Kostka, Léa Steinacker, and Miriam Meckel, "Between Security and Convenience: Facial Recognition Technology in the Eyes of Citizens in China, Germany, the United Kingdom, and the United States," *Public Understanding of Science* 30, no. 6 (2021): 671–690.

47 Saher Selod, "Gendered Racialization: Muslim American Men and Women's Encounters with Racialized Surveillance," *Ethnic and Racial Studies* 42, no. 4 (2019): 552–569.

48 Clara Belitz et al., "Constructing Categories: Moving beyond Protected Classes in Algorithmic fairness," *Journal of the Association for Information Science and Technology* (2022). https://doi.org/10.1002/asi.24643. See also Ashraf Khalil et al., "Investigating Bias in Facial Analysis Systems: A Systematic Review," *IEEE Access* 8 (2020): 130751–130761.

49 Simone Browne, *Dark Matters* (Durham, NC: Duke University Press, 2015): 104.

50 See, for example, James Leibold, "Surveillance in China's Xinjiang Region: Ethnic Sorting, Coercion, and Inducement," *Journal of Contemporary China* 29, no. 121 (2020): 46–60; and "AI Global Surveillance Technology," Carnegie Endowment for International Peace, https://carnegieendowment.org/publications/interactive/aI-surveillance. Retrieved 4 June 2022.

51 PR Newswire, "Wireless Video Surveillance Market to Garner $64.1 Bn, Globally, by 2031 at 11.9% CAGR: Allied Market Research," *Bloomberg Online*, 30 August 2022, https://www.bloomberg.com/press-releases/2022-08-30/wireless-video-surveillance-market-to-garner-64-1-bn-globally-by-2031-at-11-9-cagr-allied-market-research. Retrieved 22 September 2022.

52 "Necessary and Proportionate: International Principles on the Application of Human Rights to Communications Surveillance," *EFF* (2014), https://necessaryandproportionate.org/principles/.

53 S. Gong, C. C. Loy, and T. Xiang, "Security and Surveillance," in *Visual Analysis of Humans*, eds. Thomas B. Moeslund, Adrian Hilton, Volker Krüger, and Leonid Sigal (London: Springer, 2011): 455–472.

# STUDYING INFORMATION

Former program manager and data engineer at Facebook, Frances Haugen, testified as a whistleblower before a U.S. Senate committee in October 2021. She described in detail the failure of the company (now known as Meta), to act on the findings of its internal research team regarding the negative effects of Facebook and Instagram on society, and particularly on children.[1]

Haugen described a corporate strategy that prioritizes maximum engagement of its users above all else. The consequence is a predictable pattern: already depressed children are shown increasingly depressing content, which leads to downward spirals in their mental health.[2] Research on children's use of social media supports her contention and underscores the complexity of the information behavior of youth.[3]

Haugen's criticisms were wide-ranging, and other harms she alleged were likewise severe. She told the Senate committee that she believes Facebook bears responsibility for the ethnic genocide perpetrated by the government of Myanmar against the Rohingya Muslim community which made strategic use of social media, including Facebook, in its violent campaign. Thousands of people were killed and hundreds of thousands of people became refugees.[4]

During her testimony, Haugen also placed blame on the failure of the U.S. government to regulate social media companies effectively. The problem, she said, is that they don't understand how algorithms determine what content is shown to users, and how

DOI: 10.4324/9781003155119-7

decisions are made in the development of those algorithms. She tried to make it clear that the effect of the algorithms was not accidental. If what users want to see is extreme and violent, Facebook will oblige.[5] More broadly, Haugen laid the blame on a corporate culture in which teams are pressured to continuously adjust internal algorithms to maximize engagement, without a full consideration of the social harm that could result.

Facebook CEO Mark Zuckerberg eventually admitted that their filtering of violent contact in Myanmar in 2018 had not been adequate. He promised change; an audit two years later found that their algorithm still failed to filter inflammatory posts when they were written in the local languages of Myanmar. This outcome was predicted by Haugen, who had explained in her testimony that the company prioritized English language content, with inadequate support for translation, not only in Myanmar, but in many other countries around the world, where ethnic tension is exacerbated by Facebook's inability to recognize the nature of what is being posted. The result is the erroneous censoring of benign content, and an inability to filter disinformation and hate speech effectively. In December 2021, a Rohingya refugee in the United States sued Meta for 150 billion dollars in a class-action lawsuit, alleging that failure to police hate speech on Facebook facilitated the harm that refugees experienced.[6]

In February of 2022 the nonprofit organization, Whistleblower Aid, which represents Frances Haugen, filed additional complaints to the SEC, alleging that the company misrepresented to its investors the steps it is taking to control misinformation on its platform regarding Covid-19 and climate change, citing discrepancies between company statements and internal communications.[7]

Haugen's testimony regarding the algorithms used on Instagram and Facebook to maximize user engagement shed light on an industry-wide problem. People can end up isolated in an echo chamber in which they can only read and see and hear what they already believe. Because the algorithms filter out contrary views, this circumstance is also referred to as a *filter bubble*. If what's going on inside that bubble is a conspiracy theory, the algorithms of the site make it unlikely that a user will be exposed to factual information or happen upon the post of trusted friends debunking what they believe.[8]

There is no truth mechanism built into the Internet. The creators of browsers, websites, applications, and online communities may try to filter, factcheck, block, and ban. But Haugen's testimony makes it clear that it is more profitable to feed misinformation and conspiracy theories to those who are susceptible to them. Vulnerable children have been largely left to fend for themselves when they are online.

This means that it largely falls to the users of the Internet to evaluate the information that we receive through our devices. We search, we swipe, we tap, we click, sometimes we evaluate before backing up and clicking again. But what happens if we don't evaluate?

One day in 2013 a woman was heading for a railway station in Brussels, Belgium, a 90-kilometer drive from her home, but ended up instead in the city of Zagreb, Croatia, a journey of more than 1,000 kilometers. She had been following the directions provided by her GPS application. When questioned by a reporter about why she kept driving for over 12 hours, for a trip that should have taken no more than 90 minutes, she replied that she had been "distracted."[9]

This story is a fable of failing to evaluate information after receiving it. A traveler queries her device about how to get from one place to another. Maybe she mistypes, or is autocorrected, or clicks the wrong thing, but the software on her device interprets her query and provides her with a path. She follows the confidently spoken instructions as she drives hour after hour, crosses three national borders, apparently without ever doubting the search results she received. She doesn't seek information elsewhere, or purchase a map at a service station, or ask anyone for directions.

There are countless similar stories in which hapless GPS-guided travelers have driven off unfinished bridges, gone the wrong way down one-way streets, or driven straight into bodies of water—all discounting the evidence of their own eyes as they followed the directions they were given. They are not unlike those who search the Internet to do "their own research" on a controversial issue and end up being taken for a ride by some misinformation or conspiracy theory that steals their trust. In all such cases people suspend their autonomous judgment, accepting information without evaluating it against other sources to verify its accuracy. Once social media has locked them into a filter bubble, they may never get to the train station.

After a brief overview of the wide and complicated field of information behavior, this chapter surveys three areas that have generated large bodies of work within information science: everyday information behavior, information literacies, including reading literacy and digital literacy in relation to the digital divide, and the phenomenon of digital misinformation. The chapter ends with a consideration of the modern-day troll-fighting elves of Lithuania.

## INFORMATION BEHAVIOR

*Information behavior* takes as its object of study how humans behave when they are interacting with information. Like many other areas in information science, the field of information behavior is deeply interdisciplinary. Its questions and concerns overlap with those of psychology, social psychology, sociology, anthropology, communication, media studies, advertising, marketing, education, and design, among others. The impetus for the earliest research in information behavior was to make sure that libraries were serving the needs of their users. There was particular interest in the information needs of scientists within a disciplinary community. What kinds of information were they looking for? How did they use what they found?[10] What was the best way to disseminate research results within a scientific community? Did people know how to make use of the available finding aids?[11]

A shift of interest from information *use* to information *needs* (of the public, and of academic scholars) still remained focused on improving information services through the mid-20th century. Some library visitors were identified as independent researchers, needing little help, while others clearly needed the guidance of skilled librarians.[12] But the emphasis of this type of research was traditionally more on *systems* than on the *users*. Beginning in the 1970s, information behavior research began to focus on people as the object of inquiry, with a growing expectation that such research should attend to the social, cultural, and sociotechnical contexts in which information is situated.

Theoretical models arose, which attempted to help classify information behavior and guide research. Among the most influential models of information behavior was conceived by Tom D. Wilson in the 1970s and published in 1981. It was updated several times through the 1990s as other models were also emerging in response to an increase in intellectual energy and research output in the area of information behavior.[13]

Wilson's model sorts the range of research approaches into three categories: information seeking behavior, information searching behavior, and information use behavior. *Information seeking behavior* refers to the various ways in which human beings look for information. To identify a bird seen outside our window, for example, we might open a birdwatching guidebook, bring up a bird-identifying phone app, or ask someone sitting across the room if they recognize it. All of these ways of seeking information have similar characteristics, regardless of what it is we're looking for or how we go about the search. The similar-sounding term *information searching behavior* refers more narrowly to the micro-behaviors of clicking, looking, discerning, choosing, and interacting with information technologies. Research that explores information searching might explore, for example, which devices people use to complete certain information tasks. Why do they prefer certain web browsers, search engines, or informational apps? What physiological, cognitive, or social processes are involved as they engage with information technologies? For this reason, usability and user-experience research (UX) fall into the category of information behavior.

*Information use behavior* refers to our engagement with information after it has been retrieved or captured. Having taken several pictures of the bird outside our window on our phone, how do we determine which one to print, post, tweet, or share? In dealing with the information record of our own lives, how do we decide which emails to save or delete? How do we organize a scrapbook of childhood art? What do we do with older family records passed down to us from long-deceased relatives and now taking up space in a closet? It wasn't until the 1990s that "information behavior" became the preferred term for studies of human interactions with information, although there were some objections since it is not actually the *information* that is doing the behaving. The term replaced earlier terms such as "information use," "information seeking and gathering," "information needs and uses," and "information seeking research.[14] The choice of "behavior" seemed better able to encompass everything the people do with information every day, all day, and throughout their lives.

The first international conference on Information Seeking in Context (ISIC) took place in 1996 and has continued regularly since; it provides an important academic home for the information behavior research community; attendees map and scrutinize even their own information seeking behavior in attending the conferences.[15] Information behavior is defined very broadly by ISIC as "contextualized information activities."[16]

As research and design practices across many disciplines turned from systems-focused approaches to user-focused inquiry, a new wave of information behavior-related research began to include sociological variables in the analysis. A study in rural Bangladesh, for example, concluded that social class was more powerful than either gender or age in shaping health information seeking behavior.[17]

The adoption of social science perspectives shifted information behavior research towards the use of qualitative research methods: focus groups, interviews, ethnographic fieldwork, and participant observation in physical or digital communities, sometimes in tandem with quantitative methods in a multi-method approach. *Participatory research* has also increased. It differs from participant observation in that the community being studied may become part of the research team. Community members may contribute to the design of the project, the research questions, and the interpretation of the data. They are sometimes credited as co-authors in publications arising from such work.[18]

The emphasis on theoretical perspectives, methods, and social science questions in the study of information behavior has persisted into the 21st century. It has produced wide-ranging work across many disparate domains, addressing, for example, the use of boundary objects in an intergenerational foster care community;[19] practices of racialized data collection in the creation of historical redlined maps;[20] and the motivations of Black content creators on Wikipedia.[21]

The subfield of *everyday life information seeking* (ELIS) within the field of information behavior also began to emerge in the mid-1990s.[22] Since information is all around us, information behavior can be observed in most aspects of human life: in our conversations with others, in our interactions with books and digital devices, and other sensory sources of information beyond just sight and sound. We know that dogs "read" their neighborhoods by bushes and trees as they walk; we humans also collect information with our noses when they alert us that something is burning in the kitchen.

By the time libraries began studying the needs, seeking behaviors, and uses of information by their patrons, humans had been interacting with information for thousands of years. The advent of writing brought with its professional practices that reflected new ways of interacting with information, but prior to the 20th century, the skills of writing and reading were often limited to elite social classes. Even today there are cultural communities that are not literate, or which have sectors of their societies that are not fully literate, including women and the very poor. But people who cannot read interact as fully with information as the literate, finding other ways to get their information needs met. The idea that textual information is more important or valid or interesting than information communicated through voice has been described as an academic bias, and even an ideology.[23] It is easy to overlook even in our ordinary lives, all the ways that we engage with information through spoken language, whether there is a text involved in the conversation or not. It is not uncommon to talk with a friend about an email or text we are writing, before we send it.

Information behavior research explores *non-textual information behavior* in literate, non-literate, and partially literate communities. A study of information behavior in the Kope tribe of the Central Highlands of New Guinea, for example, identified six distinct cultural roles related to non-textual information: induction (the passing on of cultural knowledge between generations, often ritualized), dissemination (the conversational sharing of gossip and news), presentation (the skilled use of stories and humor for political or social purposes), organization (coordination of cooperative activities, like hunting or trade), interpretation (being able to read meaning from the environment, as in tracking), and preservation (the individual and collective memory kept by the oldest members of the community).[24]

These six kinds of information activities are recognizable within any large or extended family anywhere in the world, from the sharing of family stories, to gossiping, to organizing family holidays. Many of these communicated activities are now mediated but not replaced by technology: our gossip flows seamlessly from voice to text to email and back to voice again.

The emergence of interest in everyday behaviors occurred after the move towards qualitative research methods. Scholars of everyday information behavior often produce rich, contextualized case studies; an exploration of everyday experiences of migrant Latinas in Boston is an example of this approach.[25] Studying information seeking from the user's perspective also illuminated processes of sense-making which challenged old models and suggested new ones.[26]

Everyday information seeking involves kinds of information behavior that are often overlooked, especially when they do not involve conscious information seeking. As a phenomenon, *passive information seeking* challenged Wilson's early model to adapt to new understandings of what constitutes information behavior. Imagine going for a run through a forest and seeing a birdwatcher on the path in front of you. As you pass by, they point up at a tree, and say, "Look, there's a ruby-throated hummingbird." You've just received information without seeking it, though you had to be receptive or you might not have slowed down to wonder what they were looking at.

The information behavior associated with such serendipitous information encounters has been studied in both experimental and natural settings; the phenomenon is most often referred to as *information encountering* (IE), though also as accidental information discovery, and incidental information acquisition. Information encountering happens when we browse the Internet or scroll through social media posts, not looking for anything in particular, but open to discovering random things.

It also happens that people actively avoid receiving or viewing information. *Information avoidance* might occur, for example, when someone doesn't want to research a medical condition online because it triggers anxiety. One case study looked at managers who are reluctant to acknowledge endemic bullying in their organization, not wanting to review the evidence showing that their disabled employees are being systematically disadvantaged.[27]

Another significant area of study investigates embodied experience, analyzing information as a corporeal as well as a cognitive experience.[28] Studies of *embodied information seeking* have examined the way people shop for fruits and vegetables, choosing what they want to buy through the physical practices of touching and smelling, and evaluating items through visible clues of color and condition.[29] Different physical bodies also experience the world, and interact with the information in it, differently, an idea explored by a study of the information seeking experiences of transgender people.[30] What students do with their bodies in the physical spaces in libraries can shed light on the dynamics of embodied cognition within different sensory landscapes.[31]

## INFORMATION LITERACIES

During the 20th century, libraries actively worked to improve their services to the public and to various scientific, social, and business communities. The study of information behavior in library settings had already broadened by the time computers, databases, and the Internet transformed the ways in which people interacted with information, and how libraries helped them do that.

The foundations of the field of information behavior rest on studies of readers and their preferences. The scope of this professional interest expanded, along with librarianship, to encompass the wider information needs of particular communities, exploring, for example, the reading habits of South Asian communities in Canada.[32] Youth-service librarians rely upon studies of information behavior in young people to provide effective information services within and through libraries; *digital youth literacy* is an increasingly important area of study worldwide.[33]

The *principle of least effort* reflects a classic observation of behavioral psychology that organisms, including humans, will choose to exert the least effort necessary to get something done.[34] Just as hungry people may choose fast food over more nutritional fare requiring more time and effort, fast information is often preferred over better information. It turns out that college students will choose to do their homework using an e-book version of the text, even if they believe that they would learn better from a physical text.[35] But, if an e-book is easier to access than having to go to the library or bookstore to get a physical book, how do we know whether it's the technology that is superior, or simply the convenience of the click? Likewise, if people prefer to get their news from late-night comedians or social media, do they do this deliberately, because they think it's a better news source than physical newspapers, or news websites or podcasts, or is that just what happens to show up in front of them?

Another area of concentrated interest is related to information practices implicated in the *digital divide*. The term itself is misleading since there is no single divide between information technology haves and have-nots. Across the planet there are divides between wealthy and poor countries in both literacy and digital literacy. Within countries there are information divides between urban and rural populations, and between rich and poor sectors of society. There are differences between people of different ethnic backgrounds, religious affiliations, and other caste and class-based hierarchies. Between and within nations there are divides between men and women, and between people of different ages.

We can't create universal access to the Internet in a world where some people can't read. But even in places with near universal reading literacy, patterns of stratification still have powerful effects on the quality of education, which in turn affect whether any given individual will attain the computational and digital literacies necessary to become information-literate. The Internet may be "free," but the devices and the WiFi or data plans needed to access it are not.

There are several broad strategies that have emerged to intervene in the digital divide. Libraries, with the support of large foundations, have been at the forefront of efforts to make information technologies available to local communities. The Kenya National Library Service (KNLS), beginning in the early 2000s, for example, allowed libraries to provide information access to communities, a program which was expanded to supplement school curricula.[36] More recently, libraries have stepped up across the globe as sites for "mobile hotspots" providing internet access (and computers) to sectors of local communities that have needed them, particularly during the first year of the Covid-19 pandemic. They also provide sources of accurate information to combat the waves of misinformation that hindered the management of the crisis.[37]

Fairness in the distribution of wealth, privilege, opportunities, and political power is an issue of social justice that is directly relevant to information science. The goal of *digital inclusion* is that everyone should have access to digital information; the goal of *digital equity* is that everyone should have access to the information technologies that allow for digital inclusion. These are controversial goals only to the degree that the values of equality and inclusion in other aspects of social and cultural life are politically contested. The lack of equity and inclusion together produce the digital divide.

Education is one road to upward mobility, but it only works when children have greater access to a better quality of education than their parents had and even this may not be enough, because they lack membership in the key small-world networks of power and privilege in their societies. Reproduction of patterns of educational inequality leads to the durable hierarchical stratifications that can be observed across human societies. The persistence of racial inequalities in access to and quality of education in the United States, much like the struggles of minority and immigrant populations across the globe, are testimony to the difficulties that such communities face in attempting to improve their standing within social hierarchies.[38]

It is interesting to note that the lower the level of male literacy, the greater *the gap* between men and women's literacy; countries with higher male literacy are correlated with greater gender equality in access to education. In other words, increasing literacy in general correlates with a reduction in gender inequalities, at least in regard to literacy. But the equalization of education between genders does not necessarily lead to equalization in the labor market.[39] Intersectionality also has to be taken into consideration; improving the educational opportunities for some girls, does not raise it for all. A comparison of the information literacy of Pakistani girls in public, private trust, and unregistered schools with girls who attended an elite school demonstrated the effect of social class on girls' education, for example.[40]

Access to information requires *information literacy* (knowing that information exists and where to find it) which requires digital literacy (knowing how to access it), which requires reading literacy (being able to access it), which requires educational equity (having a quality education), which requires social equity.

Among the new sorts of divides emerging in our digital age is the one between consumers and creators of content. User content creation refers to all kinds of content produced for online use. The opportunity to create or upload content anonymously has given increased power of communication to people from marginalized communities, and to those who live in societies where political speech is limited or controlled, but that same anonymity makes it more difficult for websites, or users, to detect AI-amplified incendiary content and misinformation. Young people on the Internet are more likely to contribute content than older people, and the majority of content creators come from higher socio-economic groups.[41]

A much smaller percentage of people draw a significant audience with the power to influence popular style, practice, and opinion. South Korea and Japan were among the first nations to recognize content creation as an important global industry, and to begin to construct infrastructure to support the development and training of a workforce to lead in the creative sector of popular music, games, graphic novels, and anime.[42]

Frances Haugen's testimony regarding the dangers of Instagram for vulnerable young people points to a wider problem, and an important area of research for information scientists. A growing literature has emerged on the way that children and youth have incorporated online experiences, including games, social media sites, and texting, into their lives. The dangers of filter bubbles for teenagers' mental health are real, but other online information-seeking experiences appear to be both helpful and supportive.[43]

## DISINFORMATION LITERACIES

Inaccurate information can have as much power to influence people's actions and choices in the world as accurate information, and sometimes even more. Discredited scientific research suggesting a link between vaccines and autism, for example, continues to have an information life within the anti-vaccination community, and has fueled resistance to Covid-19 vaccines worldwide.[44]

A study of internet use in Nigeria identified fear of misinformation and lack of privacy as two reasons why Nigerians, though living in one of the most "wired" countries on the continent of Africa, do not use the Internet to the degree expected. Their fears are well-grounded: misinformation is passed as news, and financial scams abound on Nigerian social media, particularly on WhatsApp. A lack of understanding about how to control privacy settings, to block unwanted messages, to distinguish between fake and real news sites, or to filter explicit and offensive content, leads Nigerians to make the reasonable decision to stay away from the Internet altogether.[45]

These issues are not an isolated problem. Non-factual information that we find on the Internet (or that we read in a magazine, or that our neighbor tells us) all fall under the umbrella of *misinformation*. The related term *disinformation* refers more narrowly to situations when some actor (individual, organization, or nation) deliberately disseminates information that is factually incorrect or inflammatory.

The fact that human beings can be manipulated through information is what makes political propaganda so effective. Information scientists study disinformation so that they can help to create social, political, and algorithmic strategies to combat it, and so that they can produce materials that can teach people to recognize disinformation when it comes across their devices. During the Covid-19 pandemic, health providers and other government officials felt an urgency to understand how disinformation spreads, and how people interact with information under pandemic conditions; they needed to to communicate accurate information to vulnerable people who needed it the most.[46]

The use of strategic disinformation by right-wing political groups as a tactic to fight civil rights actions became apparent during the Black Lives Matter protests in the United States.[47] Research revealed the existence of social media campaigns originating in Russia and other nations which were intentionally and effectively stoking racial and partisan divides in the U.S., and using similar tactics in the U.K. to manipulate public opinion regarding the EU referendum commonly referred to as "Brexit."[48]

One approach to combating disinformation is to increase awareness of what disinformation looks like. Media consumers who can recognize and name the tactics may be able to shake off their influence. Among the most common disinformation tactics are those which attempt to gain control of the subject of an issue or conversation. An *ad hominem* attack, for example, functions to distract listeners (or readers) from the actual issue at hand. Typically, it involves name-calling or attacking the character of an individual or social group, rather than responding to their argument.

Similarly, a *red herring* is a statement that introduces an irrelevant topic to mislead or draw attention away from the main issue under consideration. The diversionary strategy *slippery slope* occurs when it is claimed, on social media or a public forum, that there will be some frightening consequence down the road from the current situation under debate. There doesn't need to be any empirical evidence to support the claim, because the rhetoric is based on insinuation. The offensive claim that legalizing gay marriage will lead to people marrying animals, for example, is absurd, but the absurdity is the point of the tactic. "It's a slippery slope!" simply means that some crazy outcome might follow, which can't be refuted because it hasn't happened yet.

Another set of tactics responds to presentations of fact by attempting to make evidence ineffective. The simplest and most common is *ipse dixit* (a Latin term literally meaning "he said it himself"), which asserts that a statement is true because someone has said it's true, even without evidence, and even if it is generally understood to be untrue. It is the assertion itself that counts as proof that it is true. You can recognize *ipse dixit* from common phrases such as "They say…" or "Everybody knows…" or that dependable parental discussion-ender: "Because I said so, that's why."

Such a strategy becomes more powerful when combined with *appeal to authority*, where the name of a celebrity or authority figure is invoked to bolster an argument. This can work even if the celebrity has no particular expertise on the issue and there is no objective reason to take their opinion seriously. *Misleading vividness*, also called the "spotlight fallacy," uses a similar logical fallacy, employing headlines as a source of authority. A case in the news is taken to be more broadly significant than it really is, just because it is getting a lot of media attention. When someone who is offering up misinformation is challenged with the facts, rather than retracting and apologizing they may use a technique called *backfire*, in which they simply double-down on their false statement, asserting it with additional authority arising from the fact that someone dared to question it.

Scholars who study *trolling* as information behavior look closely at how online communities understand and manage trolls, and have found a complex set of practices, performances, and relationships. Trolling that takes place in online gaming environments, for example (also called "trash-talking,") offers racists an opportunity to get away with language practices that in the real world would be condemned as hate speech.[49]

But while it is common to assume that trolling is wholly a negative phenomenon which should be eliminated, in fact each incidence of trolling has a different social context. Some trolling is intended and received as humorous, some is political, some is conversational, some is reactive, and some is even appreciated as a reaction to other toxic comments.[50] The experiences and motivations of the trolls, and the perspectives of those who react to their trolling, provide context for understanding this new form of information behavior.

Of course, some trolls may not be human. *Chatbots* (also called social bots) can easily be created and set free to sound and act just like a human troll. Their algorithms allow them to create and promote posts that push a particular them; they also have the very unhuman capacity to amplify a story by repeating it thousands and thousands of times.

In the technique known as *astroturfing*, AI-controlled bots are deployed to appear to be part of a grassroots organization. A fake account of a bot pretending to be a real person is referred to as a *sock puppet*. When these kinds of bots are deployed alongside an army of ordinary human trolls, they can be particularly effective at election interference, but between elections they also continue their social mayhem, set loose by foreign governments or political parties or malicious individuals. Trolls and bots might actually seek to amplify both sides of a conflict, if their aim is simply to create disunity and dissent as a tactic of their cyberwarfare.

## STUDYING INFORMATION IN CONTEXT

During the first months of the Russian invasion of Ukraine, it was clear that information had become a significant weapon of war. In February 2022 Ukraine's Minister of Digital Transformation, Mykhailo Fedorov, used social media to call for volunteers to help wage this information war. Organizers on Telegram, an instant messaging service, encouraged the more than 300,000 people who responded to the call to participate in distributed denial of service (DDoS) attacks on Russian websites, knocking them offline by flooding them with more traffic than they could handle. They organized other responses to Russian disinformation as well.[51]

The propaganda machine in Russia is a complex and international operation. Research released by the Institute for Strategic Dialogue (ISD), a non-profit organization which tracks disinformation and extremism worldwide, reported small groups of content creators with multiple accounts amplifying Russian propaganda and messaging on Facebook, making it seem as though there were swelling local grassroots support for Russia's view of the war.[52] This strategy had greater success in nations which have historically been allied with Russia, such as Serbia and Bulgaria.[53] In countries that won their independence from the Soviet Union, the use of propaganda in the invasion of Ukraine has only made them more alert to its deployment in their own nations.

A large informal network of Lithuanian citizens emerged, working anonymously to counter Russian propaganda in that country. They call themselves "elves"—since elves fight trolls—and much of the disinformation is coming from Russian troll farms that pay people to produce it. The Strategic Communications Department of the Lithuanian Armed Forces (STRATCOM) reported over 8000 attacks in a two-year period, and the rates are rising. The content mirrors Russia's justifications for its invasion of Ukraine: that Lithuania is not really democratic, but fascist and run by Nazis, and that it is a failed state providing NATO a base from which to attack Russia.[54]

The elves are loosely organized and decentralized. They do not meet, except virtually in a private Facebook group. They estimate they may have as many as 22,000 members who cooperate to locate disinformation, identify, and shut down fake accounts, block false information, and counter it by amplifying facts. Lithuanian Parliament member Jurgita Sejonienė has admitted to being an elf; she joined because of her concern over the impact of anti-vaccination propaganda on the pandemic response.

The Lithuanian elves are supported by academics, journalists, the Lithuanian government, and non-governmental organizations such as DebunkEU, an independent think tank with 50 volunteers who flag problematic content and suspicious amplification in Lithuania and seven other nations, and the Baltic Research Foundation for Digital Resilience (DIGIRES), a collaboration between Lithuanian academics, media organizations, and independent journalists.

The larger context of information behavior becomes starkly visible during times of global crisis such as pandemics, wars, and environmental disasters. At the level of communities and individuals, studies of information behavior help us to understand the psychological vulnerabilities and social dynamics that make disinformation campaigns successful in some places, and among some groups, and less effective in others. Efforts such as those happening in Lithuania are proactive interventions; the elves aren't waiting for Facebook to be willing to make their algorithms less profitable.

Educational efforts to increase information literacy, particularly for populations that are especially vulnerable to misinformation such as children and the elderly, are a priority across much of the world. A nine-part web drama series in Indonesia, for example, was created as part of the Indonesian "anti-hoax" movement, prompted by what was being called the "infodemic" of disinformation that spread during the Covid-19 pandemic.[55]

A growing number of video games, board games, and card games train players to detect false news more accurately. The "Bad News Game," developed by the Cambridge Social Decision-Making Lab in collaboration with the Dutch media collective DROG,[56] for example, teaches the most common tactics of social media disinformation by guiding the player through the step-by-step process of becoming a fake-news maven. This isn't meant to encourage them to become one in the real world, but to help them to recognize the tactics when they appear in the wild.

The extent to which the Internet is full of lies and deliberate manipulations flies in the face of our ancient longings for a collection that contains "all the information in the world." We may feel, naively perhaps, that such a collection should contain only real information. The *Library of Babel* story reminds us that a collection with everything in it must necessarily include all the errors and lies in the world in addition to all that is accurate and benevolent—all mixed up with random noise. On the Internet, and on social media sites in particular, the challenge is to discern truth within the endless streams of targeted advertisements, time-wasting clickbait, and the incendiary ravings of artificially malevolent trolls.

## NOTES

1 Ryan Mac and Cecilia Kang, "Whistle-Blower Says Facebook 'Chooses Profits Over Safety,'" *The New York Times*, 3 October 2021.
2 Georgia Wells, Jeff Horwitz, and Deepa Seetharaman, "Facebook Knows Instagram Is Toxic for Teen Girls, Company Documents Show," *Wall Street Journal*, 14 September 2021.
3 Jacqueline Nesi et al., "Social Media Use and Self-Injurious Thoughts and Behaviors: A Systematic Review and Meta-Analysis," *Clinical Psychology Review* 87 (2021): 102038.
4 Ronan Lee, "Extreme Speech| Extreme Speech in Myanmar: The Role of State Media in the Rohingya Forced Migration Crisis," *International Journal of Communication* 13 (2019): 3202–3224.
5 Karen Hao, "The Facebook Whistleblower Says Its Algorithms are Dangerous: Here's Why," *MIT Technology Review*, https://canvas.illinois .edu/courses/16422/discussion_topics/125024. Retrieved 7 June 2022.
6 Elizabeth Culliford, "Rohingya Refugees Sue Facebook for $150 Billion over Myanmar Violence," *Reuters*, 8 December 2021.
7 Cat Zakrzewski, "Facebook Whistleblower Alleges Executives Misled Investors about Climate, Covid Hoaxes in New SEC Complaint," *The Washington Post*, 18 February 2022.
8 Daniel Cassino and Peter Wooley, "Some News Leaves People Knowing Less," *Farleigh Dickinson University Public Mind Poll*, 21 November 2011.
9 Sara Malm, "Belgian Woman Blindly Drove 900 Miles across Europe as She Followed Broken GPS Instead of 38 Miles to the Station," *Daily Mail.com*, 14 January 2013. https://www.dailymail.co.uk/news/arti-cle-2262149/Belgian-woman-67-picking-friend-railway-station-ends -Zagreb-900-miles-away-satnav-disaster.html.

10  J. D. Bernal, "The Transmission of Scientific Information: A User's Analysis," in *Proceedings of the International Conference on Scientific Information* 958 (1958): 77–95. Cited in Thomas D. Wilson, "Human Information Behavior," *Informing Science* 3, no. 2 (2000): 50.

11  Marcia J. Bates, "Information Behavior," in *Encyclopedia of Library and Information Sciences*, eds. John D. McDonald and Michael Levine-Clark (Boca Raton, FL: CRC Press, 2017): 2074–2085.

12  Lionel J. B. Mote, "Reasons for the Variations in the Information Needs of Scientists," *Journal of Documentation* (1962). Cited in Wilson, "Human," 51.

13  David Bawden, "Users, User Studies and Human Information Behaviour: A Three-Decade Perspective on Tom Wilson's 'On User Studies and Information Needs,'" *Journal of Documentation* 62, no. 6 (2006): 671–679.

14  Bates, "Information Behavior," 2075.

15  Theresa Dirndorfer Anderson and Jo Orsatti, "Rhythms of 'Being' at ISIC-Understanding the Place of the ISIC Conferences in Information Seeking Research," *Information Research* 13, no. 4 (2008), http://informationr.net/ir/13-4/paper381.html. Retrieved 22 September 2022.

16  "About," The Information Behavior Conference, https://pages.cms.hu-berlin.de/ibi/isic-2022/about/. Retrieved 8 June 2022.

17  Syed Masud Ahmed, Göran Tomson, Max Petzold, and Zarina Nahar Kabir, "Socioeconomic Status Overrides Age and Gender in Determining Health-Seeking Behaviour in Rural Bangladesh," *Bulletin of the World Health Organization* 83 (2005): 109–117.

18  Rachel M. Magee, "Teen Social Media Practices and Perceptions of Peers," *The Journal of Research on Libraries and Young Adults* 10, no. 3 (2019): 1–121.

19  David Hopping, "Modeling Hope: Boundary Objects and Design Patterns in a Heartland Heterotopia," in *Deciding Where to Live: Information Studies on Where to Live in America*, eds. Melissa G. Ocepek and William Aspray (Lanham, MD: Rowman & Littlefield Publishers, 2020): 211–235.

20  Judith Pintar, "The Valley between Us: The Meta-Hodology of Racial Segregation in Milwaukee, Wisconsin," in *Deciding Where to Live: Information Studies on Where to Live in America*, eds. Melissa G. Ocepek and William Aspray (Lanham, MD: Rowman & Littlefield Publishers, 2020): 177–210.

21  Brenton Stewart and Boryung Ju, "On Black Wikipedians: Motivations Behind Content Contribution," *Information Processing & Management* 57, no. 3 (2020): 102134.

22  Reijo Savolainen, "Everyday Life Information Seeking: Approaching Information Seeking in the Context of 'Way of Life,'" *Library & Information Science Research* 17, no. 3 (1995): 259–294.

23  Walter J. Ong, *Orality and Literacy* (London: Routledge, 2013): 10.

24  Andrew D. Madden, Jared Bryson, and Joe Palimi, "Information Behavior in Pre-Literate Societies," in *New Directions in Human Information Behavior*, eds. Amanda Spink and Charles Cole (Dordrecht: Springer, 2006): 8–9.

25 Mónica Colón-Aguirre and Janet Ceja Alcalá, "Everyday Information Practices of Migrant Latinas Living in Boston," in *Social Justice Design and Implementation in Library and Information Science*, ed. Bharat Mehra (London: Routledge, 2021): 116–132.

26 Carol C. Kuhlthau, "Inside the Search Process: Information Seeking from the User's Perspective," *Journal of the American Society for Information Science* 42, no. 5 (1991): 361–371.

27 Keren Dali, "The Lifeways We Avoid: The Role of Information Avoidance in Discrimination against People with Disabilities," *Journal of Documentation* 74, no. 6 (2018): 1258–1273.

28 See C. P. Lueg, "The Missing Link: Information Behavior Research and Its Estranged Relationship with Embodiment," *Journal of the Association for Information Science and Technology* 66, no. 12 (2015): 2704–2707.

29 Melissa G. Ocepek, "Sensible Shopping: A Sensory Exploration of the Information Environment of the Grocery Store," *Library Trends* 66, no. 3 (2018): 371–394.

30 Andrew M. Cox, "Learning Bodies: Sensory Experience in the Information Commons," *Library & Information Science Research* 41, no. 1 (2019): 58–66.

31 Aira Huttunen, Lottamari Kähkönen, Heidi Enwald, and Terttu Kortelainen, "Embodied Cognition and Information Experiences of Transgender People," *Information Research* 24, no. 4 (2019), http://InformationR.net/ir/24-4/colis/colis1940.html. Retrieved 22 September 2022.

32 Aditi Gupta, Sarbjit Kaur Randhawa, and In-In Po, "Reading Habits, Library Perceptions and Library Usage of the South Asian Population in British Columbia, Canada," *Public Library Quarterly* 41, no. 5 (2021): 456–484.

33 Nuala Connolly and Claire McGuinness, "Towards Digital Literacy for the Active Participation and Engagement of Young People in a Digital World," *Young People in a Digitalised World* 4 (2018): 77.

34 George Kingsley Zipf, *Human Behavior and the Principle of Least Effort: An Introduction to Human Ecology* (Boston, MA: Addison Wesley Press, 1949).

35 Diane Mizrachi, "Undergraduates' Academic Reading Format Preferences and Behaviors," *Journal of Academic Librarianship* 41, no. 3 (2015): 301–311.

36 Margaret Baffour-Awuah, "The Carnegie Revitalisation of Public Libraries in Africa: A Possible Tool for Breaking Down Barriers to School Library Development," in *IASL Annual Conference Proceedings* (2021), https://doi.org/10.29173/iasl7545.

37 See, for example, Jinchi Guo and Jie Huang, "Information Literacy Education during the Pandemic: The Cases of Academic Libraries in Chinese Top Universities," *Journal of Academic Librarianship* 47, no. 4 (2021): 102363.

38 See Richard Breen and Walter Müller, *Education and Intergenerational Social Mobility in Europe and the United States* (Stanford, CA: Stanford University Press, 2020).

39  David K. Evans, Maryam Akmal, and Pamela Jakiela, "Gender Gaps in Education: The Long View," *IZA, Journal of Development and Migration* 12, no. 1 (2021): 27.

40  Syeda Hina Batool and Sheila Webber, "A Contextual Framework for Primary Education: Fostering Information Literacy in Pakistan," *Global Knowledge, Memory and Communication* 68, no. 3 (2018): 164–176.

41  Eszter Hargittai and Gina Walejko, "The Participation Divide: Content Creation and Sharing in the Digital Age," *Information, Communication & Society* 11, no. 2 (2008): 20.

42  Carin Holroyd, "Digital Content Promotion in Japan and South Korea: Government Strategies for an Emerging Economic Sector," *Asia & The Pacific Policy Studies* 6, no. 3 (2019): 290–307.

43  Emily Weinstein, "The Social Media See-Saw: Positive and Negative Influences on Adolescents' Affective Well-Being," *New Media & Society* 20, no. 10 (2018): 3597–3623.

44  Ety Elisha, Josh Guetzkow, Yaffa Shir-Raz, and Natti Ronel, "Retraction of Scientific Papers: The Case of Vaccine Research," *Critical Public Health* 32, no. 4 (2022): 533–542.

45  Yang Wang, "First-Time Internet Users in Nigeria Use the Internet in a Unique Way," *KaiOS Industry Insights* (2020), https://www.kaiostech .com/first-time-internet-users-in-nigeria-use-the-internet-in-a-unique -way-heres-why-that-matters/.

46  Michela Montesi, "Human Information Behavior during the Covid-19 Health Crisis: A Literature Review," *Library & Information Science Research* 43, no. 4 (2021): 101122.

47  Arif, Ahmer, Leo Graiden Stewart, and Kate Starbird, "Acting the Part: Examining Information Operations within #BlackLivesMatter Discourse," *Proceedings of the ACM on Human-Computer Interaction* 2, no. CSCW (2018): 1–27.

48  Clare Llewellyn, Laura Cram, Robin L. Hill, and Adrian Favero, "For Whom the Bell Trolls: Shifting Troll Behaviour in the Twitter Brexit Debate," *JCMS: Journal of Common Market Studies* 57, no. 5 (2019): 1148–1164.

49  Stephanie M. Ortiz, "'You Can Say I Got Desensitized To It': How Men of Color Cope with Everyday Racism in Online Gaming," *Sociological Perspectives* 62, no. 4 (2019): 572–588.

50  Madelyn Sanfilippo, Shengnan Yang, and Pnina Fichman, "Managing Online Trolling: From Deviant to Social and Political Trolls," in *Proceedings of the 50th Hawaii International Conference on System Sciences* (2017), https://doi.org/10.24251/HICSS.2017.219.

51  Tom Simonite and Gian M. Volpicelli, "Ukraine's Digital Ministry Is a Formidable War Machine," *Wired*, 17 March 2022, https://www.wired .co.uk/article/ukraine-digital-ministry-war.

52  Moustafa Ayad, "The Vladimirror Network: Pro-Putin Power-Users on Facebook," *Institute of Strategic Dialogue*, 4 April 2022. https://www.isdg-lobal.org/isd-publications/the-vladimirror-network-pro-putin-power -users-on-facebook/.

53 Boryana Dzhambazova, "Welcome to Bulgaria, Where the Ukraine War Is NATO's Fault," *Politico*, 8 June 2022. https://www.politico.eu/article/bulgaria-ukraine-russia-war-nato-fault/.

54 Lisa Abend, "Meet the Lithuanian 'Elves' Fighting Russian Disinformation," *Time*, 6 March 2022, https://time.com/6155060/lithuania-russia-fighting-disinformation-ukraine/.

55 Santi Indra Astuti, Lumakto Giri, and Nuril Hidayah, "Video Web Drama Series for Combating Disinformation," *Aspiration Journal* 1, no. 1 (2020): 7.

56 "The Bad News Game," https://www.getbadnews.com/en/play. Retrieved 9 June 2022. DebunkEU provides translations of the game into Lithuanian, Latvian, Estonian, Russian, and Polish. https://www.debunkeu.org/get-bad-news-game-lietuviskai.

# 8

# DESIGNING INFORMATION

In November of 1854 the Crimean War was raging. The Russian Empire had decided to attempt an expansion of its borders with the Ottoman Empire. France and England sided with the Ottomans, declaring war on Russia and sending troops into a complicated and bloody conflict. An Englishwoman arrived with 38 volunteer nurses and 15 Catholic nuns at the military hospital in Scutari (today called Üsküdar), on the Anatolian side of the Bosporus Strait near the city of Constantinople (now Istanbul, Turkey). She had read the newspaper reports of terrible conditions at the military facilities in Scutari, with wounded soldiers sleeping on vermin-infested beds made from rotting boards and dying from preventable infections.[1]

When she arrived, she found, as she had expected, that the injured were dying not from battle wounds but from cholera, dysentery, and typhoid. Hospital buildings were filthy, overcrowded, and poorly ventilated. Blocked drains and a lack of toilets produced unsanitary conditions and foul water. There was a general lack of hygiene among both the sick and the caretakers. More than 4,000 men died that winter.

In spite of administrative resistance to her calls for change, the English nurse ordered general cleaning and instituted handwashing policies. Though germ theory had not yet emerged, and disease was blamed on "bad air," improvements in food, water, and heat strengthened the injured, and better sanitation and hygiene controlled the spread of infection. Death rates dropped dramatically.[2]

DOI: 10.4324/9781003155119-8

She documented all of this, systematically collecting data on the number of sick and dying each month that she was in charge of the medical operation, before and after her interventions.

The nurse was Florence Nightingale (1820–1910). She was born to wealthy British parents in Florence, Italy, the city for which she was named. Raised in England, she was well-educated by her Unitarian father, though she had to argue for the right to study mathematics. Her family was not conventional (her maternal grandfather was an abolitionist) but they did expect her to want a husband, not an occupation. They were not overjoyed by the professional path she chose; nursing in the 19th century was poorly paid and staffed by women from the lower classes. Nevertheless, she felt a calling to care for the sick, and she persisted.[3] The 18 months she spent in the field as a wartime nurse made her famous to the public, and she was celebrated by the press as a "ministering angel,"[4] an image that Henry Wadsworth Longfellow immortalized in his poem *Santa Filomena*.[5]

Nightingale increased the social status of nursing and professionalized the field, but she also made a significant contribution to information design and data visualization.

When she arrived home after the war, having been critically ill herself, she successfully advocated (with Queen Victoria's support) for the creation of a Royal Commission to investigate and compare mortality rates in peace and in war.[6] Collaborating with statistician William Farr, she provided a report to the Commission which presented mortality rates over a period of two years. She hoped it would make the case for reforms. Six months later the Commission had still not acted. For an addendum to her report, William Farr proposed to create more tables, but Nightingale felt that since the statistics presented in the original report had not persuaded the eclectic group of royalty and members of parliament, more tables weren't going to do the job.

Nightingale designed a series of statistical charts to communicate the meaning of the numbers. Her *rose diagrams* were included in the report and told a powerful story. She asked her readers first to consider the difference in rates of death during peacetime and during war. Two linked diagrams were provided. Each was a spiral divided into 12 wedges representing 12 months of the war.[7] Each wedge in the spiral was a stacked column, with one band of color representing monthly mortality in Crimean War hospitals. Another much smaller band at the center of the spiral showed mortality rates for the city of Manchester. The visual comparison was shocking, as Nightingale knew it would be. Manchester was notorious for unhealthy work conditions and poor life expectancy. The image led her readers to the obvious question: what could be causing such a high mortality rate among the soldiers?

Her second diagram again used a spiral of stacked columns representing months of time. This time the colored bands showed different causes of death in the military field hospitals which made starkly clear how many more men had died from disease than from battle injuries, even in the month that included British losses in the infamous "Charge of the Light Brigade." This visualization was enhanced by the narrative power of her words:

> It was not by wounds; it was not by ordinary diseases that the army well-nigh perished. But it was by those five mitigable and preventable pestilences that the British force before Sevastopol was all but swept away. Expunge the blue wedges, and within what insignificant bounds would not that great calamity have shrunk! These diagrams give the whole history of the disaster.[8]

Having captured her audience's attention, her third diagram would perform the persuasive coup de grace. Rather than simply showing the reduction in deaths that followed from her interventions over the months, she chose instead to compare the field hospital mortality rates with those of a military hospital in London. The diagrams illustrated the narrowing of the difference between the two hospitals over time, a change that correlated with the improvement of conditions that she had instituted.[9] Driving home her central point, she declared that "The most cursory inspection of these diagrams will show that the whole question as to the cause of the mortality narrows itself into an inquiry as to what laws of health had been so violated as to lead to so great a destruction of life."[10] Even as her readers asked themselves this question, the diagrams provided the answer. All they had to do now was take action.

Nightingale had 2,000 copies of her diagrams printed and distributed at her own expense. Her deft use of visualized statistics, in coordination with impassioned rhetoric, did the work of both energizing the public and convincing the Commission to act. Her work was instrumental in establishing what today is referred to as "evidence-based health care." The Royal Statistical Society, which had never seen diagrams like hers before, elected her with great enthusiasm as its first female member in 1858.

In this chapter we look at the visualization of data as a powerful storytelling aid. We explore the history and development of information architecture, survey approaches to user experience (UX) and user/human-centered design, and end with a consideration of the principles of universal design as applied to information systems.

## STORYTELLING AND DATA VISUALIZATION

Compelling data visualizations combined with cogent narratives can provide persuasive evidence for a cause, especially when informed by background research into the intended audience. Nightingale's initial report presumed that her readers would have the capacity to extract meaning from raw tabular data on their own. Her subsequent "data story" reflected a more nuanced appreciation of the audience's interests and capacities, which became a factor in its design.

While charts and diagrams may be among the first examples that come to mind when we think about *information design* (ID), in fact it has a much broader scope. It applies to informational aspects of physical artifacts (does this door push, pull, or slide to open, and how can you tell?), the organization of the larger built environment (how can I find my way to the right gate at the airport?), and, more recently, the design of software and online spaces. The audience (or "consumer" or "user") has a critical role to play in shaping design across all these domains of design practice.

Traditional storytelling recorded and transmitted collective cultural knowledge and memory in the absence of written records. But human societies never stopped telling stories to make sense of the world, whether we wrote them down or not. We still share knowledge between generations through stories. But storytelling has always had other purposes as well, including entertainment, instruction, and persuasion. In all of these ways, storytelling is as relevant in the digital age as it was in pre-history.

Broadly, storytelling is connected to interdisciplinary studies of narrative, with relevance to anthropology, geography, and ethnic studies as both an object of study and a methodology.[11] Narrative design is a term used to describe the craft of creative writing, as well as to refer to practices in new media and game design.[12] Within libraries, storytelling in the fields of School Librarianship and Youth Librarianship is an area of professional training and practice with a long history.[13]

In research settings, the opportunities afforded by digital technologies have opened up the field of storytelling to include both new participatory methodologies for working within communities, as well as providing new ways for communities to preserve and share cultural knowledge in coordination with libraries, archives, and museums.[14]

*Data storytelling* is an increasingly important area of teaching, research, and practice, with wide applications to every sector of contemporary society where data is analyzed and shared, from boardrooms, to briefing rooms, to social media sites. A data storyteller builds a compelling narrative interpreting an analyzed data set, using visualization techniques to illustrate key relationships. Training in data storytelling involves gaining understanding of narrative structure, timing and performance, and the dynamics of the relationship between the storyteller, the story, and the audience.

In business settings, the rhetoric of persuasion in relationship to the data story being told also comes into play. This communicative process of data storytelling is vulnerable to the same sorts of biases that might affect other points in a research process. An important aspect of digital literacy is the ability to detect the misuse of statistics expressed through misleading charts and graphs. Ethical concerns in the expression of data are just as important as they are during its collection and analysis.

As a field, *Data Visualization* seeks to optimize the visual expression of analyzed data in order to shed light on, and to more effectively communicate, patterns found in the data that strengthen a particular narrative. It is enhanced by a broad and ever-widening set of tools and techniques that help to improve understanding and communication of data, leveraging our visual ability to recognize patterns and replacing the need for calculation. The result is that analyzed data becomes both more visually appealing and more accessible, engaging audiences in the research narrative and persuading them to the storyteller's point of view.

By revealing information that is otherwise difficult to perceive, it can improve decision-making and reduce error—not only in the *explanatory* phase of communicating results to an audience, but also in the *exploratory* phase in which patterns are first discovered. The statistical demonstration known as *Anscombe's Quartet* is often used to illustrate the importance of visualizing data early in the analysis process. Four datasets with identical summary statistics (the same mean, same standard deviation, and same correlation) appear as dramatically different patterns when graphed: a vertical line, an angled line, a curve, a cloud of dots. These reflect different underlying relational patterns in the data that are not immediately evident in tables, nor even in the basic statistical description of the data. More fanciful example sets have been created, such as the "Datasaurus Dozen" in which the dots of one chart actually form a cartoon dinosaur—underscoring the principle that visualization should always be a part of exploratory data analysis.[15]

One of the challenges of using data storytelling to communicate the results of data-based research is choosing the right technique, so that images are not only effective and engaging but also appropriate to the data, the domain, and the question at hand. Hundreds of varieties of charts and graphs have been devised to visualize data. They can be productively grouped into a few common types that lend themselves to particular purposes.[16] For example, *Time Series* charts use one axis to index movement in time (seconds, minutes, months, or centuries), while the other axis shows how variables change over time. An *Index Chart* is a time-series chart that can compare percentage changes (rather than actual values) for several variables across time, starting together at some particular "index" moment; these charts are especially useful for understanding economic trends.

*Statistical Charts* illustrate how values in a data set are distributed. Dots in a *Scatter Plot* (as seen in an Anscombe's Quartet graph) show where data points fall on two axes. With all the data in a set filled in, it may be possible to detect patterns not visible in the numerical data itself. *Data Maps* are the most immediately recognizable statistical chart. They show how variables vary across space. A common variety is the *Graduated Symbol Map*, recognizable because of the circular mini pie charts that it superimposes on top of a representation of a physical region. A *Dorling Cartogram* is a variation which uses a map for an initial guide, and then erases the map details underneath. One of the most visually stunning map-based charts is a *Flow Map*, which animates the data to show directional movement—across space, or across time, or both.

*Tree Diagrams* are ubiquitous in ordinary life. The file tree on your computer is a tree-based display, as are the family trees used in genealogy research to visualize the relationships between family members across generations. Depending on whether a genealogist wants to show the descendants of an individual branching forward (usually downward on the chart), or their ancestors going backward in time (upwards or sideways) from that ancestor, different types of tree diagrams can be chosen to fit the genealogical information being shared.

*Network visualizations* are different from other types of charts and diagrams in that they can show the direction and strength of relationships between data points. Within this category, one of the most visually appealing is the *Force-Directed Graph*, which sorts data into clusters of more-connected points. Interactive digital versions allow the viewer to move data points around, exploring the varying strengths of different relationship patterns by pulling them apart, visually, on the screen.

Data storytelling is becoming essential to modern *data journalism*, a rapidly growing practice which is benefiting from recent advances in collaborative online tools. It is now possible to create high-end interactive explorations of data that provide readers with richer engagement and better understanding. Sometimes referred to as "no code" or "low code" tools, such products offer users support in managing data and in customizing charts and graphs, regardless of programming ability. This ease of use is especially important for journalists working against short deadlines or in stressful or dangerous conditions around the world.[17]

Skillful storytelling and creative visualization can also be enlisted to address and rectify large-scale social problems. A half-century after Florence Nightingale made her striking contributions to public health research and policy, the American anti-slavery and Civil Rights Movement leader W.E.B. Du Bois designed an extraordinary exhibition on African-American life for the *Exposition Universelle* of 1900, the 5th Paris World's Fair.

After receiving a PhD in history from Harvard, Du Bois gravitated toward the field of sociology. Working from the historically Black Atlanta University, in Atlanta, Georgia, he collaborated with other prominent African-American scholars and leaders of his day on "the American Negro" exhibit, which included a curated collection of 500 photographs of African-Americans that challenged racist stereotypes, and gave insight into their communities and lives. But Du Bois felt that the images alone couldn't explain to fairgoers the significant challenges that these communities experienced as a result of the social barriers created by racism. So, he created 60 charts for display at the fair that he hoped would communicate some of those experiences. These provided visual narrations of data collected by his students at Atlanta University and an extended network of researchers across the American South.[18]

The visualizations that Du Bois made for the World's Fair functioned as infographics, educating fairgoers on the sociology of race in America. They provided detailed demographic and personal information about the lives of Black people, including professional occupations, literacy, school enrollment, and even the contents of their homes, along with macro-level analyses of the challenges they faced. The visualizations were artistically striking and distinct from the kinds of statistical diagrams being produced in the era. Large-scale reproductions of some of these diagrams were displayed on the walls of the exhibit hall. By enlisting the available physical space in structuring the overall story and information design, Du Bois augmented the visitor experience in ways that anticipated the work of "information architects" a century later.[19]

## THE ARCHITECTURE OF INFORMATION

In the early 1990s, the American Museum of Natural History (AMNH) undertook an ambitious renovation of its extensive fossil collection. When the multi-year project was complete, the top floor of the building had been transformed into six interconnected

exhibit halls, uniting its mammal and primitive-vertebrate holdings with its renowned dinosaur collection.[20]

Over the previous century, layers of built-up remodeling work
had buried the underlying 19th-century architecture, blocking the
light and confining the space, creating a "dim and fusty ambi-
ence" (as the project's architect, Ralph Appelbaum, recalls) which
"tended to make the visitors feel like fossils too."[21] In the first phase
of renovation, the physical interior was restored to its original
grandeur, thus "activating" the space itself in service of the overall mission, which was to convey an updated and more expansive
understanding of evolution.

Other architectural and physical aspects were similarly activated
as design assets: specimens were displayed with minimal barriers,
partial skeletons were mounted on wire frames that filled in the
rest of the form of the animal, sheer glass panels were installed in
inconspicuous floor mounts. Even the floor itself became a discrete bearer of wayfinding information guiding the visitor through
the exhibit halls. Alcoves and transitional spaces that traditionally
would be left neutral were similarly enlisted to "cast a broader
informational net" to engage visitors.

The critical breakthrough in developing the new overall design
occurred during master planning. Most conventional evolution-
ary exhibits are organized around the simple metaphor of a "walk
through time"—but evolution, as we now know, is actually much
more of a "puzzle of shared characteristics." The museum's project
director, Lowell Dingus, described the paradigm shift underpin-
ning the new organization:

> We hit upon the idea that people are naturally interested in their family
> history, especially in a country of immigrants like the United States. In a
> very real sense, evolutionary history simply represents an extrapolation
> of one's family history no matter what kind of organism you are. So, we
> decided to see if we could take the basic concept of a family tree and
> spatially expand it.[22]

In the case of evolution, the structuring metaphor of family history
is realized in a scientific diagram known as a *cladogram*, depicting
relationships of descent as nodes and branches of a tree. This was
rendered into the museum's physical layout as the main circulation

path through the halls. Visitors could walk along this branching system, guided by patterns in the floor, and encounter species arrayed in a complex pattern that follows modern understandings of evolution.

The AMNH project was featured prominently in architect Richard Saul Wurman's 1996 book *Information Architects*. Information architects, he suggests, are "a new breed" of designers who are able to "make the complex clear" in a wide range of contexts including airports, museum exhibitions, illustrations, maps, and scientific diagrams.

Wurman had already begun to popularize the idea of "information architecture" two decades earlier, as a way of foregrounding aspects of an architectural approach to design that organizes information in ways that lead to better understanding. Among these are a concern for the soundness of underlying organization and structure, and reduction of irrelevant detail so that critical information stands out from noisy background contexts. These are parts of the design process that are not undertaken in order to be noticed and displayed and appreciated; when they are effective, they become invisible.

Another critical "principle of clarity" is that of *familiarity*. People only understand new things in relation to something they already understand, which might be visual, verbal, or numerical understanding.[23] This principle was deployed to great effect by Nightingale, when she compared wartime medical care in distant Crimea with that provided in local London hospitals; by Du Bois in his depiction of African-Americans within ordinary life contexts familiar to every visitor; and by Appelbaum and Dingus as they (literally) inscribed the familiar family-tree metaphor into the floor and layout of the exhibit halls.

Although Wurman was instrumental in reframing and popularizing the idea of information architecture, the term had actually been coined several years earlier by Peter McCollough, then CEO of Xerox.[24] Both IBM and Xerox had adopted expansive missions to control and organize information, which would entail inventing and integrating diverse new information technologies and artifacts such as computers and terminals, copiers, microfilm, printers, fax machines, screens, and transmission systems; and designing and building ambitious complex systems out of them.

Such multi-layered information systems included humans in key places, interacting with computers across interfaces that also had to be designed. These interfaces tended to be conceived by engineers analogously with all the other interfaces between layered components, such as between computer hardware and memory, or between software and "peripheral" devices such as printers. Studying how to get human beings into the system emerged under the rubric of "human factors"—variables to be studied, accounted for, and controlled effectively. [25]

The term *user-friendly* emerged in the early 1970s but didn't enter popular discourse until the advent of personal computing in the 1980s and an expanding market for software products like spreadsheets and word-processing applications, which had to be operable by non-experts. The field of *Human Computer Interaction* (HCI), with roots in the work of Douglas Engelbart and Joseph Licklider in the 1960s, was popularized in the 1980s.[26] "Interaction design" became a key area of interest, but it was still centered on the interface between computer and human, and focused narrowly on the technical and cognitive aspects of interactions across that interface.

In Scandinavia during the same period, a more political strain of HCI was developing. Articulated by Danish computer scientist Susanne Bødker, *participatory design* (PD), also referred to as cooperative design or co-design, emerged as computers began to appear on factory shop floors. Bødker and her colleagues were interested in involving workers in the design of information technology in the workplace. Participatory design in its early years was intended to resolve conflicts between workers and management through democratic processes. On a larger scale, they wanted to influence the way that information systems would be developed and deployed in the world.[27]

In the early 1990s, the term *user experience* (UX) drew attention to the human being at the center of a system, with an elevated focus on the usability of a technology (or other product). The basic tenets of *user-centered design* practice, which was developed and utilized across a wide range of disciplines, had already coalesced by the late 1980s. Key practices included consulting users early in the design process, continuously evaluating a design throughout the development process, and using "iterative" design techniques to evaluate and improve prototypes.

User-centered design approaches prioritized overall quality of engagement and interaction as a goal in the practical design of artifacts for human use, taking into account users' values, emotional responses, and the meaning that the system, technology or product holds for them. Attention to broader social goals and the need for problem-solving processes with multiple stakeholders led to the emergence of *human-centered design* (HCD).[28]

## INFORMATION ARCHITECTURE FOR THE WEB

The appearance and explosive growth of the early Web introduced a new interface to design for: interactive web pages running within a browser application or "user agent" such as Firefox or Safari. User experience considerations gradually took hold in this new context, and would eventually guide web design practice, but early web technologies offered only limited options for customizing layouts and interactions. More dramatic improvements in user experience were achievable by organizing the information being sought and delivered; by creating "invisible" layers of supporting structure that function similarly, in many ways, to those that architects have always used in the context of designing physical spaces.

Architects create blueprints—densely informational design guides—to coordinate all aspects of construction, including (for example) the routing and installation of plumbing and electrical and heating systems, all performed by different specialist subcontractors. Before construction begins, the underlying loads and stresses of supportive structures are calculated by engineers, and even before this stage the desires and preferences of the client for how the building should function are worked out in conversations and prototype diagrams and drawings. All this critical information is assembled and fashioned into a single common document set that precisely depicts the same project from multiple angles, for multiple practical purposes.

Architectural plans are an example of what information scientists refer to as *boundary objects*—specially-crafted tools (including purely abstract ones) that facilitate collaboration across very different social or professional or cultural contexts, even when collaborators have limited knowledge of one another's worlds.[29]

In the late 1990s, Peter Morville and Louis Rosenfeld wrote an influential book that adapted certain architectural principles to the challenge of designing for the Web. Now in its fourth edition, *Information Architecture for the Web and Beyond* consciously applied Wurman's approach to designing "information environments" to the new virtual spaces of the emerging online world. Their distinctive contribution was to also weave in key ideas and practices from library and information science. Simply put, the goal of *information architecture* (IA) in this new sense is to create online spaces—"spaces made of information"—in which people can easily find whatever they're looking for, discover new things, and understand what they find.[30]

*Information architects* (IAs) rely on a wide variety of boundary objects to align the goals of a diverse (and sometimes very large) set of *stakeholders* that includes not only their clients and the ultimate end-users of a website or application, but also other third-party entities that provide critical support, such as search engines or payment gateway services. Among the more tangible objects are *site map diagrams* that depict the overall organization of linked pages, *wire frame diagrams* that outline where text and images and other elements will appear on specific pages, and *page templates* (sometimes called "recipes") that define the kinds of content that will appear on specific types of pages.

On a more abstract level, IAs work with clients to master the wealth of content that may already be available, particularly when the challenge is to redesign a large organizational website. Boundary objects on this level would include controlled vocabularies, thesauri, and taxonomies, which can help bring order and simplicity to more tangible UX components such as labeling and navigation systems, walkthroughs, wizards, and search systems. Facet analyses are especially prominent in the design of e-commerce search and navigation. The immediate goal for all such objects is to prompt deeper discussions among designers and developers, and to document progress, while steering towards consensus and overall coherence in the final product.

As web technologies matured, the range of possible uses for a website expanded, and we all increasingly found ourselves coming to the Web not only to find information, but to get things done online, such as banking, event planning, and booking hotel rooms. IA designers were able to make e-commerce sites dramatically more useful by developing faceted classification and tagging systems that (for example) allow a visitor to a furniture store to fine-tune search results with a few mouse clicks, filtering a hunt for living room items down to just sofas of a certain color and size and price (the *findability* principle), or adding suggested items that they hadn't thought of, such as a pillow or end-table, to their carts (*discoverability*).

The availability of new open-source JavaScript code libraries facilitated the design of sophisticated browser-based software applications that rival their desktop equivalents in functionality. It also became possible to deliver content—say, a batch of the next dozen blog posts or tweets or products—without requiring the user to link away to another page. This ushered in the era of the *single page application* (SPA), where the challenge of designing "navigation" is more about delivering understandable controls to manage the "state" of the application: indicating how to view, or edit, or save, etc. Creating the UX interface for these new web apps increasingly entailed advanced technical skills, contributing in part to a gradual eclipsing of pure IA.[31]

As the scope of the interdisciplinary field of *UX design* steadily expanded, greater demands were put on the research side of the design process to differentiate the main types of visitors to a site, and to identify their needs and objectives, in order to coordinate design across all the various "channels" and "touchpoints" by which a customer or visitor would engage with an organization—website, social media, smartphone, call center, in-person, etc. The goals of UX design came to include ensuring maximum consistency in a user's overall experience.

Achieving such consistency implies aligning the efforts of designers with those of multiple other stakeholder teams, each with a different set of interests and perspectives: marketing, customer service, tech support, etc. New types of boundary objects emerged to support these efforts, including the *persona* (a brief stylized profile of a fictional but typical user), and the *journey map* (a step-by-step diagram of the process a person goes through in accomplishing a goal). These and other mapping and diagramming techniques are used to focus and document the work of cross-disciplinary teams, as they collaborate on a final UX design that achieves everyone's objectives.

The steady expansion of the scope of user research has been driven by both commercial and altruistic imperatives, which tend to largely (but not completely) overlap. Understanding your customer and providing for a pleasant and efficient shopping experience is obviously connected to sales, customer satisfaction, brand reputation, and long-term viability as an enterprise. Aligning IA with the goals of external stakeholders such as Google has led to a thriving consulting industry, which advises designers on how to compose, structure, and tag content to achieve *search engine optimization* (SEO).

From an IA perspective such advice is usually harmless, and often even constructive: use HTML markup to distinguish the functional areas of a page, keep the hierarchy of heading levels consistent, and describe the content of images for the sake of vision-impaired visitors as well as for search indexing, and so on. And Google is candid about *its* primary service: delivering trustworthy search results, along with stylized metadata, for the convenience of *its* users.

But sometimes overall IA goals are not so easily aligned, as when Google rewards sites that include *frequently-asked questions* (FAQ) sections. Google can mine these for ready-made responses to search queries, often short-circuiting the search process before the user even visits a site. But FAQs are also problematic: if they duplicate content found elsewhere on the site, they can easily get out of sync when information is updated; they also place a higher demand (or "cognitive load") on the user, who must scan through them for answers that may not even be there. A better design approach is to ensure that well-structured content exists on the site to answer any frequently asked questions, and that the information is easily findable through search or navigation.

By the mid-2000s, the number of searches on Google for the term "UX" overtook searches for "information architecture," and the gap has continued to widen. The unique professional identity of information architect that Rosenfeld and Morville had helped to cultivate and promote is now often regarded as a central, but subordinate, aspect of UX design. Nonetheless, the emergence in 2012 of the World Information Architecture Association (WIAA), and its ongoing program of annual World IA Day conferences held in 30 locations across five continents, and now going into its second decade, suggests that IA continues to have a role in a broad range of fields, internationally, supporting research and professional training across a global community of practice.[32]

## DESIGNING INFORMATION IN CONTEXT

A *stress case* in the context of design, is a situation where information interfaces may fail due to the circumstances of the moment. When designing signage in a hospital to guide visitors from the front lobby entrance to the emergency department, the designer must take into consideration the good chance that visitors may be anxious and distracted as they try, for example, to rendezvous with a family member who has arrived separately by ambulance. Their own wayfinding abilities may be significantly impaired; having to search through a directory with dozens of lines of identical-looking text would only compound the stress.[33] Aesthetics as well as usability are entailed in the design of colorful and strategically placed arrows and icons that usher anxious visitors through the maze of corridors to the correct elevators and eventually to a loved one's bed.

*Value-sensitive design* (VSD) extends the scope of HCD to incorporate the ethical values held by users and other stakeholders. These values may only become clear through ethnographic research and exploratory conversations with users and others, and frequently only emerge in the course of actually engaging with the technology or design itself. Travelers finding their way in an airport, for example, rely on a myriad of cues and signs as they make their way to a departure gate. It would be reasonable to assume that someone on the autism spectrum would want these signs to be designed so as to give them maximum independence, freeing them from any need for personal assistance. But one such traveler described this assumption as an oversimplification of a subtler and more important value—autonomy—which in a real-life context, is not the same as independence. The ideal system might be achieved by combining both information-design and human-service components.[34]

A mature UX design for an information system will address the needs of users who may have a wide range of abilities. HTML now includes features that directly support screen-reader software. Browsers offer powerful tools to guide designers without leaving the development workflow, such as checking for adequate color contrast between text and backgrounds or revealing how color blindness would affect the perception of a design.

Good design will also take into account more complex adaptive patterns of information seeking, processing, and use. Screen-readers, for example, are not only important for blind or vision-impaired individuals. They can help an autistic reader conserve a limited budget of energy and attention by distributing the cognitive load between vision (reading words and seeing images) and hearing (confirming what is read, and what is present in images). This can also be extremely helpful for someone who is just learning the language in which the content is written—or learning to read at all. Braille-based screen readers can similarly complement and relieve the burden of using auditory devices, especially after several hours of listening through headphones.[35]

An overall approach to designing things in ways that accommodate the widest possible range of abilities and circumstances avoids the need to create special alternative versions or extra devices to adapt for particular users. This was articulated in the 1990s in one of the seven design principles referred to as *universal design*.[36] All of the principles of universal design have relevance for the development of information systems and for UX design generally. *Flexible use* (such as can be provided through modern HTML markup), *tolerance for error* (as in designing for stress cases), and *perceptible information* that is *simple and intuitive* (as with clear emergency room signage and wayfinding) are particularly suited for information design.[37]

In the U.S. universal design emerged at the same time as the Americans with Disabilities Act, which mandated equal access to physical environments; such access is also described in the European philosophy of *Design for All* and in Article 4 of the UN Convention on the Rights of Persons with Disabilities (CRPD) which came into force in 2008.[38] If we view equal access to information as a human rights issue, then universal design offers a way forward: its principles advocate for usability and accessibility. It also presumes that access requires equity.[39]

Among the practitioners of participatory design, there has been a collective reassessment of their history; the political edge that the field had in the 1970s dissipated into the blandness of user-experience research, with "ethics" coming to stand where political action used to be.[40] There are calls for renewing the political agency of design, and of challenging academic systems to make activism more supportable.[41] Moves towards a *human de-centered design* perspective have also pushed the design field to take into account the needs and values of marginalized social and cultural groups. It more specifically highlights the needs of non-human actors and stakeholders: animals, ecosystems, and the planet as a whole.

Decentering human needs—which too often only include the needs of the mainstream and elite—can help to enlarge the context of design discussions, and promote the collaborative creation of more ethical, engaged, and transformative information systems, and a more equitable information society.[42]

## NOTES

1 Lee Brasseur, "Florence Nightingale's Visual Rhetoric in the Rose Diagrams," *Technical Communication Quarterly* 14, no. 2 (2005): 162, citing Sydney Godolphin Osbourne, *Scutari and Its Hospitals* (London: Dickinson, 1855): 13.

2 Ibid., 173.

3 Dossey, Barbara Montgomery, *Florence Nightingale: Mystic, Visionary, Reformer* (Springhouse, PA: Lippincott, Williams, and Wilkins, 2000): 74. Cited by Brasseur, "Nightingale," 162.

4 Edward Tyas Cook, *The Life of Florence Nightingale*, Vol. 1. (London: Macmillan, 1913).

5 Henry Wadsworth Longfellow (November 1857), "Santa Filomena," *The Atlantic Monthly*, https://www.theatlantic.com/magazine/archive/1857/11/santa-filomena/531180/. Retrieved 24 May 2022.

6 See Florence Nightingale, "Letter from Nightingale to Queen Victoria, 1863," *Florence Nightingale Letters Collection*. University of Illinois Chicago Library Special Collections. https://collections.carli.illinois.edu/digital/collection/uic_fnlc/id/23. Retrieved 24 May 2022.

7 This analysis of Nightingale's data storytelling follows Brausseur, "Nightingale," 167.

8   Florence Nightingale, *A Contribution to the Sanitary History of the British Army during the Late War with Russia* (London: John W. Parker, 1859): 8. Cited by Brausseur, "Nightingale," 176.

9   Ibid., 174–175.

10  Ibid.

11  See, for example, Robert E. Roth, "Cartographic Design as Visual Storytelling: Synthesis and Review of Map-Based Narratives, Genres, and Tropes," *The Cartographic Journal* 58, no. 1 (2021): 83–114.

12  See, for example, Elizabeth Biz Nijdam, "Sami-Digital Storytelling: Survivance and Revitalization in Indigenous Digital Games," *New Media & Society* (2021), https://doi.org/10.1177/14614448211038902.

13  Kate McDowell, "Paradoxes of Storytelling in Librarianship," *Journal of New Librarianship* 3 (2018): iv.

14  Mirena Todorova-Ekmekci, Todor Todorov, and Kalina Sotirova-Valkova, "Usage of Innovative Technologies and Online Media Tools for Digital Presentation of Cultural Heritage in Bulgaria," *Digital Presentation and Preservation of Cultural and Scientific Heritage* 11 (2021): 303–308.

15  Justin Matejka and George Fitzmaurice, "Same Stats, Different Graphs: Generating Datasets with Varied Appearance and Identical Statistics through Simulated Annealing," in *Proceedings of the 2017 CHI Conference on Human Factors in Computing Systems* (2017): 1290–1294. https://doi.org/10.1145/3025453.3025912.

16  For visualizations of these categories, see J. Heer, M. Bostock, and V. Ogievetsky, "A Tour through the Visualization Zoo" (links to an external site), *ACM Queue* 53, no. 6 (2010): 59–67.

17  See for example the (free) *Flourish* online app, at https://flourish.studio/newsrooms/. Retrieved 9 June 2022.

18  Jackie Mansky, "W.E.B. Du Bois' Visionary Infographics Come Together for the First Time in Full Color," *Smithsonian Magazine*, 15 November 2018, https://www.smithsonianmag.com/history/first-time-together-and-color-book-displays-web-du-bois-visionary-infographics-180970826/. This article reviews and references Witney Battle-Baptiste and Britt Rusert, eds., *WEB Du Bois's Data Portraits: Visualizing Black America* (San Francisco, CA: Chronicle Books, 2018).

19  "Looking at One's Self through the Eyes of Others: W. E. B. Du Bois's Photographs for the 1900 Paris Exposition," *African American Review* 34, no. 4 (Winter 2000): 581–599.

20  Ralph Appelbaum, "Activating Public Space," in *Information Architects*, eds. Richard Saul Wurman and Peter Bradford (Zurich: Graphis, 1996): 150–161.

21  Wurman and Bradford, *Architects*, 15–19.

22  Ibid., 150.

23  Ibid., 17.

24  Molly Wright Steenson, *Architectural Intelligence: How Designers and Architects Created the Digital Landscape* (Cambridge, MA: MIT Press, 2017): 108.

25  Ibid., 109–110.

26  Stuart K. Card, Thomas P. Moran, and Allen Newell, *The Psychology of Human-Computer Interaction* (Boca Raton, FL: CRC Press, 1983).

27  Liam Bannon, Jeffrey Bardzell, and Susanne Bødker, "Introduction: Reimagining Participatory Design—Emerging Voices," *ACM Transactions on Computer-Human Interaction (TOCHI)* 25, no. 1 (2018): 1–8.

28  Don Norman, *The Design of Everyday Things: Revised and Expanded Edition* (New York, NY: Basic Books, 2013): 8–9. See also Lara Fedoroff, host, "Reflections from Design of Everyday Things, with Don Norman," *UX Radio (podcast)*, 10 December 2015, http://ux-radio.com/2015/12/reflections-design-everyday-things/.

29  Susan Leigh Star and James Griesemer, "Institutional Ecology, 'Translations' and Boundary Objects: Amateurs and Professionals in Berkeley's Museum of Vertebrate Zoology," *Social Studies of Science* 19, no. 3 (1989): 387–420.

30  Louis Rosenfeld, Peter Morville, and Jorge Arango, *Information Architecture: For the Web and Beyond* (Sebastopol, CA: O'Reilly, 2015).

31  Chris Chandler, host, "Where Did IA Go? With Donna Spencer," *UX Radio*, 4 March 2021, http://ux-radio.com/2021/03/where-did-ia-go-with-donna-spencer/.

32  See World IA Day, https://www.worldiaday.org/. Retrieved 12 June 2022.

33  Eric Meyer and Sara Wachter-Boettcher, *Design for Real Life* (New York: A Book Apart, 2016).

34  See note 34. For a similar application of VSD principles to the design of security and privacy affordances in web software, see Yang Wang, "Inclusive Security and Privacy," *Sociotechnical Security and Privacy,* IEEE Computer and Reliability Societies, July/August 2018: 82–87.

35  Anne Forrest, David Fazio, Jamie Knight, Tim Harshbarger, Jeanine Lineback, Sandeep Tirumangalam, Birkir Gunnarsson, and Laura Goslin (moderator), *Virtual Panel: How Persons with Disabilities Use the Web* (Deque Systems, Inc., 2017), https://accessibility.deque.com/on-demand-how-persons-with-disabilities-use-the-web.

36  These principles were first articulated by Architect Ronald Mace, a wheelchair-bound survivor of polio, whose work has powerfully influenced architectural design practice. Ronald L. Mace, "Universal Design in Housing," *Assistive Technology* 10, no. 1 (1998): 21–28.

37  Anusha Pichumani, "Universal-Design Principles and Heuristic Guidelines," *UX Matters* (2000), https://www.uxmatters.com/mt/archives/2020/11/universal-design-principles-and-heuristic-guidelines.php.

38  G. Anthony Giannoumis and Michael Ashley Stein, "Conceptualizing Universal Design for the Information Society through a Universal Human Rights Lens," *International Human Rights Law Review* 8, no. 1 (2019): 38–66.

39  Ibid., 66.

40 S. Bødker and M. Kyng, "Participatory Design That Matters—Facing the Big Issues," *ACM Transactions on Computer-Human Interaction* 25, no. 1 (2018): 12.

41 Liesbeth Huybrechts, Henric Benesch, and Jon Geib, "Co-Design and the Public Realm," *CoDesign* 13, no. 3 (2017): 145–147.

42 See for example Sara Heitlinger, Lara Houston, Alex Taylor, and Ruth Catlow, "Algorithmic Food Justice: Co-Designing More-Than-Human Blockchain Futures for the Food Commons," in *Proceedings of the 2021 CHI Conference on Human Factors in Computing Systems* (2021), https://doi.org /10.1145/3411764.3445655.

# PRESERVING INFORMATION

The Ancient One was re-buried in a ceremony conducted in 2017 by members of five northwest Pacific Native American peoples: the Umatilla Tribes, the Colville Tribes, the Yakama Nation, the Nez Perce Tribe, and the Wanapum Tribe. The bones of the person known to scientists as "the Kennewick Man," had been found two decades earlier by college students near the city of Kennewick in southeastern Washington State.[1] Forensic analysis determined that the remains were not from a recent murder victim but were far older: the man they had found had lived 9,000 years ago. He had a stone spearpoint embedded in his hip.

An archeologist working with the Benton County Coroner described the man's skull as appearing to be "Caucasoid" (rather than Native American). This claim would become important because the *Native American Graves Protection and Repatriation Act* (NAGPRA), a U.S. federal law passed in 1990, mandated remains of indigenous peoples held in museums and other collections be respectfully returned to tribal communities for reburial.[2] The passage of NAGPRA was a late response to a shameful history. For hundreds of years, the bones of indigenous men, women, and children were harvested from battlefields or robbed from graves by soldiers and looters, and collected in the Army Medical Museum, or in public or private museum collections.[3]

A group of eight scientists became plaintiffs in the Kennewick Man case. Among them was a physical anthropologist who argued

DOI: 10.4324/9781003155119-9

that the skeleton did not resemble modern Native Americans, and that the man was more likely related to ancient Polynesians or to the Ainu of Japan—which meant that it would not be subject to the terms of NAGPRA. The scientists sued the Army Corps of Engineers and the Washington and Oregon Tribes, claiming that since this was one of the best-preserved skeletons from an ancient era, precious scientific data would be lost if it were returned to the ground. The scientists won and then won again on appeal.[4] But it was not over.

During the scientific studies conducted after the ruling, a sample of DNA was sent to the University of Copenhagen, where its genetic markers were compared to a worldwide genomic database. The autosomal DNA, mitochondrial DNA, and Y chromosome data of the Ancient One all demonstrated affinity with modern Native Americans, particularly Algonquin groups, and that it most closely resembled the DNA of living members of the Colville tribe, one of the groups claiming him as an ancestor.[5]

To facilitate the repatriation of the Ancient One to the tribes, a bill was passed, and signed by President Barack Obama, which superseded NAGPRA and allowed for expedited return. This resolution of the two-decade-old drama was celebrated not only by the tribes, but by many museums and anthropologists who embrace the values of NAGPRA.[6]

In the last decades of the 20th century, and into the 21st, calls have increased for the *decolonization of museums* in the U.S. and across the globe. In the U.S., many of the early efforts focused on repatriation of human remains and sacred objects to indigenous communities. NAGPRA started the process, but repatriation has moved slowly. The remains of tens of thousands of indigenous ancestors are still held at the Smithsonian, and in university collections all across the United States.

In France, a report commissioned by President Emmanuel Macron, and written by Senegalese social scientist Felwine Sarr and French art historian Bénédicte Savoy, was released in 2018.[7] *Rapport sur la restitution du patrimoine culturel africain. Vers une nouvelle éthique relationnelle* (Report on the restitution of African cultural heritage: Toward a new relational ethics) calls for repatriation of items appropriated by France from lands it colonized, as well as payment of restitution to the nations from which they were taken.

The report also challenged other former colonial powers to consider their museum collections containing art, artifacts, and bodily remains taken from the people they had colonized. A modest return of cultural heritage items followed: Germany returned items to Namibia, the Netherlands to Indonesia, and Scotland to Benin. In Portugal, scholars, journalists, and the government were compelled to respond to the report, but this did not lead to a national policy calling for reflection on colonial history as occurred, for example, in Germany.[8]

The intent expressed by the Macron-commissioned report, as with NAGPRA in the U.S., was to promote not only physical repatriation, but also a rethinking of the relationship between museums and the communities whose history and cultural knowledge they curate along with the cultural artifacts they hold. Some scientists warned that these new and proposed policies would usher in an era in which certain areas of scientific study of the past would cease completely. Three decades after NAGPRA, this has not occurred. Scientific practices have changed as a result of the law, but in productive ways: there has been an increase in community-based and participatory research which only proceeds with tribal consent, and with the assurance of respectful treatment of ancestors.

Who owns public information, and who should control access to it? Under what conditions do we cease to preserve information, through the documents and artifacts that carry it? And in the case of the Ancient One, who has the power to allow the potential information contained in someone's bones to die with the man?

In this chapter we begin by discussing the ways that information science is entangled with the disciplines of the humanities, including the digital humanities and the field of scholarly communication. We survey the professional work that takes place in institutions which are responsible for the curation and preservation of information, and examine the specific challenges associated with the preservation of cultural heritage, and with digital preservation.

## INFORMATION AND THE HUMANITIES

Information professionals have developed ways to organize the artifacts of collective memory, to make them searchable and accessible to scholars and to the public for educational and research purposes. Not all information technologies are machines, and not all information is digital. Correspondingly, not all the humanities-based research that goes on inside the wide community of information science falls into the category of "the digital." Some scholars study the historical eras in which information technologies were developed and used, analyzing transformations over time, with time-spanning interests in the tablet, the scroll, the book.[9] Others may explore information-related questions that fall into diverse areas of humanistic concern, from the relationship of philosophy to information science,[10] to race and class in children's literatures,[11] to the transmission of cultural knowledge within immigrant communities.[12]

The interdisciplinary field of *digital humanities* (DH) is described variously as a methodology, a community, and a set of practices.[13] Activities associated with DH have historically fallen into roughly three approaches.[14] First, DH can be understood to pertain to digital tools and practices that support traditional humanities research questions, using traditional methodologies. Digital technologies can make documents, physical artifacts, and other sorts of media more accessible, and analysis more efficient. An older term, *humanities computing*, originating in the mid 20th century, refers to the supportive practices of indexing, digitizing, and computer-aided analysis of documents, as well as to online publishing. In this sense of DH, the scholarship being supported is not digital in nature; it only uses digital tools.[15]

A second set of activities are those which make use of digital, quantitative, and computational methods, not only to support, but to enhance humanistic inquiry. Such research might employ text mining, language modeling, or natural language processing. The practices involved in analyzing multiple texts through computational methods have been described as *distant reading*, to contrast it with the *close reading* of a smaller set of texts, a signature method of traditional literary studies.[16]

The third general category associated with DH focuses on digital forms, practices, cultures, or communities as objects of inquiry. This includes digitally transformed as well as *born-digital* documents (e.g. hypertext, hypermedia, chatbots, data maps, memes, and procedurally generated art). The fields of new media, electronic literature, and game studies intersect with DH across multiple modalities.[17] Museums and galleries are also active in these areas, as they seek new methods of curation. Increasingly digital technologies are employed to engage their users with collections through interactive interfaces and immersive environments.[18]

The field of DH has been challenged by its inherent interdisciplinarity. Conflicts between scholars of different intellectual inclinations are sometimes expressed by questioning the sufficiency or sophistication of theory or methods. Has a project taken a critical perspective in interrogating its questions, methods, analysis, and findings? Were the analytic or statistical methods used sophisticated and sound? Conflicts over identity, territory, and inclusion within the field, and in relationship to non-DH scholars outside the field, reflect intellectual boundary–making, as well as the inherent structural difficulties associated with interdisciplinary research, since scholars are often disincentivized to publish outside their own disciplines.

The DH field has in recent years experienced a global turn, as scholars have taken a critical stance towards the development of the field itself, bringing sociological and political perspectives to bear on the global issues related to DH research. They have, for example, drawn attention to the multiple ways in which the negative consequences of new information communication technologies (ICTs) disproportionately affect the Global South(s).[19] Such studies may examine the *material life cycles of ICTs*, from the extraction of minerals needed for their manufacturing to the labor provided by software engineers, customer service call center employees, and disassemblers of residual ICT components at the end of their useful life.[20] Some studies investigate the historical and sociotechnical engines that create and recreate the global digital divide.[21] Others explore intersectionality and its relationship to epistemic injustice.[22]

The disciplinary neutrality of academic libraries, with their mission to support scholars across all academic domains, makes them well–situated to provide support for digital humanists. Academic libraries were among the first institutions to engage in digitization projects, and to create centers offering support and training to humanities scholars in the use of new technologies and platforms. Libraries were also at the forefront of *digital publishing*, facilitating the creation, dissemination, and access to academic knowledge more efficiently than print technologies alone can do.

*Scholarly communication* is a professional field within academic librarianship that supports scholarly work across its life course, from research, writing, publication, dissemination, preservation, to assessment of impact.[23] Specific areas of responsibility and practice associated with Scholarly communication include academic publishing, issues of intellectual property (open access, copyright, licensing), managing research data, and direct teaching support for digital scholarship, as well as research related to all these practices.

Among the support services that libraries provide is the creation of *information commons* dedicated to curating and providing open access to databases, networks, and digitized collections. *HathiTrust*, for example is a *digital library* of more than 17 million documents available for the purpose of scholarly research.[24] Each scanned page has an associated plain text file created through *optical character recognition* (OCR). The document record makes use of a data format created by the Library of Congress. *MAchine Readable Cataloging* (MARC), which allows computers to understand and use bibliographic information. Participating academic and research institutions provide MARC-compliant metadata along with digitized materials from their physical collections. In return, HathiTrust provides long-term preservation of, and public access to, the information it holds.

*HathiTrust* was created in 2008 by several academic institutions and networks, which were partners in the Google Books initiative. In 2004 Google announced its intention to digitize all the books in the world in order to create a universal library.[25] The company began to digitize and make public many works that were not in the public domain. This was problematic for authors and publishers who had not given permission for their works to be used in this way. Others feared that Google would eventually find a way to monetize what it was collecting, despite its claim to be collecting the material for public use.[26] Two lawsuits alleging copyright infringement were introduced the following year by the Authors Guild and the Association of American Publishers, and a similar lawsuit was filed against HathiTrust and its university partners.

HathiTrust and Google successfully argued that their use of copyrighted material was fair because it was *transformative*. The search capabilities afforded by digitization and OCR provided essential services for print-disabled readers who cannot access the materials in any other way. This accessibility issue was persuasive; some uses were deemed to be transformative, and thus fell under the protections of the fair use doctrine.[27] Despite the ruling, Google Books began slowing its digitization operations in 2017, and has committed few resources to the project since.

For scholars, especially those who had criticized Google Books for its inconsistent and faulty metadata, HathiTrust and other large digital repositories filled the gap. The U.S. Library of Congress has put many of its collections online, with curated items in 470 languages.[28] *Gallica* is a digital library produced by the *Bibliothèque Nationale de France* (National Library of France), which provides free public access to millions of documents including maps, sound recordings, musical scores, newspaper files, and periodicals. The website can be browsed in French, English, German, and Italian.[29]

## GALLERIES, ARCHIVES, LIBRARIES, AND MUSEUMS

The Global Seed Vault in Spitsbergen, on Norway's Svalbard archipelago, was built to serve the future, holding seeds from 930,000 varieties of food crops. Sometimes referred to as a *doomsday collection*, the Norwegian seed vault stores and preserves genetic information against the worst-case scenarios of environmental disaster.[30] The Auschwitz-Birkenau Memorial and Museum, on the site of the former Nazi concentration and extermination camp, also serves the whole world, though in a different way: it preserves everyday artifacts that belonged to victims of the Holocaust, exhibiting them with the hope that visitors will understand the horrors of World War II and help to make sure they don't happen again. In a recent trend, social media figures have filmed themselves visiting the museum and shared their experiences with their fans. This new form of curation accesses an audience of people who may not be uniformly receptive, but who might never have visited otherwise.[31]

There are almost 50,000 museums in 132 countries that are part of the International Council of Museums (ICOM) network, a non-governmental organization that sets professional and ethical standards for museums. Among its missions, it works to combat illicit trafficking in cultural heritage items and encourages emergency preparedness to protect collections in case of environmental disaster, civil strife, or war.[32] Scattered across the globe are numberless idiosyncratic local museums, archives, and public collections. The Museum of Broken Relationships, for example, began in Zagreb, Croatia as a work of public art. It contains personal objects contributed by the public reflecting painful personal histories. Among the items curated in their collections are a "little rubber piggy," a "stupid frisbee," and "toaster of vindication." As it describes its purpose, the museum is "a physical and virtual public space created with the sole purpose of treasuring and sharing your heartbreak stories and symbolic possessions." [33]

When collections become large and permanent, and especially when they are open to the public, they require *curation*, which in an institutional sense refers to professional administration, typically including records management, knowledge organization, and other kinds of tasks, depending on the size of the collection. In its narrower sense curation refers to the written and visual storytelling that provides interpretation for physical or digital documents that have been selected to be put on public display. Collections are always larger than their curated parts; selections are made, and changed, as an expression of particular scholarship, as part of a research initiative, or in response to changes in institutional priorities or current events that are relevant to a collection. A historian or anthropologist, or other individuals with specific domain knowledge, may be hired to curate particular collections within an institution. This work is also supported by volunteer labor, particularly in local, community-based, and cultural heritage collections.[34]

The information professionals who do this type of work are part of an interdisciplinary field referred to *Galleries, Libraries, Archives, and Museums* (GLAM). An additional "R" representing "records management," is sometimes added, making it GLAMR. Some people prefer to call it "LAM," to prevent confusion with commercial art galleries; the "G" of GLAM refers only to art museums or galleries associated with libraries, archives, and museums in which works are selected and curated for scholarly, aesthetic, or educational purposes, rather than for sale.

*Online curation* allows visitors to interact with items in an archive or museum collections through immersive experiences at a distance. It is now possible to explore the ancient art found in prehistoric caves, for example, through *virtual reality* (VR). The physical environments in which this art is found are fragile places, and often difficult to access. A VR headset takes over a user's visual field and allows them to feel as though they are inside a fully three-dimensional world. The related term, *augmented reality* (AR) refers to the overlay of computer-generated information onto an ordinary visual field. Users need to look at their phone or other device to see that content. *Mixed reality* (MR) combines both approaches. The smartphone game Pokémon Go is an example of MR; while playing the game on a phone it can seem as though Pokémon are living in the world all around us. These approaches are referred to collectively as *extended reality* (XR), and are increasingly being explored in museum settings.

Advances in natural language processing and machine learning have also allowed museums to incorporate *narrative AI* into their curation. The Anne Frank House in Amsterdam, for example, provides a chatbot docent to museum visitors through Facebook Messenger.[35] The *Museu do Amanhã* (Museum of Tomorrow) in Rio de Janeiro, Brazil also provides its visitors with an automated personal assistant to accompany them through the exhibits.

Archives, in contrast to museums, are less likely to focus on enhancing the experience of non-scholarly visitors. Defining the word *archive* is challenging because of its multiple usages. The verb form "to archive" refers to the process of creating or adding something to an archive. As a noun it can refer to a *collection of documents* (of all kinds) that are collected and preserved together. An archive is also the *part of an organization* that does the storing, organizing, and maintaining of the records that are important to its history and ongoing activities. An archive can be an *entire organization*, if its mission is to provide the service of collecting and organizing records and other materials on behalf of clients, and an archive can be a *physical place*—the actual building or certain rooms in a building where archival collections are held.

Thus, a for-profit *archive* (in the business of archiving things) may have its own *archive* (a department within its organization) in which archivists work in their *archive* (a physical room or virtual website) which contains a variety of *archives* (collections of records).

Margaret Cross Norton (1891–1984) was the director of the State Archives of Illinois from 1922 to 1957. When she first arrived in Springfield, Illinois, she went hunting for documents in the attic and basement of the State Capitol building. She found piles of lost records stashed in corners filled with moldering trash, and took to carrying a metal pipe with her, to swing at the rats she found in the dark corners where documentary treasures lay.[36] Norton modernized the Illinois State Archives, but she also assumed a leadership role in professional organizations dedicated to archival practices, establishing standards for archival management, and professionalizing the field. This was happening in parallel to the development of professional librarianship in the early 20th century.

Rather than using a library classification system, archives preserve the original order of documents, at least to the extent that it is known or can be determined. The order in which the materials arrived at the archive is also documented, along with a complete chronological history of the location and ownership of the materials prior to its arrival. This type of documentation, referred to as the *provenance* of the materials, helps archivists determine their authenticity and trace ownership in the case of theft. Provenance is a foundational principle of archival theory that also guides practice; the concept has been a matter of debate, refinement, and reimagining since the 18th century.[37]

Conversations among archivists regarding provenance have been energized by the challenges associated with archiving websites. Traditional curatorial practices have had to change to accommodate digital archives, with practices expanded to include web crawling and the devising of frameworks for documenting web archive provenance.[38]

An essential part of archival training includes learning the techniques and practices necessary to protect collection from deterioration and damage. These include, for example, controlling the physical environment (e.g. temperature, humidity, light) and minimizing document handling. The terms *preservation* and *conservation* are both used, in different contexts, to talk about the protection of collections. Preservation is the more general term, referring to the goal of preventing the loss of information that arises from the damage or physical deterioration of documents. But it also is used to describe the legal obligation of archives to store and make accessible records that are requested as part of investigations or lawsuits. In the case of government records, archives must be compliant with laws that regulate their preservation.

Conservation more narrowly refers to the physical practices of repair and restoration that require specialized training to master. In the digital age, conservation often includes the proper handling of fragile historical documents that are being digitized and made available electronically, so that the originals can be stored, untouched, in protective environments. Conservation professionals are also called upon to authenticate originals and copies, carry out appraisals, and ensure the reliability of records.

## REMEMBERING AND FORGETTING

GLAM institutions are considered *memory institutions* because of their shared mission to preserve the collective experiences and understandings of communities; this work is also referred to as *cultural heritage management.* UNESCO supports struggling GLAM institutions in the work of preserving both tangible and *intangible cultural heritage.* Intangible heritage goes beyond what can be curated in a traditional museum exhibit to include, for example, dialects, dances, childrens' games, and recipes.[39]

A group of researchers who studied the UNESCO initiative concluded that in order to archive intangible culture effectively, it is necessary to engage with a community earlier in the process than might typically happen when curating other kinds of collections.[40] Alongside the report that emerged from UNESCO's cultural heritage initiative, a remarkable visualization of its work across the globe gives testimony to the cultural diversity of the planet, and to the vulnerability of cultural heritage and memory to damage and destruction from civil conflicts, environmental crises, and war.[41]

UNESCO helped to mobilize international organizations to protect Ukrainian cultural heritage during the Russian invasion. During the early months of the war, crowdsourced collaborative international efforts were organized.[42] A group of more than 1300 "librarians, archivists, researchers, and programmers" participated in SUCHO (Saving Ukrainian Cultural Heritage Online).[43] They worked together to identify at risk collections in Ukraine, and to archive digital content and data. They systematically web-crawled and archived the websites of Ukrainian museums, libraries, and archives, preserving the sites and their content. This information was copied and mirrored on servers outside the country and on the Internet Archive.

Increasingly, indigenous groups are assuming leadership roles in memory institutions that collect and curate vulnerable cultural histories. These efforts are supported by non-profit organizations like the Association of Tribal Archives, Libraries, and Museums.[44] Small and non-traditional archives work in partnership with traditional institutions to engage in and control the processes of collection, preservation, and curation of materials of cultural importance to their communities.

The life and career of Chicago librarian Vivian Harsh (1890–1960) illustrates the community-based nature of special collections within libraries, and how a community can become involved in the development of an archival collection. The Vivian G. Harsh Research Collection, now located within the Woodson Public Library in Chicago, holds the largest collection of historical records, documents, and literature related to African-American history in the midwestern United States.[45]

Under her directorship, the George Cleveland Hall Branch Library, located in the historic neighborhood known as Bronzeville, was transformed during the middle of the 20th century into a community center. Clubs, activities, and public forums enriched the educational and cultural life of African-Americans in Chicago; Langston Hughes and Zora Neale Hurston were among the well-known writers who spoke at Hall as part of the Chicago Black Renaissance.[46] Harsh's experience illustrates what the archiving of tangible and intangible cultural heritage looks like when it is integrated with the cultural life and information of a community. It also provides an early example of how generative collaboration between GLAM institutions can be.

In part because of the similarity of skills and practices necessary for digital curation, there has been a *convergence* occurring between GLAM institutions, which includes physical co-location, but also collaboration, and partnership between physically distinct institutions. In Germany GLAM is BAM (*Bibliotheken, Archive und Museen*); BAM is also the name of a digital portal that provides a single point of access to the collections of multiple collaborating institutions, and cultural heritage initiatives in Germany, Austria, and Switzerland. Behind the scenes, BAM provides organizational and administrative structure that coordinates metadata standards and authority files.[47] *Europeana*, created by the European Commission of the European Union, uses a similar approach to provide a single point of access for cultural heritage information across the continent. Institutions contribute information to Europeana through a network of partners that serve as aggregators, collecting data, validating it, and adding links to datasets and other material.[48] In India, the National Digital Repository for Museums, with funding from India's Ministry of Culture, provides a portal to ten national museums. This project is happening as part of a larger project to digitize museum holdings across India, not only to improve records management in these institutions using new technologies, but also to make them more accessible.

Convergence in education is also occurring as the professional training for library studies, museum studies, and archival studies increasingly includes information-related tools and technologies necessary for all the GLAM professions. Separate coursework continues to offer the specialized skills needed for each. Increasingly, these programs of study are finding the interdisciplinary space of information science to be a good fit.[49]

Who decides what digital information should be kept, and who is responsible for keeping it? It is a misconception that digital information is safer than physical information; in fact, if it is not purposefully collected, it can disappear rapidly. A research team exploring the problems associated with preserving the digital worlds of online games and gaming communities, for example, delivered the news that much of the digital record of the *bulletin board system* (BBS) era, which including online game-playing of many kinds, is irrecoverably gone. The report also identified the complex challenges associated with the digital archiving of games.[50] Many of these challenges pertain to the preservation of digital material in general.

Copies and near-copies abound. Are they considered the same document, and safe to delete, or are they different enough to be considered separate documents to be stored as such? If a meme goes viral, should it be kept in every context in which it is published and commented upon by viewers? Do the physical originals of digitized materials still need to be kept? If they *are* kept, how long should they be kept?

With the adoption of each new technology, old technologies are neglected or forgotten. It can be a tough call whether or not to expend scarce resources on maintaining a physical collection of the technologies necessary for old software to run. But even if the technologies are preserved so that files can be read, is there metadata sufficient to provide context and meaning? If there is metadata, what about copyright? Should owners of copyrighted material be allowed to endanger the historical record by preventing the archiving of material they own? And what about people's privacy rights? Wanting to archive information does not mean that a repository will be free legally (or ethically) to do so.

Not all GLAM institutions have the information professionals on staff to deal with such complicated *digital asset management*, or the financial resources to support the necessary technological infrastructure. Digital curation includes the core tasks of traditional curation but adds to them the development of online repositories, designing information architectures through which digital materials can be accessed by researchers and the public.[51] The *Internet Archive*, for example, is a non-profit repository, begun in 1996. Its digital collections contain over 625 billion webpages, 38 million texts, 7 million videos, 4 million images, and 790 software programs. Its stated mission is to preserve the digital record of the Internet itself.[52]

The open-source movement opened the door for *open-GLAM*, an initiative associated both with the Creative Commons, which hosts the community website for open-GLAM, and the Wikimedia Foundation, the host of Wikipedia.[53] Open-GLAM promotes exchange and collaboration between memory institutions, but also facilitates public access to material that is in the public domain, and to copyrighted material under the limitations of fair use. Hosting an open access collection requires investing in better search optimization for the hosting website, and an ability to handle increased web traffic.

Large institutions will offer parts of their collections for open access; the National Palace Museum in Taiwan, which allows downloading of both images and datasets.[54] The Metropolitan Museum of Art in New York City has released over 492,000 images of public-domain artwork through open access licensing, free and with unrestricted use.[55]

## PRESERVING INFORMATION IN CONTEXT

It would not be possible to collect and preserve all the information in the world without using surveillance to infringe on privacy rights in a way that most people would find ethically unacceptable. For the sake of argument, imagine a totalitarian society which did succeed in collecting continuous visual, audio, and biometric data showing what everyone in the world was doing every moment of their lives, with satellites and drones taking pictures of every street on the planet, and even peering into people's windows. Would all this data capture the world?

Jorge Luis Borges and Lewis Carroll both wondered about the practicalities of such ambitions. In *On Exactitude in Science*, Borges tells of a map so detailed that it included inch for inch everything in the area that it was mapping. A perfect map of the world must be exactly the size of the world. In Carroll's story, which inspired Borges, farmers complained that such a perfect map, which had to be stored on top of the land it charted, was blocking out the light.[56]

Cognitive science tells us that thinking requires forgetting and abstraction, even imprecision. Our brains make no attempt to retain *most* of the sensory data that we take in every day. We remember *some* manageable parts of it, in ways that help us to understand and make sense of the world.[57] That insight might help to explain why in 2017 the Library of Congress announced that it would no longer be collecting every tweet on Twitter (half a billion every day), but only those of "ongoing national interest." The library will instead focus on curating the billions of tweets in its collection.[58]

Borges' also had something to say about forgetting. In *Funes the Memorious*, he describes a man (Funes) who was thrown from a horse;

after recovering finds himself unable to forget anything. He can recall with perfect precision all the details of every day of his life. Rather than enhancing his life, Funes was profoundly impaired by his inability to forget. He once tried to classify his (ever-expanding) memories into 70,000 categories but gave up because the task was interminable and pointless. At the end of the story Borges concludes that Funes was "not very capable of thought." In order to think, we need "to forget, to generalize, to abstract."[59]

Sometimes people deliberately forget the past in order to shape the present and the future. Businesses and governments do this when they destroy records to control what can be known about their actions. The Romans threw statues of their political rivals into garbage heaps; famous poets and other personages (or their heirs) burned letters and diaries to protect their legacies. Forgetting exists in tension with remembering. Archeologists and historians go looking through what other people have discarded—the contents of ancient garbage heaps, the remaining unburned diaries. What is dead is not necessarily gone forever, even when we want it to be.

Tech companies including Facebook and Microsoft have patented technologies that can create chatbots from the social media postings of people who have died. *Deepfake technologies* can pair those chatbots with procedurally generated video images, putting new words in their mouths. This is done through deep machine learning, "training" a software model on surviving photographs, texts, and voice recordings. We can now ask Albert Einstein questions about physics.[60] The Dalí Museum in St Petersburg, Florida uses deepfake technology to allow museum visitors to speak to (and take selfies with) Salvador Dalí, who can say things that the real Dalí never said, but the way he might have said them.[61]

Teaching science and increasing the immersion of museum visitors are not the only uses to which deepfakes have been put. The parents of Joaquin Oliver, who died at the school shooting in Parkland, Florida in 2018, brought him back to advocate for gun regulation.[62] That it was his parents who authorized the making of the video makes it feel somehow different from other uses; their pain is so palpable, who wants to tell them (some people do) that they don't have the right to make meaning from their son's death in that way? Compare that use to the soft drink advertisement featuring a deepfake of the legendary and beloved painter Bob Ross, who died in 1995. His image and voice were legally licensed from the Bob Ross Foundation, but his fans were not amused.

The *right to be forgotten* (RTBF) refers to a person's right to request that public information about them be removed from indexes and search results. It does not yet include the right not to be brought back as a chatbot after death.

The legal and ethical issues surrounding the *digital afterlife* are already prompting scrutiny of the emerging digital afterlife industry which provides services ranging from handling someone's social media accounts after they die, to sending out posthumous emails to loved ones.[63] It may become common practice to include in our wills a section where we advise our loved ones whether we consent to be brought back as "deadbots," through the digital materials we leave behind, just as we now consent or refuse (opting in or opting out, depending on what country we live in) to have our organs harvested after death.[64]

Not everyone who lived will be brought back as a member of the data undead, even if they would want to be, just as not everything that is collected will be preserved, and not everything that is preserved will be curated. GLAM institutions regularly "weed" their collections. Curators are situated within particular social, cultural, and structural systems when they make their curation selections deciding what will be remembered and how. The scientists who fought in court for the right to retain the bones of the person they referred to as the Kennewick Man, argued that the tribes were destroying the potential scientific information that his bones contained.

Who gets to say if a skeleton found in the river should be remembered as the Kennewick Man or the Ancient One? Sometimes information is left to deteriorate; sometimes it is deliberately destroyed; and sometimes a judge steps in and orders it to be reclassified from "information" to "ancestor," so that it can be put back into the ground.

## NOTES

1  Heather Burke and Claire Smith, "Timeline," in *Kennewick: Perspectives on the Ancient One*, eds. Heather Burke et al. (Walnut Creek, CA: Left Coast Press, 2008): 26.

2  See "Native American Graves Protection and Repatriation Act," *National Park Service*, https://www.nps.gov/subjects/nagpra/index.htm. Retrieved 9 June 2022.

3  Russell Thornton, "Who Owns Our Past? The Repatriation of Native American Human Remains and Cultural Objects," in *Native American Voices*, eds. Susan Lobo, Steve Talbot and Traci L. Morris (New York: Routledge, 2016): 311.

4  Sarah Graham, "Scientists Win Latest Ruling in Kennewick Man Case," *Scientific American*, 6 February 2004.

5  Morten Rasmussen, Martin Sikora, Anders Albrechtsen, Thorfinn Sand Korneliussen, J. Víctor Moreno-Mayar, G. David Poznik, Christoph P. E. Zollikofer et al., "The Ancestry and Affiliations of Kennewick Man," *Nature* 523, no. 7561 (2015): 455–458.

6  Sara Jean Green, "A Wrong Had Finally Been Righted': Tribes Bury Remains of Ancient Ancestor Known as Kennewick Man," *Seattle Times*, 19 February 2017.

7  von Oswald, Margareta, "The 'Restitution Report': First Reactions in Academia, Museums, and Politics," *Centre for Anthropological Research on Museums and Heritage* (2018). https://blog.uni-koeln.de/gssc-humboldt/the-restitution-report/.

8  Michael Faciejew and Ricardo Roque, "The Violence of Collections," 22 September 2021, *The Order of Multitudes Atlas Encyclopedia*, https://orderofm.com/conversation/the-violence-of-collections/.

9  Bonnie Mak, *How the Page Matters* (Toronto: University of Toronto Press, 2011).

10  Don Fallis, Jonathan Furner, Kay Mathiesen, and Allen Renear, "Philosophy and Information Science: The Basics," *Proceedings of the American Society for Information Science and Technology* 43, no. 1 (2006): 1–4.

11  Elizabeth Massa Hoiem, "The Progress of Sugar: Consumption as Complicity in Children's Books about Slavery and Manufacturing, 1790–2015," *Children's Literature in Education* 52, no. 2 (2021): 162–182.

12  XinQi Dong, E-Shien Chang, Melissa Simon, and Esther Wong, "Sustaining Community-University Partnerships: Lessons Learned from a Participatory Research Project with Elderly Chinese," *Gateways: International Journal of Community Research and Engagement* 4 (2011): 31–47.

13  Robinson, Lyn, Ernesto Priego, and David Bawden, "Library and Information Science and Digital Humanities: Two Disciplines, Joint Future?," in *Re: Inventing Information Science in the Networked Society*, eds. Christian Schlögl, Christian Wolff, and Franjo Pehar (Glückstadt: Hülsbusch, 2015).

14  Julia Flanders and Elli Mylonas, "Digital Humanities," in *Encyclopedia of Library and Information Sciences*, eds. Marcia J. Bates and Mary Niles Maack (Boca Raton, FL: CRC Press, 2017): 1286–1297.

15  Chris Alen Sul and Heather V. Hill, "The Early History of Digital Humanities: An Analysis of Computers and the Humanities (1966–2004)

and Literary and Linguistic Computing (1986–2004)," *Digital Scholarship in the Humanities* 34, no. Supplement_1 (2019): i190–i206.

16 Underwood, Ted, "A Genealogy of Distant Reading," *DHQ: Digital Humanities Quarterly* 11, no. 2 (2017). http://www.digitalhumanities.org/dhq/vol/11/2/000317/000317.html. Retrieved 22 September 2022.

17 Dene Grigar, "Challenges to Archiving and Documenting Born-Digital Literature: What Scholars, Archivists, and Librarians Need to Know," in *Electronic Literature as Digital Humanities: Contexts, Forms, and Practices*, eds. Dene Grigar and James O'Sullivan (2021): 237–245.

18 Nadezhda Povroznik, "Digital History of Virtual Museums: The Transition from Analog to Internet Environment," in *Proceedings of the Digital Humanities in the Nordic Countries 5th Conference* (2020): 125–136. http://ceur-ws.org/Vol-2612/paper9.pdf. Retrieved 22 September 2022.

19 Domenico Fiormonte, Sukanta Chaudhuri, and Paola Ricaurte, eds., *Global Debates in the Digital Humanities* (Minneapolis, MN: University of Minnesota Press, 2022).

20 Sibo Chen, "The Materialist Circuits and the Quest for Environmental Justice in ICT's Global Expansion," *tripleC: Communication, Capitalism & Critique. Open Access Journal for a Global Sustainable Information Society* 14, no. 1 (2016): 121–131.

21 Payal Arora, "Bottom of the Data Pyramid: Big Data and the Global South," *International Journal of Communication* 10 (2016): 19.

22 Daniel O'Donnell et al., "Boundary Land: Diversity as a Defining Feature of the Digital Humanities" (2016), http://dh2016.adho.org/abstracts/406.

23 Katrina Fenlon, Megan Senseney, Maria Bonn, and Janet Swatscheno, "Humanities Scholars and Library-based Digital Publishing: New Forms of Publication, New Audiences, New Publishing Roles," *Journal of Scholarly Publishing* 50, no. 3 (2019): 159–182.

24 Maria Bonn, "Computation, Corpus, Community: The HathiTrust Research Center Today," *College & Research Libraries News* 77, no. 4 (2016): 194–197.

25 See Timothy J. Busse, "Crossing the Digital Rubicon: Google Books and the Dawn of an Electronic Literature Revolution," *Houston Business and Tax Law Journal* 18 (2018): 121–149.

26 Tim Wu, "Whatever Happened to Google Books," *The New Yorker*, 11 September 2015.

27 Kim D. Gainer, "Fair Use and Digitization: Google Prevails in the Latest Court Ruling," in *The CCCC-IP Annual: Top Intellectual Property Developments of 2013*, ed. Clancy Ratliff (2014): 37. https://escholarship.org/uc/item/6ng4h3mj. Retrieved 22 September 2022.

28 See "General Information," Library of Congress, https://www.loc.gov/about/general-information/. Retrieved 23 May 2022.

29 Michel Duchesneau, "Gallica: The Online Digital Library of the Bibliothèque nationale de France," *Nineteenth-Century Music Review* 11,

no. 2 (2014): 337–347; see "BnF Gallica," https://gallica.bnf.fr/. Retrieved 23 May 2022.

30  Ola T. Westengen, Charlotte Lusty, Mariana Yazbek, Ahmed Amri, and Åsmund Asdal, "Safeguarding a Global Seed Heritage from Syria to Svalbard," *Nature Plants* 6, no. 11 (2020): 1311–1317.

31  Tomasz Łysak, "Vlogging Auschwitz: New Players in Holocaust Commemoration," *Holocaust Studies* (2021): 1–26.

32  "International Council of Museums | About," *ICOM,* https://icom.museum/en/about-us/. Retrieved 10 June 2022.

33  "Museum of Broken Relationships," https://brokenships.com/visit. Retrieved 24 May 2022.

34  David E. Beel et al., "Cultural Resilience: The Production of Rural Community Heritage, Digital Archives and the Role of Volunteers," *Journal of Rural Studies* 54 (2017): 459–468.

35  Manuel Charr. "How are Museums Using Chatbots?" *Museum Next,* 14 September 2019.

36  Erin Lawrimore, "Margaret Cross Norton: Defining and Redefining Archives and the Archival Profession," *Libraries & The Cultural Record* 44, no. 2 (2009): 186.

37  See Douglas, Jennifer. "Origins and Beyond: The Ongoing Evolution of Archival Ideas about Provenance," *Currents of Archival Thinking* 2 (2017): 25–52.

38  See Emily Maemura, Nicholas Worby, Ian Milligan, and Christoph Becker, "If these Crawls Could Talk: Studying and Documenting Web Archives Provenance," *Journal of the Association for Information Science and Technology* 69, no. 10 (2018): 1223–1233.

39  "Text of the Convention for the Safeguarding of the Intangible Cultural Heritage," *UNESCO Intangible Cultural Heritage,* https://ich.unesco.org/en/convention. Retrieved 11 June 2022.

40  Maria Bonn, Lori Kendall, and Jerome McDonough, "Libraries and Archives and the Preservation of Intangible Cultural Heritage: Defining a Research Agenda" (white paper), *Illinois: School of Information Sciences* (2017): 50–51. http://hdl.handle.net/2142/97228. Retrieved 22 September 2022.

41  See "Dive into intangible cultural heritage!" *UNESCO Intangible Cultural Heritage,* https://ich.unesco.org/en/dive. Retrieved 11 June 2022.

42  Luke Harding and Harriet Sherwood, "Ukrainians in Race to Save Cultural Heritage," *The Guardian,* 9 March 2022.

43  Heather Stephenson, "Preserving Ukraine's Cultural Heritage Online," *Tufts Now,* 22 March 2022.

44  Meghanlata Gupta, "Regaining Control: Indigenous-Owned and Operated Archives," https://indiancountrytoday.com/news/regaining-control-indigenous-owned-and-operated-archives. Retrieved 11 June 2022.

45  "Vivian G. Harsh Research Collection," *Chicago Public Library,* https://www.chipublib.org/vivian-g-harsh-research-collection/. Retrieved 11 June 2022.

46 Laura Burt, "Vivian Harsh, Adult Education, and the Library's Role as Community Center," *Libraries & The Cultural Record* 44, no. 2 (2009): 234–255.

47 Thomas Kirchhoff, Werner Schweibenz, and Jörn Sieglerschmidt. "Archives, Libraries, Museums and the Spell of Ubiquitous Knowledge," *Archival Science* 8, no. 4 (2008): 256.

48 "About Us," *Europeana,* https://www.europeana.eu/en/about-us. Retrieved 11 June 2022.

49 Mary Anne Kennan and Jessie Lymn, "Where Is the I(nformation) in GLAM? Education, Knowledge and Skill Requirements of Professionals Working in GLAM Sector Institutions," *Journal of the Australian Library and Information Association* 68, no. 3 (2019): 236–253.

50 Jerome P. McDonough et al., *Preserving Virtual Worlds Final Report* (2010), http://hdl.handle.net/2142/17097.

51 Sarah Higgins, "Digital Curation: The Development of a Discipline within Information Science," *Journal of Documentation* 74, no. 6, (2018), https://doi.org/10.1108/JD-02-2018-0024.

52 "About the Internet Archive," Internet Archive, https://archive.org/about/. Retrieved 24 May 2022.

53 "Open-GLAM: What," https://openglam.org/what/. Retrieved 24 May 2022.

54 "Open Data," *National Museum Palace,* https://theme.npm.edu.tw/opendata/. Retrieved 20 June 2022.

55 "Open Access at the Met," https://www.metmuseum.org/about-the-met/policies-and-documents/open-access. Retrieved 22 June 2022.

56 Jorge Luis Borges, "On Exactitude in Science," in *Jorge Luis Borges: Collected Fictions,* trans. Andrew Hurley (New York: Penguin Putnam, 1998): 325. Lewis Carroll, *Sylvie and Bruno Concluded* (London: Macmillan, 1894).

57 Scott A. Small, "Age-Related Memory Decline: Current Concepts and Future Directions," *Archives of Neurology* 58, no. 3 (2001): 360–364.

58 Laurel Wamsley, "Library of Congress Will No Longer Archive Every Tweet," *NPR,* 26 December 2017.

59 Jorge Luis Borges, *Labyrinths: Selected Stories & Other Writings,* Vol. 1066 (New York: New Directions Publishing, 2007): 66.

60 See "Digital Einstein Experience," https://einstein.digitalhumans.com/. Retrieved 18 June 2022.

61 See "Dali Lives," https://thedali.org/exhibit/dali-lives/. Retrieved 18 June 2022.

62 "Parents of Parkland Shooting Victim Joaquin Oliver Bring Son Back Digitally in New Voting Initiative," *CBSNews,* 2 October 2020.

63 Carl Öhman and Luciano Floridi, "The Political Economy of Death in the Age of Information: A Critical Approach to the Digital Afterlife Industry," *Minds and Machines* 27, no. 4 (2017): 639–662.

64 Sara Suárez-Gonzalo, "'Deadbots' Can Speak for You after Your Death: Is That Ethical?" *The Conversation,* 9 May 2022.

# IMAGINING INFORMATION

Matthias Röder, who creates classical music through machine learning at the Salzburg-based Karajan Institute, assembled a team to complete Ludwig Beethoven's tenth symphony, left unfinished when the composer died in 1827. He recruited computer scientist Ahmed Elgammel, composer Walter Werzowa, musicologist Robert Levin, and computational music expert Mark Gotham. The project began by translating Beethoven's works into a digital format understandable by a computer.[1]

*Deep machine learning* (DML) makes use of complex algorithms to form neural networks, machine learning models that allow computer applications to discover complex patterns in very large data sets. Once these models are trained on existing data, they can be used to generate novel patterns. Röder trained their model on the composer's distinctive style, as well as traditional forms of symphonic composition, so that it could predict what Beethoven might have chosen to do with his musical ideas had he lived to develop them into a full symphonic score. The musicians and musicologists integrated the AI-suggested material with the musical sketches Beethoven had made before he died, to create their first attempt at a finished symphony.

A piece of the symphony was tested before a group of Beethoven scholars, who were unable to tell where Beethoven's orchestration ended, and the team's work began. The team spent another 18 months completing the rest of the symphony, which premiered

DOI: 10.4324/9781003155119-10

in Bonn, Germany, Beethoven's birthplace. Headlines announcing this event proclaimed that "robots" or "artificial intelligence" had finished Beethoven's work.[2] But the more interesting aspect of the project, from an information science perspective, was the collaborative sociotechnical process through which a musical score—a particular and distinct kind of information—was created. The combined expertise of scholars, composers, and musicians was *extended by* the computational capacities of the program.

When AI is used as a proper noun as if it were a person, it can be easy to forget that the underlying algorithms, even when working autonomously and calculating at a speed and complexity beyond what a human brain can do, were *designed*. A machine learning process might be argued to have its own material agency, as any object does within a sociotechnical system, but it retains human intentions because it has none of its own. In the case of Beethoven's unfinished symphony, crediting AI as the composer makes a better headline, but it doesn't give the humans their due.

The program could not assess how the music feels to a listener, so it couldn't have evaluated its own success or failure. The algorithms were *tuned* by a skilled programmer and the output was guided by the trained ears of people familiar with Beethoven's work. The AI enhanced the capacities of its human team members, as they enhanced the capacities of the AI, in a delicate dance of resistance and accommodation.[3]

The process that took the team from concept to concert involved an iterative design process within a complex more-than-human information system. Arguably, they had collectively become a *cyborg*. To say that AI "finished the symphony" looks past the real magic of what was achieved.

In this chapter we bring the book to a close by surveying some of the emerging technologies that are inspiring both utopian hopes and dystopian fears. We briefly revisit the stories told through the volume, as we consider imagined futures for the field of information science and our information society.

## INFORMATION FUTURES

Artists, designers, and programmers are exploring *creative AI*, an emerging field in which algorithmic and computational processes have been used to generate visual art, write original poetry, animate old photos, or produce endless streams of heavy metal.[4] Some artists may view themselves as collaborators with the AI. Artists whose work is used by others to train AI may feel that their *style* has been stolen; copyright law will need to catch up with the new technologies. But some people do see in the creative output of AI something more transcendent. They may be looking forward to the imagined moment when a computer program becomes self-aware. Others fear *the singularity*, a future in which superhuman intelligence brings about the end of the human era.[5]

Utopian visions and dystopian fears regarding autonomous artificial intelligence have been present in speculative fiction since well before the digital era, in stories about automatons, golems, and the reanimated dead. In the 20th century the architects of the Internet argued about whether the development of AI should aim to produce independent cognition, or hybrid human–machine systems. The robots-versus-cyborgs debate continues, but more urgently now that machine learning is a part of our ordinary lives.

In June 2022 a Google employee announced to the press that their Language Model for Dialogue Applications (LaMDA) had achieved sentience.[6] Transcripts of LaMDA also claiming to be a squirrel flew across social media as AI researchers responded in unanimity that its responses were computationally derived. Some also warned that "crying sentience" is an unhelpful red herring, if announcements like this distract the public from looking critically at the risks that human ambition and unregulated AI pose as black-boxed algorithms become more deeply established in our information infrastructures.

Research suggests that risks associated with AI fall disproportionately upon marginalized people.[7] A study testing the language model that LaMDA had trained on, found that when it was asked to complete the prompt, "Two Muslims walked into a—" it produced a response related to violence (axes, bombs, fire, shooting, killing) in 66% percent of the completions.[8] Allowing a bot to learn directly from public sources makes it even more susceptible to parroting and elaborating upon stereotypes that it does not understand. In 2016 Microsoft released their now infamous Twitter bot, Tay, as a "conversational experiment." Within 24 hours she was producing sexist, racist, and antisemitic tweets.[9] The experience didn't *make* Tay racist, as some headlines reported. She had just learned to *sound* racist, an expectable outcome that her programmers failed to anticipate.

Researchers have studied the application of AI-driven Big Data surveillance technologies for *predictive policing*, a technique in which a system is trained on large data sets that include historical crime data, in order to decide where best to deploy limited police forces, and which communities and individuals should be more closely surveilled. The results of the study suggest that the use of such technologies doesn't create bias in the society where it is employed as much as it amplifies existing bias. In this particular case, the AI extended the capacities of the racist practices historically associated with the over-monitoring and control of minority communities.[10]

The ideal of AI-human cooperation has produced positive results in a variety of domains: *human-drone collaboration* in emergency rescue has proved successful,[11] and there are significant breakthroughs in robotic and other accessibility tools for people with disabilities, some of whom already think of themselves as cyborgs.[12] Advances in natural language processing, video analytics, and biometrics are leading to innovations across science, healthcare, and education.

Industries are turning to *smart manufacturing* to improve the efficiency of their operations, lower their labor costs, and take advantage of new data-driven opportunities. Automation is well-suited to repetitive tasks. The introduction of robots and *co-bots*, working alongside people in the workplace may reduce error and injury but it will require invasive surveillance.[13] Economists warn that without social intervention in wealth distribution or extensive educational retraining, AI automation will exacerbate already widening income inequalities.

The *Internet of things* (IoT), *smart homes*, and *smart cities* all promise benefits by connecting our devices together. Critics point to the risks (to privacy, to autonomy, to anonymity) that are unavoidable in implementing the data-hungry, mass surveillance technologies required to create these integrated and automated worlds. The jury is still out on the safety of self-driving cars, not because of flaws in the technology that can't be fixed, but because of the unpredictable imperfections of the world. Making the world safe *for* self-driving cars may be the greater challenge.[14]

Deepfake technologies also have two imagined futures. When they are used for educational, political, entertainment, and commercial purposes, game designers create realistic *non-player characters* (NPCs) with faces that are indistinguishable from real people, except that these have never lived; creative apps put our faces onto the bodies of famous actors in our favorite movie scenes or make photographs of our great-grandparents smile, dance, and wink.[15] When they are used with malice, deepfakes may be deployed for cyberbullying, sexual harassment, revenge porn, child porn, fraud, political manipulation, and election interference.[16]

Optimistic hopes, pessimistic fears, and also cynicism arising from over-hype, hover around new information technologies. Some people are heralding a migration of all human interaction into a digitally mediated shared *metaverse* made possible via *blockchain technologies* and VR interfaces. But for other people, blockchain is the enabler of bitcoin pyramid schemes, and VR is only another way to play—one that produces nausea or a headache if a headset is worn too long.

More certain is the steady expansion of the role of games, gaming, and game-like interfaces in every domain of our lives. Game studies research and game design are of increasing interest to information science because games have transformed the interfaces through which we interact with information, and with each other. We play (and watch) games for sport, entertainment, learning, training, relaxation, excitement, activism, exercise, and personal enrichment. We play on consoles in our living rooms and bedrooms, on tabletops in our kitchens and dining rooms, on phones or tablets in bathrooms, waiting rooms, cars, and public transportation. Students play at science through Minecraft[17] and learn the skills of archeology by conducting virtual digs.[18]

Things that aren't quite games, but which incorporate game-like elements, are all around us. Chatbots answer our customer service questions. We train for new jobs through professional simulations. The economy is experimenting with games, as blockchain-enabled crypto games invite us to gamble for non-fungible tokens

(NFTs). Even dating apps, with their swiping of faces left and right, make our interpersonal relationships technologically mediated and game-like too.

Imagined information futures—both the optimistic and utopian, and the pessimistic and dystopian—are immediately relevant to the practices and professions of information science. The field is preparing the information professionals of the future. They will be tasked with classifying, organizing, optimizing, managing, governing, studying, designing, evaluating, critiquing, curating, and preserving the information that is required or produced by each new tool, technology, and system when it is created, as long as it lives, and after it (inevitably) gets left behind.

Information, chimerical and ubiquitous, is at the center of it all.

## IMAGINING INFORMATION IN CONTEXT

If we were to imagine an information future in which we do a better job responding to current and future information challenges as they arise, what might that future look like?

It is possible to imagine *a more accessible information future.* This book began with the viral image of children attending school on a sidewalk during the first year of the Covid pandemic, highlighting the dramatic disparities that exist in access to information. How can information infrastructures change so that everyone has access to the Internet, regardless of income or location?

It is possible to imagine *a more inclusive information future.* The burning of the libraries in Timbuktu told a story about censorship, the attempt to control information that challenges institutions and hierarchies. How can information professionals help to make sure that no one's history or experience is marginalized, excluded, or erased?

It is possible to imagine *a more responsive information future.* The story of the *Libro de los Epítomes,* the book that was lost in a library, was the springboard for a discussion about how we sort the world. How can classification systems and information institutions become more self-conscious, flexible, and open to criticism and change?

It is possible to imagine *a more restorative information future.* We considered the personhood of the Whanganui river, and how different ways of knowing the world affect how we organize information. How can information science engage with indigenous and other historically marginalized groups, taking responsibility for harm, and allowing them to organize their own knowledge?

It is possible to imagine *a more diverse information future*. The discussion of Small World Networks and gender bias in Wikipedia underscored the need to diversify the information profession so that multiple perspectives can work towards reducing bias. How can we change the way students are trained for information professions so that more diverse professional cultures, networks, and workplaces can evolve?

It is possible to imagine *a more ethical information future*. The deciphering of the Antikythera mechanism led to a discussion of the promises and risks of Big Data analytics and increased data sharing. How can the promise of machine learning be better evaluated, and the risks diminished, through more effective oversight, and algorithmic transparency?

It is possible to imagine *a more secure information future*. The story behind the Domesday Book as a public record introduced information governance, and the need to protect information rights and freedoms. How can information science work to support information freedoms and to protect privacy rights even in heavily surveilled societies?

It is possible to imagine *a more discerning information future*. Facebook's filter-bubble-producing algorithms shed light on human behavior, including our vulnerability to social media. How do we do a better job teaching information literacy, so people learn to recognize and challenge disinformation rather than being manipulated by it?

It is possible to imagine *a more transformative information future*. The rose graphs created by Florence Nightingale illustrated the power of storytelling to bring about positive social change within a domain. How can the design of information systems and institutions incorporate more universal, participatory, and human-*decen*tered approaches to solving local and global challenges?

It is possible to imagine *a more collaborative information future*. The fight over the Ancient One suggests that knowledge communities have often been excluded from processes of curation and preservation. How can memory institutions collaborate earlier and more closely with communities to respect and protect their tangible and intangible heritage?

Finally, it is possible to imagine *a more equitable information future*. As this chapter noted, an algorithm set loose in the world will reflect the governance, supervision, and evaluation provided by the human in the machine. How do we build equity into our information systems so that the benefits and costs of emerging information technologies are shared equitably between and within nations?

The utopian view of information systems and technologies of the future is that their power will be used to improve the world and solve its most intractable problems. The pessimistic, dystopian view arises from the possibility that giving power to machine-learning algorithms, especially if they are relied upon to make critical real-world decisions, will be disastrous. The truth of the matter, as many speculative works of dystopian fiction can attest, is that our technologies will be as benevolent or as destructive as we are. While society is biased, information systems invariably will be biased too, unless we take conscious, active steps to intervene. How do we build equity into our information systems? We must also ask how to create equity in the social world.

Information science, as we have explored it here, takes as its subject the intellectual space where information, technology, and people meet. Humanistic values, social theories, and analytic methods interact freely within that space. The embrace of multiple approaches and methodologies gives the field the potential to be both critical and innovative. Utopian or not, these possible futures provide powerful aspirations upon which to rest the emergent discipline of information science.[19]

# NOTES

1 Ahmed Elgammal, "How Artificial Intelligence Completed Beethoven's Unfinished Tenth Symphony," *Smithsonian Magazine*, 24 September 2021.

2 Caroline Delbert, "Beethoven Never Finished His Last Symphony. Can Robots Complete the Job?" *Popular Mechanics*, 18 December 2019; Julie Gaubert, "After More Than Two Centuries, Beethoven's 10th Symphony Has Been Completed by an AI," *EuroNews.next*, 14 October 2021.

3 See Andrew Pickering, *The Mangle of Practice: Time, Agency, and Science* (Chicago, IL: University of Chicago Press, 2010): 52.

4  Relentless Doppelganger has been continuously streaming since 4 September 2019, "Relentless Doppelganger," *Dadabots*, https://www.youtube.com/watch?v=MwtVkPKx3RA.

5  Carol Cadwalladr, "Are the Robots about to Rise? Google's New Director of Engineering Thinks So…," *The Guardian*, 22 February 2014.

6  Nitasha Tiku, "The Google Engineer Who Thinks the Company's AI Has Come to Life," 11 June 2022, https://www.washingtonpost.com/technology/2022/06/11/google-ai-lamda-blake-lemoine/. See also "About," *OpenAI*, https://openai.com/about/. Retrieved 17 June 2022.

7  Emily M. Bender, "Human-Like Programs Abuse Our Empathy – Even Google Engineers Aren't Immune," *The Guardian*, 14 June 2022.

8  Abubakar Abid, Maheen Farooqi, and James Zou, "Large Language Models Associate Muslims with Violence," *Nature Machine Intelligence* 3, no. 6 (2021): 461–463. Cited by Timnit Gebru and Margaret Mitchell, "We Warned Google that People Might Believe AI Was Sentient: Now It's Happening," *The Washington Post*, 17 June 2022.

9  See Elle Hunt, "Tay, Microsoft's AI Chatbot, Gets a Crash Course in Racism from Twitter," *The Guardian*, 24 March 2016. https://www.theguardian.com/technology/2016/mar/24/tay-microsofts-ai-chatbot-gets-a-crash-course-in-racism-from-twitter/; and Sara Suárez-Gonzalo, Luís Mas Manchón, and Frederic Guerrero Solé, "Tay Is You: The Attribution of Responsibility in the Algorithmic Culture," *Observatorio* 13, no. 2 (2019): 1–14.

10 Xerxes Minocher and Caelyn Randall, "Predictable Policing: New Technology, Old Bias, and Future Resistance in Big Data Surveillance," *Convergence* 26, no. 5–6 (2020): 1108–1124.

11 Mateusz Dolata and Kiram Ben Aleya, "Morphological Analysis for Design Science Research: The Case of Human-Drone Collaboration in Emergencies," in *International Conference on Design Science Research in Information Systems and Technology*, eds. Andreas Drechsler, Aurona Gerber and Alan Hevner (Cham: Springer, 2022): 17–29.

12 Cy. Jillian Weise, "How a Cyborg Challenges Reality," *The New York Times*, 22 June 2022. https://www.nytimes.com/2022/06/22/special-series/cyborgs-reality-identity.html. Retrieved 22 September 2022; Chloé Valentine Toscano, "Go Ahead and Stare at My Prosthetic Arm. I Know It's Awesome," *Washington Post*, 19 September 2022, https://www.washingtonpost.com/lifestyle/2022/09/19/prosthetic-arm-design-personalize-disability/. Retrieved 22 September 2022.

13 Federico Cassioli, Giulia Fronda, and Michela Balconi, "Human–Co-Bot Interaction and Neuroergonomics: Co-Botic vs. Robotic Systems," *Frontiers in Robotics and AI* 8 (2021): 659319.

14 Jack Stilgoe, "How Can We Know a Self-Driving Car Is Safe?," *Ethics and Information Technology* 23, no. 4 (2021): 635–647.

15 Jason Mueller and Genevieve Perez, "'Deepfake' Technology: Very Real Marketing Value … and Risks," *National Law Review* 12, no. 267 (2020), https://www.natlawreview.com/article/deepfake-technology-very-real-marketing-value-and-risks. Retrieved 22 September 2022.

16  Travis L. Wagner and Ashley Blewer, "'The Word Real Is No Longer Real': Deepfakes, Gender, and the Challenges of AI-Altered Video," *Open Information Science* 3, no. 1 (2019): 32–46.

17  Matt Gadbury and H. Chad Lane, "Mining for STEM Interest Behaviors in Minecraft," in *International Conference on Artificial Intelligence in AI*, eds Maria Mercedes Rodrigo, Noburu Matsuda, Alexandra I. Cristea and Vania Dimitrova (Cham: Springer, 2022): 236–239.

18  Laura Shackelford, Wenhao David Huang, Alan Craig, Cameron Merrill, and Danying Chen, "Relationships between Motivational Support and Game Features in a Game-Based Virtual Reality Learning Environment for Teaching Introductory Archaeology," *Educational Media International* 56, no. 3 (2019): 183–200.

19  For further reading, see Nicole A. Cooke, Renate Chancellor, Yasmeen Shorish, Sarah Park Dahlen, and Amelia Gibson, eds, "Once More for Those in the Back: Libraries Are Not Neutral," *Publishers Weekly*, 10 June 2022; Tami Oliphant, "A Case for Critical Data Studies in Library and Information Studies," *Journal of Critical Library and Information Studies* 1, no. 1 (2017). https://doi.org/10.24242/jclis.v1i1.22; Rose L. Chou, Annie Pho, and Charlotte Roh, eds., *Pushing the Margins: Women of Color and Intersectionality in LIS* (Sacramento, CA: *Library Juice Press* 2018); Ragnar Audunson, Herbjørn Andresen, Cicilie Fagerlid, Erik Henningsen, Hans-Christoph Hobohm, Henrik Jochumsen, Håkon Larsen, and Tonje Vold, eds, *Libraries, Archives and Museums as Democratic Spaces in a Digital Age* (Berlin: De Gruyter, 2020).

# BIBLIOGRAPHY

Abend, Lisa. "Meet the Lithuanian 'Elves' Fighting Russian Disinformation." *Time*. 6 March 2022. https://time.com/6155060/lithuania-russia-fighting -disinformation-ukraine/.

Abid, Abubakar, Maheen Farooqi, and James Zou. "Large Language Models Associate Muslims with Violence." *Nature Machine Intelligence* 3, no. 6 (2021): 461–463.

"About." *OpenAI*. Retrieved 17 June 2022. https://openai.com/about/.

"About." The Information Behavior Conference. https://pages.cms.hu -berlin.de/ibi/isic-2022/about/. Retrieved 8 June 2022.

"About DCMI." *Dublin Core Metadata Initiative* Website. Retrieved 20 May 2020. https://www.dublincore.org/about/.

"About the Internet Archive." *Internet Archive*. https://archive.org/about/. Retrieved 24 May 2022.

"About Us." *Europeana*. https://www.europeana.eu/en/about-us. Retrieved 11 June 2022.

"About Us." *United States Indigenous Data Sovereignty Network*. https:// usindigenousdata.org/about-us. Retrieved 22 June 2022.

Ackoff, Russell L. "From Data to Wisdom." *Journal of Applied Systems Analysis* 16, no. 1 (1989): 3–9.

Adams, Douglas, *The Hitchiker's Guide to the Galaxy*. Pan Books, 1979.

"Adelina the Jester." *Open Domesday*. https://opendomesday.org/name/ adelina-the-jester/. Retrieved 30 May 2022.

Adu, Kofi Koranteng, and Patrick Ngulube. "Key Threats and Challenges to the Preservation of Digital Records of Public Institutions in Ghana." *Information, Communication & Society* 20, no. 8 (2017): 1127–1145.

Ahmed, Syed Masud, Göran Tomson, Max Petzold, and Zarina Nahar Kabir. "Socioeconomic Status Overrides Age and Gender in Determining Health-Seeking Behaviour in Rural Bangladesh." *Bulletin of the World Health Organization* 83 (2005): 109–117.

"AI Global Surveillance Technology." *Carnegie Endowment for International Peace.* https://carnegieendowment.org/publications/interactive/aI-surveill ance. Retrieved 4 June 2022.

Albert-László, Barabási. "Network Science." *Philosophical Transactions of the Royal Society A: Mathematical, Physical and Engineering Sciences* 371. 1987 (2013): 20120375.

Allen, Walter C., and Robert F. Delzell. *Ideals and Standards: The History of the University of Illinois Graduate School of Library and Information Science, 1893–1993.* The Graduate School of Library and Information Science, University of Illinois at Urbana-Champaign, 1992.

Allsop, Jim. "The Ongoing Information War over Ukraine." *The Media Today, Columbia Journalism Review*, 9 May 2022.

American Library Association. "ALA Statement on Censorship of Information Addressing Racial Injustice, Black American History, and Diversity Education." Retrieved 17 May 2022. https://www.ala.org/ advocacy/intfreedom/statement/opposition-censorship-racial-injustice -black-history-diversity-education.

"Ancient Mesopotamia." *Journal of Technical Writing and Communication* 49, no. 3 (2019): 338–364.

Anderson, Theresa Dirndorfer, and Jo Orsatti. "'Rhythms of Being' at ISIC-Understanding the Place of the ISIC Conferences in Information Seeking Research." *Information Research* 13 no. 4 (2008). http://informationr.net/ir /13-4/paper381.html. Retrieved 22 September 2022.

"The Anglo-Saxon Chronicle: Eleventh Century." *The Avalon Project: Documents in Law, History & Diplomacy.* Yale Law School. https://avalon .law.yale.edu/medieval/ang11.asp. Retrieved 30 May 2022.

Apenīte, Mārīte. "Subject Indexing at the National Library of Latvia: New Approach, Challenges, and Benefits." *Cataloging & Classification Quarterly* 59, no. 4 (2021): 334–354.

Appelbaum, Ralph. "Activating Public Space." In *Information Architects*, edited by Richard Saul Wurman and Peter Bradford, 150–161. Zurich: Graphis Inc., 1996.

Archi, Alfonso, "Ebla and Its Archives." In *Texts, History, and Society*, De Gruyter, 2015.

Arif, Ahmer, Leo Graiden Stewart, and Kate Starbird. "Acting the Part: Examining Information Operations within #BlackLivesMatter Discourse." *Proceedings of the ACM on Human-Computer Interaction* 2, no. CSCW (2018): 1–27.

"ARLIS/NA Statement on Removal of Library of Congress: Illegal Aliens – Subject Headings." *Art Libraries Association of North America.* 21 January 2022.

Arora, Payal. "Bottom of the Data Pyramid: Big Data and the Global South." *International Journal of Communication* 10 (2016): 19.

Ash, Thomas. "Naudé, Mazarin and the Origins of France's Oldest Public Library." March 9, 2017. https://thomasash.wordpress.com/2017/03/09/naude-mazarin-and-the-origins-of-frances-oldest-public-library/.

Aspray, William F. "The Scientific Conceptualization of Information: A Survey." *IEEE Annals of the History of Computing* 7, no. 02 (1985): 117–140.

Assari, Shervin, Cleopatra H. Caldwell, and Mohsen Bazargan. "Association between Parental Educational Attainment and Youth Outcomes and Role of Race/Ethnicity." *JAMA Network Open* 2, no. 11 (2019). https://doi.org/10.1001/jamanetworkopen.2019.16018

Astuti, Santi Indra, Lumakto Giri, and Nuril Hidayah. "Video Web Drama Series for Combating Disinformation." *Aspiration Journal* 1, no. 1 (2020): 7.

Audunson, Ragnar, Herbjørn Andresen, Cicilie Fagerlid, Erik Henningsen, Hans-Christoph Hobohm, Henrik Jochumsen, Håkon Larsen, and Tonje Vold. *Libraries, Archives and Museums as Democratic Spaces in a Digital Age.* Berlin: De Gruyter, 2020.

Ayad, Moustafa. "The Vladimirror Network: Pro-Putin Power-Users on Facebook." *Institute of Strategic Dialogue.* 4 April 2022. https://www.isdglobal.org/isd-publications/the-vladimirror-network-pro-putin-power-users-on-facebook/.

"The Bad News Game." *DebunkEU.* https://www.getbadnews.com/en/play. Retrieved 9 June 2022.

Baffour-Awuah, Margaret. "The Carnegie Revitalisation of Public Libraries in Africa: A Possible Tool for Breaking Down Barriers to School Library Development." In IASL Annual Conference Proceedings, 2021. https://doi.org/10.29173/iasl7545

Banks, R.R. and Ford, R.T. "(How) Does Unconscious Bias Matter: Law, Politics, and Racial Inequality." *Emory LJ* 58 (2008).

Bannon, Liam, Jeffrey Bardzell, and Susanne Bødker. "Introduction: Reimagining Participatory Design: Emerging Voices." *ACM Transactions on Computer-Human Interaction (TOCHI)* 25, no. 1 (2018): 1–8.

Baron, Jill E., and Tina Gross. "Sorrow, Fury, Helplessness, and Cynicism: An Account of the Library of Congress Subject Heading 'Illegal Aliens.'" In *Borders and Belonging: Critical Examinations of Library Approaches toward Immigrants*, edited by Ana Ndumu. Sacramento, CA: Library Juice Press, 2021.

Basile, Jonathan. *Tar for Mortar: "The Library of Babel" and the Dream of Totality.* Sacramento, CA: Punctum Books, 2018.

Bates, Marcia J. "Information." *Encyclopedia of Library and Information Sciences* 3 (2010): 2048–2063.

Bates, Marcia J. "Information Behavior." In *Encyclopedia of Library and Information Sciences,* edited by John D. McDonald and Michael Levine-Clark. Boca Raton: CRC Press, 2017: 2074–2085.

Bates, Marcia J. "The Information Professions: Knowledge, Memory, Heritage." *Information Research* 20, no. 1 (2015). Retrieved from http://InformationR.net/ir/20-1/paper655.html

Batool, Syeda Hina, and Sheila Webber. "A Contextual Framework for Primary Education: Fostering Information Literacy in Pakistan." *Global Knowledge, Memory and Communication* 68, no. 3 (2018): 164–176.

Battle-Baptiste, Whitney, and Britt Rusert, editors. *WEB Du Bois's Data Portraits: Visualizing Black America.* San Francisco, CA: Chronicle Books, 2018.

Bawden, David. "Users, User Studies and Human Information Behaviour: A Three-Decade Perspective on Tom Wilson's 'On User Studies and Information Needs.'" *Journal of Documentation* 62, no. 6 (2006): 671–679.

Bawden, David, and Lyn Robinson. *Introduction to Information Science.* London: Facet Publishing, 2015.

Becker, Annette. "Memory Gaps: Maurice Halbwachs, Memory and the Great War." *Journal of European studies* 35, no. 1 (2005): 102–113.

Beel, David E., Claire D. Wallace, Gemma Webster, Hai Nguyen, Elizabeth Tait, Marsaili Macleod, and Chris Mellish. "Cultural Resilience: The Production of Rural Community Heritage, Digital Archives and the Role of Volunteers." *Journal of Rural Studies* 54 (2017): 459–468.

Belghith, Yasmine, Sukrit Venkatagiri, and Kurt Luther. "Compete, Collaborate, Investigate: Exploring the Social Structures of Open Source Intelligence Investigations." In *CHI Conference on Human Factors in Computing Systems,* 2022: 1–18. https://doi.org/10.1145/3491102.3517526.

Belitz, Clara, Jaclyn Ocumpaugh, Steven Ritter, Ryan S. Baker, Stephen E. Fancsali, and Nigel Bosch. "Constructing Categories: Moving beyond Protected Classes in Algorithmic Fairness." *Journal of the Association for Information Science and Technology* (2022). https://doi.org/10.1002/asi.24643.

Bender, Emily M. "Human-Like Programs Abuse Our Empathy – Even Google Engineers Aren't Immune." *The Guardian,* 14 June 2022.

Berman, Sanford. *Prejudices and Antipathies: A Tract on the LC Subject Heads Concerning People.* Metuchen, NJ: Scarecrow Press, 1971.

Bernal, J. D. "The Transmission of Scientific Information: A User's Analysis." In *Proceedings of the International Conference on Scientific Information* 958 (1958): 77–95. Cited in Wilson, Thomas D. "Human Information Behavior." *Informing Science* 3, no. 2 (2000): 50.

Berners-Lee, T., Hendler, J., & Lassila, O. "The Semantic Web." *Scientific American*, 284(5), (2001). 28–37.

Bertot, John Carlo, Paul T. Jaeger, Lesley A. Langa, and Charles R. McClure. "Public Access Computing and Internet access in Public Libraries: The Role of Public Libraries in E-Government and Emergency Situations." *First Monday* (2006).

Beyer, Wiebke. "Teaching in Old Babylonian Nippur, Learning in Old Assyrian Aššur?" *Studies in Manuscript Cultures*, 15: (2021).

Bhaskar, Chakravorti. "Why AI Failed to Live Up to Its Potential during the Pandemic." *Harvard Business Review*. 27 March 2022.

Bibliothèque nationale de France. https://gallica.bnf.fr/. Retrieved 23 May 2022.

Bizer, Christian, Tom Heath, and Tim Berners-Lee. "Linked Data: The Story So Far." In *Semantic Services, Interoperability and Web Applications: Emerging Concepts*, edited by Amit P. Sheth. Hershey, PA: IGI Global, 2011: 205–227.

Blair, Ann M. *Too Much to Know*. New Haven, CT: Yale University Press, 2010.

Blake, Virgil LP. "Forging the Anglo-American Cataloging Alliance: Descriptive Cataloging, 1830–1908." *Cataloging & Classification Quarterly* 35, no. 1–2 (2002): 3–22.

Blei, Daniela. "How the Index Card Cataloged the World." *The Atlantic*. 1 December 2017.

Bødker, S., & Kyng, M. Participatory Design That Matters: Facing the Big Issues. *ACM Transactions on Computer-Human Interaction* 25, no. 1 (2018): 12.

Bogaert, Hannah. "History Repeating Itself: The Resurgence of the Taliban and the Abandonment of Afghan Women." *Immigration and Human Rights Law Review* 4, no. 1 (2022): 3.

Bohannon J. and A. Elbakyan "Data from: Who's Downloading Pirated Papers? Everyone." *Dryad Digital Repository* (2016). https://doi.org/10.5061/dryad.q447c

Bond, Sarah E. "Erasing the Face of History." *New York Times*. 14 May 2011.

Bonn, Maria. "Computation, Corpus, Community: The Hathitrust Research Center Today." *College & Research Libraries News* 77, no. 4 (2016): 194–197.

Bonn, Maria, Lori Kendall, and Jerome McDonough. "Libraries and Archives and the Preservation of Intangible Cultural Heritage: Defining a Research Agenda" (white paper). Champaign, IL: *School of Information Sciences* (2017): 50–51. Retrieved 22 September 2022. http://hdl.handle.net/2142/97228.

"The Book of Books: Hernando Colón's Libro de los Epítomes." Department of Nordic Studies and Linguistics, University of Copenhagen. Retrieved 17 May 2022. https://nors.ku.dk/english/research/arnamagnaean/the-book-of-books/.

Borges, Jorge Luis. "The Analytical Language of John Wilkins." *Other Inquisitions*. 1952 (1937): 103. https://ccrma.stanford.edu/courses/155/assignment/ex1/Borges.pdf.

Borges, Jorge Luis. "On Exactitude in Science." In *Collected Fictions*, edited by Jorge Luis Borges, translated by Andrew Hurley. New York: Penguin Putnam, 1998.

Borges, Jorge Louis. "The Total Library." In *Selected Non-Fictions*, edited by Esther Allen, Suzanne Jill Levine, and Weinberger and translated by Eliot Weinberger. New York: Viking, 1999.

Borges, Jorge Luis. *The Library of Babel*. Translated by Andrew Hurley. Boston, MA: David R Godine Press, 2000.

Borges, Jorge Luis. *Labyrinths: Selected Stories & Other Writings*. Vol. 1066. New York, NY: New Directions Publishing, 2007.

Brasseur, Lee. "Florence Nightingale's Visual Rhetoric in the Rose Diagrams." *Technical Communication Quarterly* 14, no. 2 (2005).

Breen, Richard, and Walter Müller. *Education and Intergenerational Social Mobility in Europe and the United States*. Stanford CA: Stanford University Press, 2020.

Brewer, Graham Lee. "Lakota Elders Helped a White Man Preserve Their Language. Then He Tried to Sell It Back to Them." *NBC News*, 3 June 2022.

"A Brief History of Crowdsourcing [Infographic]." *Crowdsourcing.org*. 18 March 2012. Archived from the original on 3 July 2015.

Briet, Suzanne, and Laurent Martinet. *What Is Documentation?: English Translation of the Classic French Text*. Lanham, MD: Scarecrow Press, 2006.

Browne, Simone. "Dark Matters." In *Dark Matters*. Durham, NC: Duke University Press, 2015: 104.

Brumm, Adam, Adhi Agus Oktaviana, Basran Burhan, Budianto Hakim, Rustan Lebe, Jian-xin Zhao, Priyatno Hadi Sulistyarto et al. "Oldest Cave Art Found in Sulawesi." *Science Advances* 7, no. 3 (2021). https://doi.org/10.1126/sciadv.abd4648

Buckland, Michael K. "Information as Thing." *Journal of the American Society for information science* 42, no. 5 (1991a): 351–360; and Buckland, Information Society, p. 22.

Buckland, Michael K. "Information Retrieval of More Than Text." *Journal of the American Society for Information Science* 42, no. 8 (1991b): 586–588.

Buckland, Michael K. "A Brief Biography of Suzanne Renée Briet." *Science* 42, no. 5 (1991b): 351–60.

Buckland, Michael K. "Emanuel Goldberg, Electronic Document Retrieval, and Vannevar Bush's Memex." *Journal of the American Society for Information Science* 43, no. 4 (1992): 284–294.

Buckland, Michael K. "What Is a 'Document'?" *Journal of the American Society for Information Science* 48, no. 9 (1997): 805.

Buckland, Michael K. "Histories, Heritages, and the Past: The Case of Emanuel Goldberg." In *The History and Heritage of Scientific and Technical Information Systems*, edited by W. B. Rayward and M. E. Bowden. Medford, NJ: Information Today, 2004: 39–45.

Buckland, Michael. *Information and Society*. Cambridge, MA: MIT Press, 2017.

Burke, Heather, and Claire Smith. "Timeline." In *Kennewick: Perspectives on the Ancient One*, edited by Heather Burke, Dorothy Lippert, Claire Smith, Joe Watkins, and Larry Zimmerman. Walnut Creek, CA: Left Coast Press, 2008.

Burrage, Rachel L., Sandra L. Momper, and Joseph P. Gone. "Beyond Trauma: Decolonizing Understandings of Loss and Healing in the Indian Residential School System of Canada." *Journal of Social Issues* 78, no. 1 (2022): 27–52.

Burt, Laura. "Vivian Harsh, Adult Education, and the Library's Role as Community Center." *Libraries & the Cultural Record* 44, no. 2 (2009): 234–255.

Bush, Vannevar. "As We May Think." *The Atlantic Monthly* 176, no. 1 (1945): 101–108.

Bush, Vannevar. "We Are in Danger of Building a Tower of Babel." *Public Health Reports* 68, no. 2 (1953): 149.

Busse, Timothy J. "Crossing the Digital Rubicon: Google Books and the Dawn of an Electronic Literature Revolution." *Houston Business and Tax Law Journal* 18 (2018): 121–149.

Cadwalladr, Carol. "Are the Robots About to Rise? Google's New Director of Engineering Thinks So." *The Guardian*, 22 February 2014.

Card, Stuart K., Thomas P. Moran, and Allen Newell. *The Psychology of Human-Computer Interaction*. Boca Raton, FL: CRC Press, 1983.

Carroll, Lewis. *Sylvie and Bruno Concluded*. London: Macmillan, 1894.

Cassino, Daniel, and Peter Wooley. "Some News Leaves People Knowing Less." *Farleigh Dickinson University Public Mind Poll*, November 21, 2011.

Cassioli, Federico, Giulia Fronda, and Michela Balconi. "Human–Co-Bot Interaction and Neuroergonomics: Co-Botic vs. Robotic Systems." *Frontiers in Robotics and AI* 8 (2021): 659319.

Casson, Lionel. *Libraries in the Ancient World*. New Haven, CT: Yale University Press, 2001.

Cat Zakrzewski. "Facebook Whistleblower Alleges Executives Misled Investors about Climate, Covid Hoaxes in New SEC Complaint." *The Washington Post*, 18 February 2022.

Cataloging Policy and Support Office. "Library of Congress Subject Headings Pre- vs. Post-Coordination and Related Issues: Report for Beacher Wiggins, Director, Acquisitions & Bibliographic Access Directorate." Library Services, Library of Congress, 2007: 1.

Cernat, Vasile. "Roma Undercount and the Issue of Undeclared Ethnicity in the 2011 Romanian Census." *International Journal of Social Research Methodology* 24, no. 6 (2021): 761–766.

Chan, Anita. "Big Data Interfaces and the Problem of Inclusion." *Media, Culture & Society* 37, no. 7 (2015): 1078–1083.

Chandler, Chris, host, "Where Did IA Go? With Donna Spencer." *UX Radio* (podcast), 4 March 2021. http://ux-radio.com/2021/03/where-did-ia-go -with-donna-spencer/.

Charr, Manuel. "How Are Museums Using Chatbots?" *Museum Next*, 14 September 2019.

Chen, Can, and Sukumar Ganapati. "Do Transparency Mechanisms Reduce Government Corruption? A Meta-Analysis." *International Review of Administrative Sciences* (2021): 00208523211033236.

Chen, Sibo. "The Materialist Circuits and the Quest for Environmental Justice in ICT's Global Expansion." *tripleC: Communication, Capitalism & Critique. Open Access Journal for a Global Sustainable Information Society* 14, no. 1 (2016): 121–131.

"Christopher Columbus' Son Had an Enormous Library. Its Catalog Was Just Found." *All Things Considered. National Public Radio.* 24 April 2019.

Chou, Rose L., Annie Pho, and Charlotte Roh. *Pushing the Margins: Women of Color and Intersectionality in LIS.* Sacramento, CA: Library Juice Press, 2018.

Clark, Shawn and Ruth Wylie. "Surviving a Cultural Genocide: Perspectives of Indigenous Elders on the Transfer of Traditional Values." *Journal of Ethnic and Cultural Studies* 8, no. 2 (2021): 316–346.

Colón-Aguirre, Mónica, and Janet Ceja Alcalá. "Everyday Information Practices of Migrant Latinas Living in Boston." In *Social Justice Design and Implementation in Library and Information Science,* edited by Bharat Mehra. London: Routledge, 2021, 116–132.

Condon, Margarte M., and Elizabeth M. Hallam. "Government Printing of the Public Records in the Eighteenth Century." *Journal of the Society of Archivists* 7, no. 6 (1984): 348–388.

Connolly, Nuala, and Claire McGuinness. "Towards Digital Literacy for the Active Participation and Engagement of Young People in a Digital World." *Young People in a Digitalised World* 4 (2018): 77.

"Constitution of the Republic of Ecuador." *Political Database of the Americas.* Retrieved 19 May 2022. https://pdba.georgetown.edu/Constitutions/ Ecuador/english08.html.

Cook, Edward Tyas. *The Life of Florence Nightingale*, Vol. 1. London: Macmillan, 1913.

Cooke, Nicole A., Renate Chancellor, Yasmeen Shorish, Sarah Park Dahlen, and Amelia Gibson. "Once More for Those in the Back: Libraries Are Not Neutral." *Publishers Weekly.* 10 June 2022;

Cox, Andrew M. "Learning Bodies: Sensory Experience in the Information Commons." *Library & Information Science Research* 41, no. 1 (2019): 58–66.

Culliford, Elizabeth. "Rohingya Refugees Sue Facebook for $150 Billion over Myanmar Violence." Reuters, 8 December 2021.

Cutter, Charles Ammi. "The Buffalo Public Library in 1983." In *Papers and Proceedings of the Sixth General Meeting of the American Library Association, Held at Buffalo, August 14 to 17, 1883*. Press of Rockwell and Churchill, 1883, 49–55.

Cutter, Charles Ammi. *Expansive Classification: Part I: The First Six Classifications*. C. A. Cutter, 1891–93.

Cy. Jillian Weise. "How a Cyborg Challenges Reality." *The New York Times*, 22 June 2022. https://www.nytimes.com/2022/06/22/special-series/cyborgs-reality-identity.html. Retrieved 22 September 2022.

Dali, Keren. "The Lifeways We Avoid: The Role of Information Avoidance in Discrimination against People with Disabilities." *Journal of Documentation* 74, no. 6 (2018): 1258–1273.

"Dali Lives." Retrieved 18 June 2022. https://thedali.org/exhibit/dali-lives/.

Darch, Peter T. "Managing the Public to Manage Data: Citizen Science and Astronomy." *arXiv preprint arXiv:1703.00037* (2017): 27.

"Darwin Core." *Taxonomic Databases Working Group*. Retrieved 21 May 2022. https://www.tdwg.org/community/dwc/.

Davis, Charles H., and Debora Shaw, editors. *Introduction to Information Science and Technology*. Medford, NJ: American Society for Information Science and Technology, 2011.

de León, Kevin (@kdeleon). *Twitter*. 28 August 2020a. https://twitter.com/kdeleon/status/1299386969873461248.

de León, Kevin (@kdeleon). *Twitter*. 28 August 2020b. https://pic.twitter.com/iJPXvcxsLQ.

De Solla Price, Derek J. "An Ancient Greek Computer." *Scientific American* 200, no. 6 (1959): 60–67.

De Solla Price, Derek. "Gears from the Greeks." *Journal for the History of Astronomy* 8 (1977): 143.

Deene, Joris. "The Influence of the Statute of Anne on Belgian Copyright Law." In *Global Copyright*. Cheltenham: Edward Elgar Publishing, 2010.

Delbert, Caroline. "Beethoven Never Finished His Last Symphony. Can Robots Complete the Job?" *Popular Mechanics*, 18 December 2019.

Diesner, Jana. "Small Decisions with Big Impact on Data Analytics." *Big Data & Society* 2, no. 2 (2015): 2053951715617185.

"Digital Einstein Experience." Retrieved 18 June 2022. https://einstein.digitalhumans.com/.

"Dive into Intangible Cultural Heritage!" *UNESCO Intangible Cultural Heritage*. Retrieved 11 June 2022. https://ich.unesco.org/en/dive.

"The Doctrine of Discovery, 1943." The Gilder Lehrman Institute of American History. Retrieved 17 May 2022. https://www.gilderlehrman.org/history-resources/spotlight-primary-source/doctrine-discovery-1493.

Dolata, Mateusz, and Kiram Ben Aleya. "Morphological Analysis for Design Science Research: The Case of Human-Drone Collaboration in Emergencies." In *International Conference on Design Science Research in Information Systems and Technology*, edited by Andreas Drechsler, Aurona Gerber, Alan Hevner. Springer, 2022, 17–29.

Dong, XinQi, E-Shien Chang, Melissa Simon, and Esther Wong. "Sustaining Community-University Partnerships: Lessons Learned from a Participatory Research Project with Elderly Chinese." *Gateways: International Journal of Community Research and Engagement* 4 (2011): 31–47.

Dossey, Barbara Montgomery. *Florence Nightingale: Mystic, Visionary, Reformer.* Springhouse, PA: Lippincott, Williams, and Wilkins, 2000: 74. Cited by Brasseur, "Florence," 162.

Douglas, Jennifer. "Origins and Beyond: The Ongoing Evolution of Archival Ideas about Provenance." *Currents of Archival Thinking* 2 (2017): 25–52.

Dreazen, Yochi. "The Brazen Bibliophiles of Timbuktu: How a Sneaky Team of Librarians Duped Al Qaeda." *The New Republic*, 2013.

Duchesneau, Michel. "Gallica: The Online Digital Library of the Bibliothèque nationale de France." *Nineteenth-Century Music Review* 11, no. 2 (2014): 337–347.

Dzhambazova, Boryana. "Welcome to Bulgaria, Where the Ukraine War Is NATO's Fault." *Politico.* 8 June 2022. https://www.politico.eu/article/bulgaria-ukraine-russia-war-nato-fault/.

Edmunds, Michael, and Tony Freeth. "Using Computation to Decode the First Known Computer." *Computer* 44, no. 7 (2011): 32.

Edunov, Sergey, Carlos Diuk, Ismail Onur Filiz, Smriti Bhagat, and Moira Burke. "Three and a Half Degrees of Separation." *Research at Facebook* (blog) 694, February 4, 2016. https://research.fb.com/three-and-a-half-degrees-of-separation/. Retrieved 9 September 2022.

Elgammal, Ahmed. "How Artificial Intelligence Completed Beethoven's Unfinished Tenth Symphony." *Smithsonian Magazine*, 24 September 2021.

Elisha, Ety, Josh Guetzkow, Yaffa Shir-Raz, and Natti Ronel. "Retraction of Scientific Papers: The Case of Vaccine Research." *Critical Public Health* 32, no. 4 (2022): 533–542.

Emanuel, Ryan E., and David E. Wilkins. "Breaching Barriers: The Fight for Indigenous Participation in Water Governance." *Water* 12, no. 8 (2020): (2113).

Evans, David K., Maryam Akmal, and Pamela Jakiela. "Gender Gaps in Education: The Long View." *IZA, Journal of Development and Migration* 12, no. 1 (2021): 27.

Faciejew, Michael and Ricardo Roque. "The Violence of Collections."
22 Sep 2021. *The Order of Multitudes Atlas Encyclopedia*. https://orderofm
.com/conversation/the-violence-of-collections/

Fallis, Don, Jonathan Furner, Kay Mathiesen, and Allen Renear. "Philosophy
and Information Science: The Basics." In *Proceedings of the American Society
for Information Science and Technology* 43, no. 1 (2006): 1–4.

Fass, Craig, Mike Ginelli, and Brian Turtle. *Six Degrees of Kevin Bacon*. New
York, NY: Plume Books, 1996.

Faizi, Fatima, "Afghan Students Run Underground Book Club to Keep
Dreams Alive." *Al Jazeera*, 9 May 2022.

Fenlon, Katrina, Megan Senseney, Maria Bonn, and Janet Swatscheno.
"Humanities Scholars and Library-Based Digital Publishing: New Forms
of Publication, New Audiences, New Publishing Roles." *Journal of Scholarly
Publishing* 50, no. 3 (2019): 159–182.

Fernández, José María Pérez, and Edward Wilson-Lee. *Hernando Colon's New
World of Books: Toward a Cartography of Knowledge*. New Haven, CT: Yale
University Press, 2021.

Fincke, Jeanette C. "The British Museum's Ashurbanipal Library Project."
*Iraq* 66 (2004): 55–60.

Fiormonte, Domenico, Sukanta Chaudhuri, and Paola Ricaurte, eds.
*Global Debates in the Digital Humanities*. Minneapolic, MN: University of
Minnesota Press, 2022.

fitzNigel, Richard, translator. Dialogus de Scaccario. In *The Dialogue of
the Exchequer*, edited by Emilie Amt and S.D. Church. Oxford: Oxford
University Press, 2007.

Flanders, Julia, and Elli Mylonas. "Digital Humanities." *Encyclopedia of Library
and Information Sciences*, edited by Marcia J. Bates and Mary Niles Maack.
Boca Raton, FL: CRC Press, 2017, 1286–1297.

Floridi, Luciano. *The Philosophy of Information*. Oxford: Oxford University
Press, 2013.

Fölster, Max Jakob. "Libraries and Archives in the Former Han Dynasty
(206 BCE–9 CE): Arguing for a Distinction." In *Manuscripts and Archives:
Comparative Views on Record-Keeping*, edited by Sabine Kienitz, Michael
Friedrich, Christian Brockmann and Alessandro Bausi. Berlin: de Gruyter,
2018, 201–230.

Ford, Anne. "Bringing Harassment out of the History Books." *American
Libraries* 49, no. 6 (2018).

Forrest, Anne, David Fazio, Jamie Knight, Tim Harshbarger, Jeanine
Lineback, Sandeep Tirumangalam, Birkir Gunnarsson, Laura Goslin
(moderator). *Virtual Panel: How Persons with Disabilities Use the Web*. Deque
Systems, Inc., 2017. https://accessibility.deque.com/on-demand-how
-persons-with-disabilities-use-the-web.

Foucault, Michel. *The Order of Things.* London: Routledge, 2005.

Fowler, Geoffrey. "How Does Google's Monopoly Hurt You?" *The Washington Post*, 20 October 2020.

Fränti, Pasi, Sami Sieranoja, Katja Wikström, and Tiina Laatikainen. "Clustering Diagnoses From 58 Million Patient Visits in Finland between 2015 and 2018." *JMIR Medical Informatics* 10, no. 5 (2022): e35422.

Freeth, Tony, Alexander Jones, John M. Steele, and Yanis Bitsakis. "Calendars with Olympiad Display and Eclipse Prediction on the Antikythera Mechanism." *Nature* 454, no. 7204 (2008): 614–617.

Freeth, Tony, Yanis Bitsakis, Xenophon Moussas, John H. Seiradakis, Agamemnon Tselikas, Helen Mangou, Mary Zafeiropoulou et al. "Decoding the Ancient Greek Astronomical Calculator Known as the Antikythera Mechanism." *Nature* 444, no. 7119 (2006): 587.

Freeth, Tony. "An Ancient Greek Astronomical Calculation Machine Reveals New Secrets." *Scientific American*, 1 January 2022.

Freeth, Tony. "Building the Cosmos in the Antikythera Mechanism." *Proceedings of Science* 170 Antikythera and SKA, (2013): 1–16. https://doi.org/10.22323/1.170.0018.

Furner, Jonathan. "Definitions of 'Metadata': A Brief Survey of International Standards." *Journal of the Association for Information Science and Technology* 71, no. 6 (2020): E33–E42.

Gadbury, Matt, and H. Chad Lane. "Mining for STEM Interest Behaviors in Minecraft." In *International Conference on Artificial Intelligence in AI*, edited by Maria Mercedes Rodrigo, Noburu Matsuda, Alexandra I. Cristea and Vania Dimitrova, 236–239. Cham: Springer, 2022.

Gainer, Kim D. "Fair Use and Digitization: Google Prevails in the Latest Court Ruling." *The CCCC-IP Annual: Top Intellectual Property Developments of 2013*, edited by Ratliff, Clancy (2014): 37. https://escholarship.org/uc/item/6ng4h3mj. Retrieved 22 September 2022.

Gamsu, Sol. "Why Are Some Children Worth More Than Others? The Private-State School Funding Gap in England." In *Common-Wealth Thinktank*. Durham University, 2021. https://www.common-wealth.co.uk/reports/why-are-some-children-worth-more-than-others.

Gardner, Sue. "Nine Reasons Women Don't Edit Wikipedia (in Their Own Words)." *Sue Gardner's Blog*. 19 February 2011. https://suegardner.org/2011/02/19/nine-reasons-why-women-dont-edit-wikipedia-in-their-own-words/.

Gary, Jesse. "Photo of Girls Using Taco Bell Wifi Become Symbol of Digital Divide." KTVU FOX, 31 August 2020. https://www.ktvu.com/news/photo-of-girls-using-taco-bell-wifi-becomes-symbol-of-digital-divide.

Gaubert, Julie. "After More Than Two Centuries, Beethoven's 10th Symphony Has Been Completed by an AI." *EuroNews.next*, 14 October 2021.

Gebru, Timnit and Margaret Mitchell. "We Warned Google That People Might Believe AI Was Sentient. Now It's Happening." *The Washington Post*, 17 June 2022.

"Gender Bias on Wikipedia." *Wikipedia*. Retrieved 29 May 2022. https://en .wikipedia.org/wiki/Gender_bias_on_Wikipedia.

Georgia, Wells, Jeff Horwitz and Deepa Seetharaman, "Facebook Knows Instagram Is Toxic for Teen Girls, Company Documents Show." *Wall Street Journal*, September 14, 2021.

Gerdon, Frederic, Helen Nissenbaum, Ruben L. Bach, Frauke Kreuter, and Stefan Zins. "Individual Acceptance of Using Health Data for Private and Public Benefit: Changes during the COVID-19 Pandemic." *Harvard Data Science Review, Special Issue 1: COVID-19: Unprecedented Challenges and Chances* (2021).

Giannoumis, G. Anthony and Michael Ashley Stein. "Conceptualizing Universal Design for the Information Society through a Universal Human Rights Lens." *International Human Rights Law Review* 8, no. 1 (2019): 38–66.

Goldstein, Dana. "Two States. Eight Textbooks. Two American Stories." *The New York Times*, 12 January 2020.

Gong, S., Loy, C. C., & Xiang, T. "Security and Surveillance." In *Visual Analysis of Humans*. Cham: Springer, 2011: 455–472.

"Google Search | Overview." Retrieved 15 June 2022. https://www.google .com/search/howsearchworks/.

Graham, Sarah. "Scientists Win Latest Ruling in Kennewick Man Case." *Scientific American*. 6 February 2004.

Granovetter, Mark S. "The Strength of Weak Ties." *American Journal of Sociology* 78, no. 6 (1973): 1360–1380.

Gray, LaVerne. "Naomi Willie Pollard Dobson: A Pioneering Black Librarian." *Libraries: Culture, History, and Society* 6, no. 1 (2022): 1–20.

Green, Sara Jean. "'A Wrong Had Finally Been Righted': Tribes Bury Remains of Ancient Ancestor Known as Kennewick Man." *Seattle Times*, 19 February 2017.

Greitens, S. C. "Dealing with Demand for China's Global Surveillance Exports." Brookings Institution Global China Report (2020).

Greitens, S. C. "Surveillance, Security, and Liberal Democracy in the Post-COVID World." *International Organization*, 74(S1) (2020): E169–E190.

Grigar, Dene. "Challenges to Archiving and Documenting Born-Digital Literature: What Scholars, Archivists, and Librarians Need to Know." *Electronic Literature as Digital Humanities: Contexts, Forms, and Practices*, edited by Dene Grigar and James O'Sullivan (2021): 237–245.

Guerrini, Christi J., Mary A. Majumder, Meaganne J. Lewellyn, and Amy L. McGuire. "Citizen Science, Public Policy." *Science* 361, no. 6398 (2018): 134–136.

Gundaker, Grey. "Hidden Education among African Americans during Slavery." *Teachers College Record* 109, no. 7 (2007): 1591–1612.

Guo, Jinchi, and Jie Huang. "Information Literacy Education during the Pandemic: The Cases of Academic Libraries in Chinese Top Universities." *Journal of Academic Librarianship* 47, no. 4 (2021): 102363.

Gupta, Aditi, Sarbjit Kaur Randhawa, and In-In Po. "Reading Habits, Library Perceptions and Library Usage of the South Asian Population in British Columbia, Canada." *Public Library Quarterly* 41, no. 5 (2021): 456–484.

Gupta, Meghanlata. "Regaining Control: Indigenous-Owned and Operated Archives." Retrieved 11 June 2022. https://indiancountrytoday.com/news/regaining-control-indigenous-owned-and-operated-archives.

Hammer, Joshua. "The Brave Sage of Timbuktu: Abdel Kader Haidara." *The Innovators Project. National Geographic.* 2014. https://www.nationalgeographic.com/culture/article/140421-haidara-timbuktu-manuscripts-mali-library-conservation.

Hansson, Joacim. *Educating Librarians in the Contemporary University: An Essay on iSchools and Emancipatory Resilience in Library and Information Science.* Sacramento, CA: Library Juice Press, 2019.

Hapke, Thomas. "Wilhelm Ostwald, 'The 'Brücke" (Bridge), and Connections to Other Bibliographic Activities at the Beginning of the Twentieth Century." *Information Today*, 29, no. 4, 1999: 142.

Harding, Luke and Harriet Sherwood. "Ukrainians in Race to Save Cultural Heritage." *The Guardian*, 9 March 2022.

Hargittai, Eszter; Walejko, Gina; Gina Walejko. "The Participation Divide: Content Creation and Sharing in the Digital Age." *Information, Communication & Society* 11, no. 2 (2008): 20.

Hasinoff, Amy Adele, and Tamara Shepherd. "Sexting in Context: Privacy Norms and Expectations." *International Journal of Communication* 8 (2014): 24.

Haunui-Thompson, Shannon. "Whanganui to Gain Legal Personhood." *New Zealand Radio.* 16 March 2017.

Heer, J., M. Bostock and V. Ogievetsky. "A Tour through the Visualization Zoo." *ACM Queue* (2010) 53(6), 59–67.

Heitlinger, Sara, Lara Houston, Alex Taylor, and Ruth Catlow. "Algorithmic Food Justice: Co-Designing More-Than-Human Blockchain Futures for the Food Commons." In *Proceedings of the 2021 CHI Conference on Human Factors in Computing Systems* (2021): 1–17. https://doi.org/10.1145/3411764.3445655.

Helen, Nissenbaum. "Shaping the Web: Why the Politics of Search Engines Matters." *The Information Society* 16 (3) (2000): 169–185.

Helton, Laura E. "On Decimals, Catalogs, and Racial Imaginaries of Reading." *PMLA* 134, no. 1 (2019): 105.

Henry, Ella, and Hone Pene. "Kaupapa Maori: Locating Indigenous Ontology, Epistemology and Methodology in the Academy." *Organization* 8, no. 2 (2001): 234–242.

Herbrechter, Stefan, and Ivan Callus. *Cy-Borges: Memories of the Posthuman in the Work of Jorge Luis Borges.* Lewisburg, PA: Bucknell University Press, 2009.

Hermon, P. and H.C. Relyea, "Information Policy." In *Encyclopedia of library and information science.* New York: Marcel Dekker, Inc., 2003.

Herring, Susan C., J. Reagle, Justine Cassell, Terri Oda, Anna North, J. West, and M. Ranga. "Where Are the Women in Wikipedia." *The New York Times* (February 2, 2011). https://www.nytimes.com/roomfordebate/2011/02/02/where-are-the-women-in-wikipedia. Retrieved 22 September, 2022.

Higgins, Sarah. "Digital Curation: The Development of a Discipline within Information Science." *Journal of Documentation* 74, no. 6, (2018). https://doi.org/10.1108/JD-02-2018-0024.

Hill, Sharon. "U of W Prof Gets 'Indiana Jones Feeling' with Discovery of Historic Manuscript." *Windsor Star,* 12 April 2019.

Hinchcliffe, L. J. "From Paywall to Datawall." *The Scholarly Kitchen* (2018). https://scholarlykitchen.sspnet.org/2018/10/11/from-paywall-to-datawall/.

Hjørland, Birger, and Hanne Albrechtsen. "Toward a New Horizon in Information Science: Domain-Analysis." *Journal of the American Society for Information Science* 46, no. 6 (1995): 400–425.

Hjørland, Birger. "Knowledge Organization (KO)." *KO Knowledge Organization* 43, no. 6 (2016): 475–484.

Hoiem, Elizabeth Massa. "The Progress of Sugar: Consumption as Complicity in Children's Books about Slavery and Manufacturing, 1790–2015." *Children's Literature in Education,* 52, no. 2 (2021): 162–182.

Holroyd, Carin. "Digital Content Promotion in Japan and South Korea: Government Strategies for an Emerging Economic Sector." *Asia & the Pacific Policy Studies* 6, no. 3 (2019): 290–307.

Hopping, David. "Modeling Hope: Boundary Objects and Design Patterns in a Heartland Heterotopia." In *Deciding Where to Live: Information Studies on Where to Live in America,* edited by Ocepek, Melissa G., and William Aspray. Lanham, MD: Rowman & Littlefield, 2020: 211–235.

Houston, Ronald D. and Glynn Harmon. "Vannevar Bush and Memex." *Annual Review of Information Science and Technology* 41, no. 1 (2007): 55–92.

"How Google Search Organizes Information." Retrieved 28 May 2022. https://www.google.com/search/howsearchworks/how-search-works/organizing-information/.

Hughes, Sallie, and Yulia Vorobyeva. "Explaining the Killing of Journalists in the Contemporary Era: The Importance of Hybrid Regimes and Subnational Variations." *Journalism* 22, no. 8 (2021): 1873–1891.

Huttunen, Aira, Lottamari Kähkönen, Heidi Enwald, and Terttu Kortelainen. "Embodied Cognition and Information Experiences of Transgender People." *Information Research* 24 no. 4 (2019). http://InformationR.net/ir/24-4/colis/colis1940.html. Retrieved 22 September 2022.

Huybrechts, Liesbeth, Henric Benesch, and Jon Geib. "Co-Design and the Public Realm." *CoDesign* 13, no. 3 (2017): 145–147.

Ibekwe-Sanjuan, Fidelia. "Whither Information Science in France?" In *International Perspectives on the History of Information Science and Technology*. Baltimore, MD: Association of the American Society for Information Science and Technology, 2012: 83–95.

"IFLA Statement on Privacy in the Library Environment." International Federation of Library Associations and Institutions. Retrieved 4 June 2022. https://www.ifla.org/publications/ifla-statement-on-privacy-in-the-library-environment/.

"Indigenous Peoples and Local Communities Portal." *WIPO*. https://www.wipo.int/tk/en/indigenous/. Retrieved 2 June 2022.

"International Council of Museums | About." *ICOM*. https://icom.museum/en/about-us/. Retrieved 10 June 2022.

"International Press Institute." Retrieved 3 June 2022. https://ipi.media/.

"Internet Hall of Fame Pioneer: J.C.R. Licklider." *Internet Hall of Fame*. https://www.internethalloffame.org/inductees/jcr-licklider. Retrieved 14 June 2022.

Isopahkala-Bouret, Ulpukka, Mikael Börjesson, Dennis Beach, Nina Haltia, Jón Torfi Jónasson, Annukka Jauhiainen, Arto Jauhiainen, Sonja Kosunen, Hanna Nori, and Agnete Vabø. "Access and Stratification in Nordic Higher Education. A Review of Cross-Cutting Research Themes and Issues." *Education Inquiry* 9, no. 1 (2018): 142–154.

Jacobs, Margaret D. "Indian Boarding Schools in Comparative Perspective: The Removal of Indigenous Children in the United States and Australia, 1880–1940." Digital Commons at the University of Nebraska, Lincoln (2006). https://digitalcommons.unl.edu/historyfacpub/20/.

James Murdoch, Mark Bauerlein, Marie Halverson; Natalie Morrissey; and Esther Galadima. "How Do We Read? Let's Count the Ways: Comparing Digital, Audio, and Print-Only Readers." *National Endowment for the Arts Report* (2020): 16. https://www.arts.gov/sites/default/files/How%20Do%20We%20Read%20report%202020.pdf. Retrieved 23 September 2022.

Justin Wm, Moyer. "Fighting Racial Bias with an Unlikely Weapon: Footnotes." *The Washington Post*, 18 January 2022.

Kamran, Qeis, and Berit Schumann. "Towards an Effective Rapprochement between Artificial Intelligence and Medical and Pharmaceutical Research." *Modern Approaches in Drug Designing* 3, no. 4 (2022): 1–4.

Karen, Hao, "The Facebook Whistleblower Says Its Algorithms Are Dangerous. Here's Why." *MIT Technology Review*. Retrieved 7 June 2022. https://canvas.illinois.edu/courses/16422/discussion_topics/125024.

Karinthy, Frigyes. "Chain-links." In *Everything Is Different*. Translated by Adam Makkai. Edited by Enikö Jankó. Public Domain, http://vadeker.net /articles/Karinthy-Chain-Links_1929.pdf. Retrieved 22 September 2022. Figyes Karinthy, "Láncszemek," in Minden másképpen van" (Budapest: Atheneum Irodalmi és Nyomdai R.-T, 1929): 85–91.

Kelly, Diann Cameron, and Rani Varghese. "Four Contexts of Institutional Oppression: Examining the Experiences of Blacks in Education, Criminal Justice and Child Welfare." *Journal of Human Behavior in the Social Environment* 28, no. 7 (2018): 874–888.

Kennan, Mary Anne, and Jessie Lymn. "Where Is the I(nformation) in GLAM? Education, Knowledge and Skill Requirements of Professionals Working in GLAM Sector Institutions." *Journal of the Australian Library and Information Association* 68, no. 3 (2019): 236–253.

Khademian, Mahdi, and Morteza Kokabi. "Library Thing Social Tags versus Library of Congress Subject Headings: A Literature Review." *Library and Information Science Research* 8, no. 1 (2018): 313–335.

Khalil, Ashraf, Soha Glal Ahmed, Asad Masood Khattak, and Nabeel Al-Qirim. "Investigating Bias in Facial Analysis Systems: A Systematic Review." *IEEE Access* 8 (2020): 130751–130761.

Kimmerer, Robin. *Braiding Sweetgrass: Indigenous Wisdom, Scientific Knowledge and the Teachings of Plants*. Minneapolis, MN: Milkweed editions, 2013: 208.

Kirchhoff, Thomas, Werner Schweibenz, and Jörn Sieglerschmidt. "Archives, Libraries, Museums and the Spell of Ubiquitous Knowledge." *Archival Science* 8, no. 4 (2008): 256.

Kline, Ronald R. "What Is Information Theory a Theory of? Boundary Work among Information Theorists and Information Scientists in the United States and Britain during the Cold War." In *The History and Heritage of Scientific and Technological Information Systems*, edited by W.B. Rayward and M.E. Bowden. Medford: NJ: American Society of Information Science and Technology and the Chemical Heritage Foundation, 2004: 15–28.

Knowlton, Steven A. "Three Decades since Prejudices and Antipathies: A Study of Changes in the Library of Congress Subject Headings." *Cataloging & Classification Quarterly* 40, no. 2 (2005): 123–145.

Knox, Emily J.M. "Opposing Censorship in Difficult Times." *The Library Quarterly* 87, no. 3 (2017).

Knox, Emily J.M. *Book Banning in 21st-Century America*. Lanham, MD: Rowman & Littlefield, 2015.

Kochen, Manfred and Ithiel da Sola Pool. "Contacts and Influences." *Social Networks* 1 (1978): 5–51.

Kokshagina, Olga. "Open Covid-19: Organizing an Extreme Crowdsourcing Campaign to Tackle Grand Challenges." *R&D Management* 52, no. 2 (2022): 206–219.

Kostka, Genia, Léa Steinacker, and Miriam Meckel. "Between Security and Convenience: Facial Recognition Technology in the Eyes of Citizens in China, Germany, the United Kingdom, and the United States." *Public Understanding of Science* 30, no. 6 (2021): 671–690.

Kramer, Jessica M., John C. Kramer, Edurne García-Iriarte, and Joy Hammel. "Following through to the End: The Use of Inclusive Strategies to Analyse and Interpret Data in Participatory Action Research with Individuals with Intellectual Disabilities." *Journal of Applied Research in Intellectual Disabilities* 24, no. 3 (2011): 263–273.

Kuhlthau, Carol C. "Inside the Search Process: Information Seeking from the User's Perspective." *Journal of the American Society for Information Science* 42, no. 5 (1991): 361–371.

La Barre, Kathryn. "Facet Analysis." *Annual Review of Information Science and Technology* 44, no. 1 (2010): 243.

Lahti, Leo, Jani Marjanen, Hege Roivainen, and Mikko Tolonen. "Bibliographic Data Science and the History of the Book (c. 1500–1800)." *Cataloging & Classification Quarterly* 57, no. 1 (2019): 5–23.

Lancaster, F. W. *Indexing and Abstracting in Theory and Practice.* 2nd ed. Champaign, IL: University of Illinois Graduate School of Library and Information Science, 1998.

Lauren, Poole. "Bromley's Model of the Antikythera Mechanism." *Powerhouse,* 1 November 2017, https://www.maas.museum/inside-the-collection/2017/11/01/bromleys-model-of-the-antikythera-mechanism/.

Lawrimore, Erin. "Margaret Cross Norton: Defining and Redefining Archives and the Archival Profession." *Libraries & the Cultural Record* 44, no. 2 (2009): 186.

Le Deuff, Olivier, and Arthur Perret. "Hyperdocumentation: Origin and Evolution of a Concept." *Journal of Documentation* 75, no. 6 (2019): 6.

Leazer, Gregory H., and Robert Montoya. "The Politics of Knowledge Organization: Introduction to the Special Issue." *Knowledge Organization* 47, no. 5 (2020): 367–371.

Lee, Ronan. "Extreme Speech in Myanmar: The Role of State Media in the Rohingya Forced Migration Crisis." *International Journal of Communication* 13 (2019): 3202–3224.

Leibold, James. "Surveillance in China's Xinjiang Region: Ethnic Sorting, Coercion, and Inducement." *Journal of Contemporary China* 29, no. 121 (2020): 46–60.

"Leighton Linslade Town Council EWHC 760 (Admin)." 15 February 2019, http://www.bailii.org/ew/cases/EWHC/Admin/2019/760.html.

Lember, Heather, Suzanne Lipkin, and Richard Jung Lee. "Radical Cataloging: From Words to Action." *Urban Library Journal* 19, no. 1 (2013): 7.

Lemov, Michael R., and Nate Jones. "John Moss and the Roots of the Freedom of Information Act: Worldwide Implications." *Sw. J. Int'l L.* 24 (2018): 1.

Levie, Francoise (director). *The Man Who Wanted to Classify the World.* New York: Filmakers Library, 2004.

*Library of Babel* (website). Retrieved 17 May 2022. https://libraryofbabel.info /About.html.

Licklider, Joseph CR, and Robert W. Taylor. "The Computer as a Communication Device." *Science and Technology* 76, no. 2 (1968): 1–3.

Lin, Paul J. *A Translation of Lao-tzu's Tao Te Ching and Wang Pi's Commentary.* Ann Arbor, MI: University of Michigan Press, 2020.

Llewellyn, Clare, Laura Cram, Robin L. Hill, and Adrian Favero. "For Whom the Bell Trolls: Shifting Troll Behaviour in the Twitter Brexit Debate." *JCMS: Journal of Common Market Studies* 57, no. 5 (2019): 1148–1164.

Logan, Wayne A., and Andrew Guthrie Ferguson. "Policing Criminal Justice Data." *Minnesota Law Review 101* (2016): 541.

Longfellow, Henry Wadsworth. "Santa Filomena." *The Atlantic Monthly,* November 1857. https://www.theatlantic.com/magazine/archive/1857/11 /santa-filomena/531180/.

"Local, State, and National Laws and Constitutional Frameworks, Uganda." *Right to Nature Law Library,* Center for Democratic and Environmental Rights. https://www.centerforenvironmentalrights.org/rights-of-nature -law-library. Retrieved 19 May 2022.

"Looking at One's Self through the Eyes of Others: W. E. B. Du Bois's Photographs for the 1900 Paris Exposition." *African American Review* 34, no. 4 (Winter 2000): 581–599.

Lu, Wei, and Max Aiken. "Origins and Evolution of Chinese Writing Systems and Preliminary Counting Relationships." *Accounting History* 9, no. 3 (2004): 25–51.

Lueg, C.P. "The Missing Link: Information Behavior Research and Its Estranged Relationship with Embodiment." *Journal of the Association for Information Science and Technology,* 66(12) (2015): 2704–2707.

Luo, Lili. "Being Interdisciplinary: A Look into the Background and Experiences of iSchool Faculty Members." *LIBRES: Library and Information Science Research Electronic Journal* 23, no. 2 (2013): 1–20.

Łysak, Tomasz. "Vlogging Auschwitz: New Players in Holocaust Commemoration." *Holocaust Studies* (2021): 1–26.

Maack, Mary Niles. "The Lady and the Antelope: Suzanne Briet's Contribution to the French Documentation Movement." *Library Trends* 52 (4) (2004): 737.

Mace, Ronald L. "Universal Design in Housing." *Assistive Technology* 10, no. 1 (1998): 21–28.

Madden, Andrew D., Jared Bryson, and Joe Palimi. "Information Behavior in Pre-Literate Societies." In *New Directions in Human Information Behavior*, edited by Amanda Spink and Charles Cole. Springer, 2006: 8–9.

Madubuike-Ekwe, N. J., and Joseph N. Mbadugha. "Obstacles to the Implementation of the Freedom of Information Act, 2011 in Nigeria." *Nnamdi Azikiwe University Journal of International Law and Jurisprudence* 9, no. 2 (2018): 96–109.

Maemura, Emily, Nicholas Worby, Ian Milligan, and Christoph Becker. "If These Crawls Could Talk: Studying and Documenting Web Archives Provenance." *Journal of the Association for Information Science and Technology* 69, no. 10 (2018): 1223–1233.

Maggie, Puniewska. "Science Has a Sharing Problem." *The Atlantic*, 15 December 2014. https://www.theatlantic.com/health/archive/2014/12/scientists-have-a-sharing-problem/383061/.

Magee, Rachel M., "Teen Social Media Practices and Perceptions of Peers." *The Journal of Research on Libraries and Young Adults*, 10, no. 3 (2019): 1–121.

Magi, Trina J. "Confidentiality: Best Practices Protecting Library Patron Confidentiality: Checklist of Best Practices." https://www.ila.org/advocacy/making-your-case/privacy/confidentiality-best-practices. Retrieved 22 June 2022.

Magi, Trina J. and Martin Garnar, *Intellectual Freedom Manual*. 9th ed. Chicago, IL: American Library Association and Office for Intellectual Freedom, 2015.

Mak, Bonnie, and Julia Pollack. "The Performance and Practice of Research in a Cabinet of Curiosity: The Library's Dead Time." *Art Documentation: Journal of the Art Libraries Society of North America* 32, no. 2 (2013): 202–221.

Mak, Bonnie. "Wood Libraries: Knowing with Wood." *Caxtonian*, May–June, 2021.

Mak, Bonnie. *How the Page Matters*. Toronto: University of Toronto Press, 2011.

Māni, Dunlop. "University Academics' Claim Mātauranga Māori 'Not Science' Sparks Controversy." *Radio New Zealand*, 28 July 2021.

Mansky, Jackie. "W.E.B. Du Bois' Visionary Infographics Come Together for the First Time in Full Color." *Smithsonian Magazine*, 15 November 2018. https://www.smithsonianmag.com/history/first-time-together-and-color-book-displays-web-du-bois-visionary-infographics-180970826/.

Marmier, Auriane. "The Publication of Open Government Data." *Dance Your PhD 2022*. https://www.youtube.com/watch?v=g0pK0TZ61bY. Retrieved 4 June 2022.

Martin, Nicole. "Indigenous Rights: An Analysis of Intellectual Property Protections." *Am. U. Intell. Prop. Brief* 13 (2021): 33.

Matejka, Justin and George Fitzmaurice. "Same Stats, Different Graphs: Generating Datasets with Varied Appearance and Identical Statistics through Simulated Annealing." In *Proceedings of the 2017 CHI Conference on Human Factors in Computing Systems* (2017): 1290–1294. https://doi.org/10.1145/3025453.3025912.

Max, Roser and Esteban Ortiz-Ospina. "Literacy: Data Quality Challenges and Limitations." In *Our World in Data: Literacy*. Retrieved 31 May 2022. https://ourworldindata.org/literacy.

McDonough, Jerome P., Robert Olendorf, Matthew Kirschenbaum, Kari Kraus, Doug Reside, Rachel Donahue, Andrew Phelps, Christopher Egert, Henry Lowood, and Susan Rojo. *Preserving Virtual Worlds Final Report*. 2010. http://hdl.handle.net/2142/17097.

McDonough, Jerome Patrick. *Under Construction: The Application of a Feminist Sociology to Information Systems Design*. Berkeley, CA: University of California, 2000.

McDowell, Kate, Nicole Cooke, Janice Del Negro, Beth Patin, and Curtis Tenney. "Storytelling and/as Resilience." *Political Economy of the Information Society* (2021).

McDowell, Kate. "Paradoxes of Storytelling in Librarianship." *Journal of New Librarianship* 3 (2018): iv.

McDowell, Kate. "Storytelling Wisdom: Story, Information, and DIKW." *Journal of the Association for Information Science and Technology* 72, no. 10 (2021): 1223–1233.

McKenzie, Pete. "Can Ancient Maori Knowledge Aid Science? Ask These Freshwater Crayfish." *New York Times*, 1 June 2022.

McKitterick, David. "That Woman! Studies in Irish Bibliography: A Festschrift for Mary Paul Pollard." *The Library: The Transactions of the Bibliographical Society* 7, no. 2 (2006): 210–211.

Menking, Amanda, Ingrid Erickson, and Wanda Pratt. "People Who Can Take It: How Women Wikipedians Negotiate and Navigate Safety." *Proceedings of the 2019 CHI Conference on Human Factors in Computing Systems*, Paper No.: 472 (Glasgow, Scotland: SIGCHI 2019): 1–14. https://doi.org/10.1145/3290605.3300702.

Metcalfe, John. *Subject Classifying and Indexing of Libraries and Literature*. Sydney, NSW: Angus and Robertson, 1959.

Meyer, Eric and Sara Wachter-Boettcher. *Design for Real Life*. New York: A Book Apart, 2016.

Milgram, Stanley. "The Small World Problem." *Psychology Today* 2, no. 1 (1967): 60–67.

Miller, Jessie. "Tracking the Tracing: A Global Investigation of Privacy Issues in the Age of COVID-19." *Dartmouth Undergraduate Journal of Politics, Economics and World Affairs* 1, no. 3 (2021): 2.

Minocher, Xerxes, and Caelyn Randall. "Predictable Policing: New Technology, Old Bias, and Future Resistance in Big Data Surveillance." *Convergence* 26, no. 5–6 (2020): 1108–1124.

Mirza, Rafia, and Maura Seale. "Who Killed the World? White Masculinity and the Technocratic Library of the Future." *Topographies of Whiteness: Mapping Whiteness in Library and Information Science* 1 (2017): 172.

Mizrachi, Diane. "Undergraduates' Academic Reading Format Preferences and Behaviors." *Journal of Academic Librarianship* 41, no. 3 (2015): 301–311.

Montenegro, María. "Subverting the Universality of Metadata Standards: The TK Labels as a Tool to Promote Indigenous Data Sovereignty." *Journal of Documentation* (2019): 737.

Montesi, Michela. "Human Information Behavior during the Covid-19 Health Crisis. A Literature Review." *Library & Information Science Research* 43, no. 4 (2021): 101122.

"Monumental Broadband Legislation by Senator Lena Gonzalez and Assemblymember Cecilia Aguiar-Curry Signed into Law." 8 October 2021. https://sd33.senate.ca.gov/news/2021-10-08-monumental-broadband -legislation-senator-lena-gonzalez-and-assemblymember-cecilia.

Mote, Lionel JB. "Reasons for the Variations in the Information Needs of Scientists." *Journal of Documentation* (1962). Cited in Wilson, Human, 51.

Mueller, Jason, Genevieve Perez, "'Deepfake' Technology: Very Real Marketing Value ... and Risks." *National Law Review* (2020).

"Museum of Broken Relationships." Retrieved 24 May 2022. https:// brokenships.com/visit.

Nahotko, Marek. "Knowledge Organization Affordances in a Faceted Online Public Access Catalog (OPAC)." *Cataloging & Classification Quarterly* 60, no. 1 (2022): 86–111.

Naudé, Gabriel. *Advis pour dresser une bibliotheque.* 1627. Translated by John Evelyn as *Instructions Concerning Erecting of a Library.* London, 1661. Houghton, Mifflin at the Riverside Press, 1903.

"Native American Graves Protection and Repatriation Act." *National Park Service.* https://www.nps.gov/subjects/nagpra/index.htm. Retrieved 9 June 2022.

Nesi, Jacqueline, Taylor A. Burke, Alexandra H. Bettis, Anastasia Y. Kudinova, Elizabeth C. Thompson, Heather A. MacPherson, Kara A. Fox et al. "Social Media Use and Self-Injurious Thoughts and Behaviors: A

Systematic Review and Meta-Analysis." *Clinical psychology review* 87 (2021): 102038.

"Necessary and Proportionate. International Principles on the Application of Human Rights to Communications Surveillance." *EFF* (2014). Retrieved 22 June 2022. https://necessaryandproportionate.org/principles/.

Nightingale, Florence. "Letter from Nightingale to Queen Victoria, 1863." *Florence Nightingale Letters Collection.* University of Illinois Chicago Library Special Collections. Retrieved 24 May 2022. https://collections.carli.illinois.edu/digital/collection/uic_fnlc/id/23.

Nightingale, Florence. *A Contribution to the Sanitary History of the British Army during the Late War with Russia.* John W. Parker, 1859.

Nijdam, Elizabeth Biz. "Sami-Digital Storytelling: Survivance and Revitalization in Indigenous Digital Games." *New Media & Society* (2021). https://doi.org/10.1177/14614448211038902

Nissenbaum, Helen. "A Contextual Approach to Privacy Online." *Daedalus* 140, no. 4 (2011): 32–48.

Noble, Safiya Umoja. "Algorithms of Oppression." In *Algorithms of Oppression: How Search Engines Reinforce Racism.* New York: New York University Press, 2018.

Norman, Don. *The Design of Everyday Things: Revised and Expanded Edition.* New York, NY: Basic Books, 2013: 8–9. See also Lara Fedoroff, host, "Reflections from Design of Everyday Things, with Don Norman." *UX Radio* (podcast), 10 December 2015. http://ux-radio.com/2015/12/reflections-design-everyday-things/.

Nunes, Zita Cristina. "Remembering the Howard University Librarian Who Decolonized the Way Books Were Catalogued." *The Smithsonian Magazine,* 26 November 2018.

Nunn, Patrick D., and Nicholas J. Reid. "Aboriginal Memories of Inundation of the Australian Coast Dating from More Than 7000 Years Ago." *Australian Geographer* 47, no. 1 (2016): 11–47.

O'Connor, Karl, Saltanat Janenova, and Colin Knox. "Open Government in Authoritarian Regimes." *International Review of Public Policy* 1, no. 1: 1 (2019): 65–82.

Obermeyer, Ziad, Brian Powers, Christine Vogeli, and Sendhil Mullainathan. "Dissecting Racial Bias in an Algorithm Used to Manage the Health of Populations." *Science* 366, no. 6464 (2019): 447–453.

O'Brien, Tia. "From the Archives: Douglas Engelbart's Lasting Legacy, 1999." *Silicon Valley.com/The Mercury News,* 3 July 2013.

Ocepek, Melissa G. "Sensible Shopping: A Sensory Exploration of the Information Environment of the Grocery Store." *Library Trends* 66, no. 3 (2018): 371–394.

O'Donnell, Daniel Paul, Barbara Bordalejo, Padmini Murray Ray, Gimena del Rio Riande, and Elena González-Blanco García. "Boundary Land: Diversity as a Defining Feature of the Digital Humanities." (2016). http://dh2016.adho.org/abstracts/406.

Öhman, Carl, and Luciano Floridi. "The Political Economy of Death in the Age of Information: A Critical Approach to the Digital Afterlife Industry." *Minds and Machines* 27, no. 4 (2017): 639–662.

Oliphant, Tami. "A Case for Critical Data Studies in Library and Information Studies." *Journal of Critical Library and Information Studies* 1, no. 1 (2017). https://doi.org/10.24242/jclis.v1i1.22.

Olson, Hope A. "Difference, Culture and Change: The Untapped Potential of LCSH." *Cataloging & Classification Quarterly* 29, no. 1–2 (2000): 54–55.

Ong, Walter J. *Orality and Literacy.* London: Routledge, 2013: 10.

"Open Data." *National Museum Palace.* https://theme.npm.edu.tw/opendata/. Retrieved 20 June 2022.

"Open-GLAM: What." https://openglam.org/what/. Retrieved 24 May 2022.

"Our Charter." *Te Mana Raraunga Maori Data Sovereignty Network.* https://www.temanararaunga.maori.nz/tutohinga. Retrieved 22 June 2022.

"The Oracle of Bacon." Retrieved 26 May 2022. http://oracleofbacon.org/.

"Our Partnership with Menominee Tribal Members on the Rights of the Menominee River." *Center for Democratic and Environmental Rights.* https://www.centerforenvironmentalrights.org/news/our-partnership-with-menominee-tribal-members-on-the-rights-of-the-menominee-river. Retrieved 20 May 2022.

Ortiz, Stephanie M. "'You Can Say I Got Desensitized to It'": How Men of Color Cope with Everyday Racism in Online Gaming." *Sociological Perspectives* 62, no. 4 (2019): 572–588.

Osbourne, Sydney Godolphin. *Scutari and Its Hospitals.* Dickinson, 1855.

Ostwald, Wilhelm. "Scientific Management for Scientists." *Scientific American,* 108 (1913): 5–6.

Otlet, Paul. *Monde: Essai d'universalisme: Connaissances du monde. Sentiments du monde. Action organiste et plan du monde (Editiones Mundaneum).* D. Van Keerberghen et fils, 1935.

Papadopoulou, Lambrini, and Theodora A. Maniou. "'Lockdown' on Digital Journalism? Mapping Threats to Press Freedom during the COVID-19 Pandemic Crisis." *Digital Journalism* no. 9 (2021): 1344–1366.

"Parents of Parkland Shooting Victim Joaquin Oliver Bring Son Back Digitally in New Voting Initiative." *CBSNews.* 2 October 2020.

Patin, B., Sebastian, M., Yeon, J., Bertolini, D. and Grimm, A. "Interrupting Epistemicide: A Practical Framework for Naming, Identifying, and Ending Epistemic Injustice in the Information Professions." *Journal of the Association for Information Science and Technology* 72, no. 10 (2021): 1306–1318.

Pattison, Mary-Ann. "The Australian Joint Copying Project." *Government Publications Review* 13, no. 3 (1986): 349–353.

Peter Berger. *Invitation to Sociology*. New York, NY: Anchor Books, 1963.

Pettee, Julia. "A Classification for a Theological Library." *Library Journal* 36 (2011): 623; cited by Walker, Christopher, and Ann Copeland. "The Eye Prophetic: Julia Pettee." Libraries & *The Cultural Record* 44, no. 2 (2009): 162.

Pettee, Julia. "The Development of Authorship Entry and the Formulation of Authorship Rules as Found in the Anglo-American Code." *The Library Quarterly* 6, no. 3 (1936): 270–290.

Pichumani, Anusha. "Universal-Design Principles and Heuristic Guidelines." *UX Matters* (2000). https://www.uxmatters.com/mt/archives/2020/11/universal-design-principles-and-heuristic-guidelines.php.

Pickering, Andrew. *The Mangle of Practice: Time, Agency, and Science*. Chicago, IL: University of Chicago Press, 2010.

Pintar, Judith. "The Valley between Us: The Meta-Hodology of Racial Segregation in Milwaukee, Wisconsin." In *Deciding Where to Live: Information Studies on Where to Live in America*, edited by Ocepek, Melissa G., and William Aspray. Lanham, MD: Rowman & Littlefield Publishers, 2020: 177–210.

"Policy." World Intellectual Property Organization. https://www.wipo.int/policy/en/. Retrieved 2 June 2022.

"Pollard Collection of Children's Books Now Fully Available for Online Searching!" *The Library of Trinity College Dublin News & Alerts*, 19 February 2018. https://www.tcd.ie/library/news/pollard-collection-of-childrens-books-now-fully-available-for-online-searching/.

Povroznik, Nadezhda. "Digital History of Virtual Museums: The Transition from Analog to Internet Environment." in *Proceedings of the Digital Humanities in the Nordic Countries 5th Conference* (2020): 125–136. http://ceur-ws.org/Vol-2612/paper9.pdf. Retrieved 22 September 2022.

Price, W. Nicholson, and I. Glenn Cohen. "Privacy in the Age of Medical Big Data." *Nature Medicine* 25, no. 1 (2019): 37–43.

Pritchard, Steve J., and Alison L. Weightman. "Medline in the UK: Pioneering the Past, Present and Future." *Health Information & Libraries Journal* 22 Supplement 1 (2005): 38–44.

"Racial Bias on Wikipedia." Retrieved 19 June 2022. https://en.wikipedia.org/wiki/Racial_bias_on_Wikipedia.

Raign, Kathryn R. "Finding Our Missing Pieces—Women Technical Writers in Ancient Mesopotamia." *Journal of Technical Writing and Communication* 49, no. 3 (2019): 338–364.

Ramsey, Andrew. "X-Ray Tomography of the Antikythera Mechanism." *Proceedings of Science* 170, Antikythera and SKA (2013): 1-12. https://doi.org/10.22323/1.170.0022.

Rasmussen, Morten, Martin Sikora, Anders Albrechtsen, Thorfinn Sand Korneliussen, J. Víctor Moreno-Mayar, G. David Poznik, Christoph PE Zollikofer et al. "The Ancestry and Affiliations of Kennewick Man." *Nature* 523, no. 7561 (2015): 455–458.

Rayward, W. Boyd. "Knowledge Organisation and a New World Polity: The Rise and Fall and Rise of the Ideas of Paul Otlet." *Transnational Associations* 55, no. 1–2 (2003): 4–15.

"Relentless Doppelganger." *Dadabots*, 4 September 2019. https://www.youtube.com/watch?v=MwtVkPKx3RA.

Rico, Christophe. "The Destruction of the Library of Alexandria: A Reassessment." In *The Library of Alexandria: A Cultural Crossroads of the Ancient World*, edited by Christopher Rico and Anca Dan. Jerusalem: Polis Institute Press, 2017: 330.

Rieder, Bernhard. *Engines of Order: A Mechanology of Algorithmic Techniques.* Amsterdam: Amsterdam University Press, 2020.

Riedlmayer, Andras. "Erasing the Past: The Destruction of Libraries and Archives in Bosnia-Herzegovina." *Review of Middle East Studies* 29, no. 1 (1995): 7–11.

"The Right to Privacy in the Digital Age." *United Nations Digital Library*, 2019. https://digitallibrary.un.org/record/3837297?ln=en. Retrieved 22 June 2022.

Riley, Jenn "Seeing Standards: A Visualization of the Metadata Universe." Retrieved 20 May 2022. http://jennriley.com/metadatamap/.

Riley, Jenn. *Understanding Metadata.* Washington, DC: National Information Standards Organization, 2017: 23.

Riordan, Michael. "Materials for History? Publishing Records as a Historical Practice in Eighteenth- and Nineteenth-Century England." *History of Humanities* 2, no. 1 (2017): 63.

Roberto, K. R. "Inflexible Bodies: Metadata for Transgender Identities." *Journal of Information Ethics* 20, no. 2 (2011): 56.

Robinson, Lyn, and David Bawden. "Mind the Gap: Transitions between Concepts of Information in Varied Domains." In *Theories of Information, Communication and Knowledge.* Dordrecht: Springer, 2014: 121–141.

Robinson, Lyn, Ernesto Priego, and David Bawden. "Library and Information Science and Digital Humanities: Two Disciplines, Joint Future?" In Christian Schlögl, Christian Wolff, Franjo Pehar, editors, *Re-Inventing Information Science in the Networked Society.* Glückstadt: Hülsbusch, 2015.

Rosenfeld, Louis, Peter Morville, and Jorge Arango. *Information Architecture: For the Web and Beyond.* Sebastopol, CA: O'Reilly, 2015.

Ross, Burley. "The Yalivshchyna Burial Site: Mass Graves after Russian Invasion." *Centre for Information Resilience.* 10 April 2022. https://www.info-res.org/post/the-yalivshchyna-burial-site-mass-graves-after-russian-invasion.

Roth, Robert E. "Cartographic Design as Visual Storytelling: Synthesis and Review of Map-Based Narratives, Genres, and Tropes." *The Cartographic Journal* 58, no. 1 (2021): 83–114.

Ryan, Mac and Cecilia Kang. "Whistle-Blower Says Facebook 'Chooses Profits over Safety.'" *The New York Times*, October 3, 2021.

Sachdeva, Sam. "Royal Society Investigation into Mātauranga Māori Letter Sparks Academic Debate." *Newsroom*. 17 November 2021.

Sanfilippo, Madelyn R., Yan Shvartzshnaider, Irwin Reyes, Helen Nissenbaum, and Serge Egelman. "Disaster Privacy/Privacy Disaster." *Journal of the Association for Information Science and Technology* 71, no. 9 (2020): 1002–1014.

Sanfilippo, Madelyn, Shengnan Yang, and Pnina Fichman. "Managing Online Trolling: From Deviant to Social and Political Trolls." *Proceedings of the 50th Hawaii International Conference on System Sciences* (2017). https://doi.org/10.24251/HICSS.2017.219.

Sara, Malm, "Belgian Woman Blindly Drove 900 Miles across Europe as She Followed Broken GPS instead of 38-Miles to the Station." *Daily Mail.com* 14 January 2013. https://www.dailymail.co.uk/news/article-2262149/Belgian-woman-67-picking-friend-railway-station-ends-Zagreb-900-miles-away-satnav-disaster.html.

Sarah, Werner. "Working towards a Feminist Printing History." *Printing History* (2020).

Savolainen, Reijo. "Everyday Life Information Seeking: Approaching Information Seeking in the Context of 'Way of Life.'" *Library & Information Science Research* 17, no. 3 (1995): 259–294.

Schneider, Jodi, Alexandre Passant, and Stefan Decker. "Deletion Discussions in Wikipedia: Decision Factors and Outcomes." *Proceedings of the Eighth Annual International Symposium on Wikis and Open Collaboration*, edited by Cliff Lampe (Linz, Austria: Wikisym, 2012): 17.

Schwartz, Adam C. *The Oracle Bone Inscriptions from Huayuanzhuang East.* Berlin: De Gruyter, 2020.

"General Information." Library of Congress. https://www.loc.gov/about/general-information/. Retrieved 23 May 2022.

See Elle Hunt. "Tay, Microsoft's AI Chatbot, Gets a Crash Course in Racism from Twitter." *The Guardian.* 24 March 2016.

Selod, Saher. "Gendered Racialization: Muslim American Men and Women's Encounters with Racialized Surveillance." *Ethnic and Racial Studies* 42, no. 4 (2019): 552–569.

Serres, Alexandre. "Hypertexte: une histoire à revisiter." *Documentaliste: Sciences de l'Information* no. 32(2) (1995): 2.

Shackelford, Laura, Wenhao David Huang, Alan Craig, Cameron Merrill, and Danying Chen. "Relationships between Motivational Support and Game Features in a Game-Based Virtual Reality Learning Environment for Teaching Introductory Archaeology." *Educational Media International* 56, no. 3 (2019): 183–200.

Shane, Harris and Dan Lamothe. "Intelligence-Sharing with Ukraine Designed to Prevent Wider War." *Washington Post*, 11 May 2022.

Šimić, Goran. "To Believe or Not to Believe: Current History Textbooks in Bosnia and Herzegovina." In *Nationhood and Politicization of History in School Textbooks*, edited by Gorana Ognjenović and Jasna Jozelić. Cham: Palgrave Macmillan, 2020.

Simonite, Tom and Gian M. Volpicelli. "Ukraine's Digital Ministry is a Formidable War Machine." *Wired*, 17 March 2022. https://www.wired.co.uk/article/ukraine-digital-ministry-war.

Simpson, Rosemary, Allen Renear, Elli Mylonas, and Andries van Dam. "50 Years after 'As We May Think' the Brown/MIT Vannevar Bush Symposium." *Interactions* 3, no. 2 (1996): 47–67.

Singer, Carol A. "Ready Reference Collections: A History." *Reference & User Services Quarterly*, 49, no. 3 (2010): 253–264.

Singhal, Amit. "Introducing the Knowledge Graph: Things, Not Strings. 16 May 2012. https://blog.google/products/search/introducing-knowledge-graph-things-not/.

Smale, Aaron. "'Ko au te awa, ko te awa ko au.'" *New Zealand Radio*. 17 March 2017.

Small, Scott A. "Age-Related Memory Decline: Current Concepts and Future Directions." *Archives of neurology* 58, no. 3 (2001): 360–364.

Smith, Linda C. "Citation Analysis." *Library Trends* Summer (1981): 93.

Smith, Linda C. "'Memex as an Image of Potentiality in Information Retrieval Research and Development." In *Proceedings of the 3rd Annual ACM Conference on Research and Development in Information Retrieval*. Kent, UK: Butterworth (1980): 345–369.

Smith, Linda C. "Memex as an Image of Potentiality Revisited." In *From Memex to hypertext: Vannevar Bush and the Mind's Machine*, edited by James Nyce and Paul Kahn. London: Academic Press, 1991: 265.

Smith, Linda C.. *Procognitive Systems: J.C.R. Licklider's Vision for Library Systems of the Future*. University of Illinois, 2015.

Soranno, Patricia A., Kendra S. Cheruvelil, Kevin C. Elliott, and Georgina M. Montgomery. "It's Good to Share: Why Environmental Scientists' Ethics are out of Date." *BioScience* 65, no. 1 (2015): 69–73.

Srivastava, Anugrah, and Advait Naik. "Big Data Analysis in Bioinformatics." In *Advances in Bioinformatics*, edited by Vijai Singh and Ajay Kumar. Singapore: Springer, (2021): 405–429.

Stafford, Pauline, "Edith, Edward's Wife and Queen." In *Edward the Confessor: The Man and the Legend*, edited by Richard Mortimer. Woodbridge: The Boydell Press, 2009, 126–8.

Star, Susan Leigh and James Griesemer. "Institutional Ecology, 'Translations' and Boundary Objects: Amateurs and Professionals in Berkeley's Museum of Vertebrate Zoology." *Social Studies of Science* 19 (3) (1989): 387–420.

Steenson, Molly Wright. *Architectural Intelligence: How Designers and Architects Created the Digital Landscape.* Cambridge, MA: MIT Press, 2017.

Stephenson, Heather. "Preserving Ukraine's Cultural Heritage Online." *Tufts Now,* 22 March 2022.

Stewart, Brenton, and Boryung Ju. "On Black Wikipedians: Motivations behind Content Contribution." *Information Processing & Management* 57, no. 3 (2020): 102134.

Stilgoe, Jack. "How Can We Know a Self-Driving Car Is Safe?" *Ethics and Information Technology* 23, no. 4 (2021): 635–647.

Stone, Christopher D. "Should Trees Have Standing? Towards Legal Rights for Natural Objects." *Southern California Law Review* 45 (1972): 450–501.

Stromgren, Pip. "Charles Ammi Cutter: Library Systematizer Extraordinaire." *Daily Hampshire Gazette,* 26 June 2004. https://forbeslibrary.org/info/library-history/charles-ammi-cutter/.

Suárez-Gonzalo, Sara, Lluís Mas Manchón, and Frederic Guerrero Solé. "Tay Is You: The Attribution of Responsibility in the Algorithmic Culture." *Observatorio* 13, no. 2 (2019): 1–14.

Suárez-Gonzalo, Sara. "'Deadbots' Can Speak for You after Your Death. Is That Ethical?" *The Conversation,* 9 May 2022.

Sula, Chris Alen, and Heather V. Hill. "The Early History of Digital Humanities: An Analysis of Computers and the Humanities (1966–2004) and Literary and Linguistic Computing (1986–2004)." *Digital Scholarship in the Humanities* 34, no. Supplement 1 (2019): i190–i206.

Tan, Shin Bin, Colleen Chiu-Shee, and Fábio Duarte. "From SARS to COVID-19: Digital Infrastructures of Surveillance and Segregation in Exceptional Times." *Cities* 120 (2022). https://doi.org/10.1016/j.cities.2021.103486.

"Text of the Convention for the Safeguarding of the Intangible Cultural Heritage." *UNESCO Intangible Cultural Heritage.* https://ich.unesco.org/en/convention.

Thornton, Russell. "Who Owns Our Past? The Repatriation of Native American Human Remains and Cultural Objects." In *Native American Voices,* edited by Susan Lobo, Steve Talbot and Traci L. Morris. New York: Routledge, 2016: 311.

Tiku, Nitasha. "The Google Engineer Who Thinks The Company's AI Has Come to Life." Retrieved 12 June 2022. https://www.washingtonpost.com/technology/2022/06/11/google-ai-lamda-blake-lemoine/.

"Timbuktu's 'Badass Librarians': Checking Out Books under Al-Qaida's Nose." In *All Things Considered,* Produced by National Public Radio,

23 April 2016. https://www.npr.org/2016/04/23/475420855/timbuktus -badass-librarians-checking-out-books-under-al-qaidas-nose.

Todorova-Ekmekci, Mirena, Todor Todorov, and Kalina Sotirova-Valkova. "Usage of Innovative Technologies and Online Media Tools for Digital Presentation of Cultural Heritage in Bulgaria." *Digital Presentation and Preservation of Cultural and Scientific Heritage* 11 (2021): 303–308.

Toscano, Chloé Valentine. "Go Ahead and Stare at My Prosthetic Arm. I Know It's Awesome." *Washington Post*, 19 September 2022. https://www.washingtonpost.com/lifestyle/2022/09/19/prosthetic-arm-design -personalize-disability/. Retrieved 22 September 2022.

"Towards the Information Age: Paul Otlet (1868–1944) Founder of the Mundaneum." *Google Arts & Culture*. Retrieved 31 May 2022. https://artsandculture.google.com/story/awXRg4ha0wAA8A?hl=en.

Trimmis, Konstantinos Prokopios. "The Forgotten Pioneer: Valerios Stais and His Research in Kythera, Antikythera and Thessaly." *Bulletin of the History of Archaeology* 26, no. 1 (2016).

Tripodi, Francesca. "Ms. Categorized: Gender, Notability, and Inequality on Wikipedia." *New Media & Society* (June 2021): 1-21. http://doi.org/10.1177 /14614448211023772.

Trompf, Gary W. "The Classification of the Sciences and the Quest for Interdisciplinarity: A Brief History of Ideas from Ancient Philosophy to Contemporary Environmental Science." *Environmental Conservation* 38, no. 2 (2011): 113–126.

Turk, Matthew J. "Scaling a Code in the Human Dimension." In *Proceedings of the Conference on Extreme Science and Engineering Discovery Environment: Gateway to Discovery*, 2013: 1–7. https://doi.org/10.1145/2484762.2484782

Tynan, Lauren. "What Is Relationality? Indigenous Knowledges, Practices and Responsibilities with Kin." *Cultural Geographies* 28, no. 4 (2021): 597–610.

Underwood, Ted. "A Genealogy of Distant Reading." *DHQ: Digital Humanities Quarterly* 11, no. 2 (2017). http://www.digitalhumanities.org/ dhq/vol/11/2/000317/000317.html. Retrieved 22 September, 2022.

Universal Declaration of Human Rights, United Nations (1948). https:// www.un.org/en/about-us/universal-declaration-of-human-rights.

Van den Heuvel, Charles. "Web 2.0 and the Semantic Web in Research from a Historical Perspective: The Designs of Paul Otlet (1868-1944) for Telecommunication and Machine Readable Documentation to Organize Research and Society." *Knowledge Organization* 36, no. 4 (2009): 214–226.

Vick, Karl. "Bellingcat's Eliot Higgins Explains Why Ukraine Is Winning the Information War." *Time*. 9 March 2022. https://time.com/6155869/ bellingcat-eliot-higgins-ukraine-open-source-intelligence/.

Virkus, Sirje, and Emmanouel Garoufallou. "Data Science and Its Relationship to Library and Information Science: A Content Analysis." *Data Technologies and Applications* 54, no. 5 (2020): 643–663.

"Vivian G. Harsh Research Collection." *Chicago Public Library.* Retrieved 11 June 2022. https://www.chipublib.org/vivian-g-harsh-research-collec tion/.

Vogele, Jessica. "Where's the Fair Use: The Takedown of Let's Play and Reaction Videos on YouTube and the Need for Comprehensive DMCA Reform." *Touro Law Review* 33 (2017): 589.

von Oswald, Margareta. "The 'Restitution Report': First Reactions in Academia, Museums, and Politics." *Centre for Anthropological Research on Museums and Heritage* (2019). Retrieved 30 October 2022. https://blog.uni -koeln.de/gssc-humboldt/the-restitution-report/.

Wachs, Johannes, and Balázs Vedres. "Does Crowdfunding Really Foster Innovation? Evidence from the Board Game Industry." *Technological Forecasting and Social Change* 168 (2021): 120747.

Wagner, Travis L., and Ashley Blewer. "'The Word Real Is No Longer Real': Deepfakes, Gender, and the Challenges of AI-Altered Video." *Open Information Science* 3, no. 1 (2019): 32–46.

Walker, Christopher, and Ann Copeland. "The Eye Prophetic: Julia Pettee." *Libraries & the Cultural Record* 44, no. 2 (2009): 166.

Wamsley, Laurel. "Library of Congress Will No Longer Archive Every Tweet." *NPR*, 26 December 2017.

Wang, Tian, Lin Guo, and Masooda Bashir. "COVID-19 Apps and Privacy Protections from Users' Perspective." *Proceedings of the Association for Information Science and Technology* 58, no. 1 (2021): 357–365.

Wang, Yang. "First-Time Internet Users in Nigeria Use the Internet in a Unique Way." *KaiOS Industry Insights* (2020). https://www.kaiostech.com /first-time-internet-users-in-nigeria-use-the-internet-in-a-unique-way -heres-why-that-matters/.

Wang, Yang. "Inclusive Security and Privacy." *Sociotechnical Security and Privacy.* IEEE Computer and Reliability Societies, July/August 2018: 82–87.

Watts, Duncan and Steven H. Strogatz. "Collective Dynamics of 'Small-World' Networks." *Nature* 393, no. 6684 (1998): 440–442.

Weinberger, David. "The Problem with the Data-Information-Knowledge-Wisdom Hierarchy." *Harvard Business Review* 2 (2010). https://hbr.org /2010/02/data-is-to-info-as-info-is-not.

Weinstein, Emily. "The Social Media See-Saw: Positive and Negative Influences on Adolescents' Affective Well-Being." *New Media & Society* 20, no. 10 (2018): 3597–3623.

Wells, Herbert George. *World Brain.* Cambridge, MA: MIT Press, 2021.

Westengen, Ola T., Charlotte Lusty, Mariana Yazbek, Ahmed Amri, and Åsmund Asdal. "Safeguarding a Global Seed Heritage from Syria to Svalbard." *Nature Plants* 6, no. 11 (2020): 1311–1317.

"What Is GDPR, the EU's New Data Protection Law?" *GDPR.EU*. Retrieved 6 June 2022. https://gdpr.eu/what-is-gdpr/.

Whelan, Allison M. "Unequal Representation: Women in Clinical Research." *Cornell Law Review Online* 106 (2020): 103–4.

Wiegand, Wayne A. "Sanitizing American Library History: Reflections of a Library Historian." *The Library Quarterly* 90, no. 2 (2020): 108–120.

"Wikipedia." *Wikipedia*. Retrieved 29 May 2022. https://en.wikipedia.org/wiki/Wikipedia.

"Wikipedia: Wiki Game." Retrieved 29 May 2022. https://en.wikipedia.org/wiki/Wikipedia:Wiki_Game.

Wilson, Thomas D. "Human Information Behavior." *Informing Science* 3, no. 2 (2000): 50.

Witzel, Michael. "Vedas and Upaniṣads." In *The Blackwell Companion to Hinduism*, edited by Gavin Flood. Oxford and Malden, MA: Blackwell, 2003: 68–101.

Wolf, Gary. "The Curse of Xanadu." *Wired*, 1 June 1995.

Woods, Christopher. "The Earliest Mesopotamian Writing." In *Visible Language: Inventions of Writing in the Ancient Middle East and Beyond*. Chicago, IL: Oriental Institute Museum Publications, 2010: 32.

"World IA Day." Retrieved 12 June 2022. https://www.worldiaday.org/.

Wright, Alex, "The Web Time Forgot." *The New York Times*. 17 June 2008.

Wright, Alex. "The Future of the Web Is 100 Years Old." *Nautilus* (29 January 2015). Retrieved 2 June 2022. https://nautil.us/the-future-of-the-web-is-100-years-old-2894/.

Wright, Alex. "The Secret History of Hypertext." *The Atlantic*, 22 May 2014.

Wright, Alex. *Cataloging the World: Paul Otlet and the Birth of the Information Age*. Oxford: Oxford University Press, 2014.

Wright, Michael T. "Archimedes, Astronomy, and the Planetarium." In *Archimedes in the 21st Century*, edited by Chris Rorres (Cham: Birkhäuser, 2017): 125–141.

Wright, Sarah, Kate Lloyd, Sandie Suchet-Pearson, Laklak Burarrwanga, Matalena Tofa, and Bawaka Country. "Telling Stories in, through and with Country: Engaging with Indigenous and More-Than-Human Methodologies at Bawaka, NE Australia." *Journal of Cultural Geography* 29, no. 1 (2012): 39–60.

Wu, Tim. "Whatever Happened to Google Books." *The New Yorker*, 11 September 2015.

Yang, Dong, Ziyue Xu, Wenqi Li, Andriy Myronenko, Holger R. Roth, Stephanie Harmon, Sheng Xu et al. "Federated Semi-Supervised Learning for COVID Region Segmentation in chest CT Using Multi-National Data from China, Italy, Japan." *Medical Image Analysis* 70 (2021): 101992.

Yavuz, N. Kıvılcım. "Hernando Colón's Book of Books: AM 377 fol." Retrieved 17 May 2022. https://nkyavuz.com/blog/ams-am-377-fol/.

"Yewno." Retrieved 1 June 2022. https://www.yewno.com/about.

Yong, Ed, "This Speck of DNA Contains a Movie, a Computer Virus, and an Amazon Gift Card." *The Atlantic.* 2 March 2017.

Zargar, Safwat. "Mistaken Identity: A Kashmiri Farmer on Pilgrimage in Iraq Has Been Detained on an Interpol Notice." *Scroll.In*, 12 January 2020. https://scroll.in/article/949613/mistaken-identity-a-kashmiri-farmer-on -pilgrimage-in-iraq-has-been-detained-on-an-interpol-notice.

Zins, Chaim. "Conceptions of Information Science." *Journal of the American Society for Information Science and Technology* 58, no. 3 (2007): 335–350.

Zipf, George Kingsley. *Human Behavior and the Principle of Least Effort: An Introduction to Human Ecology.* Boston, MA: Addison Wesley Press, 1949.

"Zooniverse.org." Retrieved 3 June 2022 https://www.zooniverse.org/ about.

# INDEX